A Wider Social Role for Sport

Sport is perceived to have the potential to alleviate a variety of social problems and generally to 'improve' both individuals and the communities in which they live. Sport is promoted as a relatively cost-effective antidote to a range of problems – often those stemming from social exclusion – including poor health, high crime levels, drug abuse and persistent youth offending, educational underachievement, lack of social cohesion and community identity and economic decline. To this end, there is increasing governmental interest in what has become known as 'sport for good'.

A Wider Social Role for Sport presents the political and historical context for this increased governmental interest in sport's potential contribution to a range of social problems. The book explores the particular social problems that governments seek to address through sport, and examines the nature and extent of the evidence for sport's positive role.

The book illustrates that, in an era of evidence-based policy-making, the cumulative evidence base for many claims for sport is relatively weak, in part because research into the precise contribution of sport faces substantial methodological problems. Drawing on worldwide research, *A Wider Social Role for Sport* explores the current state of knowledge and understanding of the presumed impacts of sport and suggests that we need to adopt a different approach to research and evaluation if sports researchers are to develop their understanding and make a substantial contribution to sports policy.

Fred Coalter is Professor of Sports Policy at the University of Stirling, UK.

A Wider Social Role for Sport

Who's keeping the score?

Fred Coalter

LONDON AND NEW YORK

First published 2007
by Routledge
2 Park Square, Milton Park, Abingdon, Oxon OX14 4RN

Simultaneously published in the USA and Canada
by Routledge
270 Madison Ave, New York, NY 10016

Routledge is an imprint of the Taylor & Francis Group, an informa business

© 2007 Fred Coalter

Typeset in Goudy by
HWA Text and Data Management, Tunbridge Wells
Printed and bound in Great Britain by
Antony Rowe Ltd, Chippenham, Wiltshire

British Library Cataloguing in Publication Data
A catalogue record for this book is available from the British Library

Library of Congress Cataloging-in-Publication Data
A catalog record for this book has been requested

ISBN10: 0–415–36349–7 (hbk)
ISBN10: 0–415–36350–0 (pbk)
ISBN10: 0–203–01461–8 (ebk)

ISBN13: 978–0–415–36349–5 (hbk)
ISBN13: 978–0–415–36350–1 (pbk)
ISBN13: 978–0–203–01461–5 (ebk)

To Eddie, Mollie and Vicki

Contents

Acknowledgements   x

1 Introduction   1
Opportunity or threat?   1
New rules?   2
Structure of the book   4
End of the warm up   6

2 From sport for all to sport for good   8
The active citizen is a responsible citizen   8
From management by objectives to objective-led management   9
Sports policy: a lottery?   14
New Labour and 'active citizenship'   14
How does sport achieve the results?   19
Standing up and being counted   23

3 Sport and social impacts: do we need new rules?   25
Evidence-based policy-making   25
But if it works, how does it work?   26
*Sport's wider social role: ill-defined interventions with hard-to-follow
     outcomes?   31*
Is it logical?   32
It's not what you do, but the way that you do it   36
Do we know what game we are playing?   38
A rational exercise that takes place in a political context   41
Final comment   46

4 Sport and social regeneration: a capital prospect   47
The Third Way and active citizenship   47
Sport and active citizenship   48

Social capital and social policy   49
Whose social capital?   50
Social capital: it depends where you look   54
Sports volunteers: the real active citizens?   55
Sports clubs and social capital   57
Sports clubs and social capital: survey evidence   62
Clubs' rules OK?   64
Can we capitalize on sport?   66

5 **Sport-in-development: sport plus**   68
A global role for sport?   68
Sport plus or plus sport?   70
From economic aid to civil society   71
Sport and gender relations   74
Developing people, creating citizens   75
The case studies   77
But are they hitting the mark?   85
Evaluation: accountability or development?   87
Participatory M&E: developing people and programmes   89
Process-led M&E: why do our programmes work?   90

6 **Sport and educational performance: scoring on the pitch
and in the classroom?**   92
Introduction   92
Failing most of the tests   93
How is sport presumed to work?   94
Maybe it is feeling better about yourself   98
Depends on your sport?   104
It's not what you do, but who you do it with   106
But at least it does no academic harm   108
Maybe it's sport plus   110
The exam results   112

7 **Sport and crime prevention: playing by the rules?**   115
Fair cop or fair play?   115
What is anti-social behaviour?   117
Theories of crime and theories of sport's processes   119
Sport plus ... again   130
Final sentencing   131

8 **The economic impacts of sport: investing in success?**   **133**
The new economic realism   133
Sport and urban regeneration   135
Large-scale sport events   141
The sports economy   150
The economic benefits of a more physically active population   153
An economy of solutions?   159

9 **From methods to logic of inquiry**   **161**
Who is listening?   161
From fuzzy snapshots to clear videos   164
It's all about families   166
From methods to logic of inquiry   167
A social vaccine?   171
Not proven   172

References   175
Index   199

Acknowledgements

I start by thanking Nick Rowe (Sport England) and Jerry Bingham (UK Sport) who commissioned me to compile the *Value of Sport Monitor*, an on-line database of research evidence of the wider impacts of sport. The work on the *Monitor* provided me with access to much of the material included in this book. Although I absolve them both from all responsibility for the contents and conclusions of this book, I hope that they explain the reasons for some of our 'discussions'. I would also like to thank Jon Best (sportscotland) for commissioning some of the reviews drawn on in this book (although I do not think that I need to distance him from my conclusions).

I would also like to thank the generous, innovative and optimistic people whom I met in Africa and India while compiling the *Sport-in-Development Monitoring and Evaluation Manual* (Coalter, 2006). They all, and especially the members of the Mathare Youth Sport Association (Nairobi), introduced me to a new way of viewing sport and its potential.

I would also like to express my sincere thanks to Samantha Grant (Routledge editor) for having the patience of Job. I am grateful to Taylor & Francis for permission to include material from Fred Coalter, 'Sports Clubs, Social Capital and Social Regeneration: "Ill-Defined Interventions with Hard-to-Follow Outcomes"?', *Sport in Society* 10(4) (2007): 537–59.

Thanks are also due to a number of authors whose work I have drawn on more than others. They will know who they are, but in case they disagree with me I will not name them here. Thanks to Derek Casey for long discussions, rarely agreeing with me and illustrating many of the tensions explored in this book. I am grateful to John Taylor for his stoical and diligent work on the *Value of Sport Monitor* and for his invaluable assistance in helping me to compile the bibliography. Thanks also to Karen Caldwell for her formatting expertise.

Finally, thanks to Vicki for listening.

1 Introduction

Opportunity or threat?

In recent years sport has achieved an increasingly high profile as part of New Labour's social inclusion agenda, based on assumptions about its potential contribution to areas such as social and economic regeneration, crime reduction, health improvement and educational achievement. However these new opportunities (welcomed by many in sport) have been accompanied by a potential threat – evidence-based policy-making. This reflects an increased emphasis on outcomes and effectiveness and an aspiration to base policy and practice on robust evidence to ensure the delivery of the government's policy goals. In pursuit of this I, and others, have been commissioned to produce several policy-oriented literature reviews to identify evidence for the presumed social and economic impacts of sport. In addition I am also responsible (with John Taylor) for the on-line research database, the *Value of Sport Monitor*, funded by Sport England and UK Sport. To the disappointment of the commissioning clients, all reviews have produced rather ambiguous and inconclusive conclusions – equivalent to the Scottish legal verdict of 'not proven'. There are no 'killer facts' and few 'best buys'.

The lack of a strong cumulative body of research evidence from which to inform policy and practice is explained by four broad factors.

(i) Conceptual weaknesses. Much available research exhibits a wide variety of frequently vague definitions of 'sport'; the nature, extent and duration of *participation*; *intermediate impacts* (i.e. the effect of sport on participants) and *outcomes* (the resulting individual behavioural or social changes – reduced 'anti-social behaviour' or increased 'social cohesion'). Such variety and lack of precision raise substantial issues of validity and comparability.

(ii) Methodological weaknesses. There is lack of systematic and robust evaluations of most programmes. In part this reflects the *mythopoeic status* of sport and the assumption of inevitably positive outcomes, with little need for monitoring and evaluation – sport works. Where research does take place, there is often an over-concentration on outputs and a failure to define precisely and measure desired intermediate impacts and outcomes; cross-sectional designs, with limited longitudinal data; convenience sampling; general lack of control groups and a failure to control for a wide range of potentially intervening and confounding variables. The number of academic articles which finish with methodological caveats about the inherent limitations of the chosen methodology is alarming. These issues raise substantial questions of reliability.

(iii) Little consideration of *sufficient conditions*. Participation in sport (itself a difficult goal among certain low participating 'target groups') is a necessary, but not sufficient condition to obtain the supposed benefits. In this regard there is a lack of information about the various mechanisms, processes and experiences associated with participation. We have little understanding about which sports and sports *processes* produce what *outcomes*, for which *participants* and in what *circumstances*. These *middle-range mechanisms* (Pawson, 2006) are a core concern of this book.

(iv) The inevitable limitations associated with such literature (or *narrative*) reviews, which are largely dependent on published materials. The material included in these sources (mostly academic journals) is inevitably selective and fails to provide information on the full complexities of programmes (and rarely provides vitally important information about failed initiatives).

It is important to note that, although this book concentrates on sports research, the weaknesses and limitations which will be highlighted are not confined to sport – evidence-based policy-making has exposed widespread limitations in many areas of research, especially their ability to inform policy (Oakley *et al.*, 2005; Faulkner *et al.*, 2006; Department of Health, 1999). The acknowledgement of these limitations has led researchers, from a range of disciplinary and subject backgrounds, to seek to develop a broader, more eclectic, definition of the world of knowledge and approaches to evidence gathering – to be less concerned with methodological purity and more with *frameworks for analysis*. Many seem increasingly to accept Hammersley's (1995: 19) argument that 'philosophy must not be seen as superordinate to empirical research ... research is a practical activity and cannot be governed in any strict way by methodological theory'.

New rules?

Within this context the book draws its intellectual inspiration, and the emphasis on process, mechanisms and programme theories, from two main sources – Pawson's (2006) writings on realist (or 'realistic') approaches to evaluation and the closely parallel work of Weiss (1997) and theory-based evaluations (TBE). Weiss (1997: 520) argues that 'the clearest call for TBE comes when prior evaluations show inconsistent results' – a situation which neatly sums up most sports-related research.

There is an emerging view that *the* major methodological limitation on producing evidence for policy-making and practice is the absence of an understanding of processes and mechanisms which either produce, or are assumed to produce, particular impacts and outcomes. In other words, there is a lack of understanding of what processes produce what effects, for which participants, in what circumstances. As all social interventions are hypotheses about relationships between programmes, participants and outcomes, understanding and evaluation requires knowledge of the *programme theories* underpinning interventions – *why* do those who fund or provide such programmes think that they will offer solutions to their policy problems? This has led to a growing interest in a loose amalgam of theories of behaviour change, realist evaluation and theory-based evaluation, in order to understand policy-makers' assumptions – their programme theories which underpin interventions. It is hoped that such an understanding will provide a basis for evaluation and an understanding of how and why interventions work for some, but not for others. Within this context our concerns with the current state of sports-related research are as follows:

- What is the nature of the evidence that participation in sport produces various *intermediate impacts* (e.g. self-efficacy; physical self-worth; self-esteem; self-confidence; aspects of social capital)?
- Do we have evidence about which sports, in what circumstances, through which mechanisms, produce what impacts, for whom?
- Even if sports interventions produce the desired *intermediate* impacts for some participants, in what circumstances do these contribute to the solution of the wider social problems?
- To what extent are sports programmes designed on the basis of an understanding of the nature and causes of the mostly complex problems to which they seek to offer a solution – lack of social cohesion, weak social capital, poor educational performance, anti-social behaviour and criminality, economic decline? To what extent can 'sport' contribute to the solution of such issues and what is the significance of the increasing use of *sport plus* approaches, in which sport's contribution is complemented and supported by a range of parallel initiatives?

The second aspect of the work of Pawson and Weiss relates to the relationship between research and policy. It concerns the nature of evidence-based policy-making and the implications of Weiss's (1993: 94) assertion that 'evaluation is a rational exercise that takes place in a political context'. The implication is that academic researchers are somewhat naive (unlike the growing band of savvy consultants) and too often confuse research with evidence, failing to recognize that research competes for attention with a range of other more influential factors – politics in all senses of the term. Where evidence is weak, where there are no killer facts, where there is little robust guidance as to a best buy, then research's or researchers' entry to the policy process will be even more restricted. Pawson and Weiss's potential solution to this is a direct consequence of a theory-based evaluation approach. This requires researchers to develop 'conversations' with policy-makers and practitioners in order to arrive at a mutual understanding of their programme theories; their assumptions about the nature of the problems which they seek to address; how these are related to programme design and delivery;

the elements and mechanisms of the programmes which are presumed to produce the desired intermediate impacts and the broader outcomes. Such an approach seeks to overcome the widespread, if somewhat crude, dichotomy between the 'engineering/political arithmetic/partisan support' view of policy-oriented research and the supposedly epistemologically (and morally) superior disciplinary-based approach of disinterested 'scholars', whose job is to enlighten rather than inform. Both Pawson and Weiss embrace a slightly different 'enlightenment' position. This is one in which the perspectives and understandings of social science are used to work with policy-makers to clarify the nature of problems, the extent to which they can be addressed by the proposed interventions and to identify those actions/ initiatives most likely to make some contribution – a position which combines both methodological modesty and political ambition. Although we do not deal with these issues in depth, they are ever-present, providing a broad backdrop against which to assess the possible relationships between the research and evaluation reviewed and the policy process, with its elements of power, organizational interests, professional repertoires and the mythopoeic status of sport.

A third aspect of the theory-based approach is that it is inherently developmental – it seeks to bring researchers, evaluators, policy-makers and practitioners (and sometimes participants) together to explore and clarify their shared and conflicting assumptions (theories). Such an approach can lead to improved coherence and effectiveness in policy, organizational and programme delivery processes. It has the potential to contribute to capacity-building, to develop a greater sense of ownership, understanding and integration and develop an organizational ability to reflect on and analyse attitudes, beliefs and behaviour.

I am not convinced that I have done the perspectives of Pawson and Weiss full justice – that would need a book on each topic. However, I can take some solace from the fact that they both regard their perspectives as *frameworks* and not the more precise and easily judged 'methods'. Hopefully the reader will spot where these broad perspectives and issues inform the description, analysis and evaluation of the material presented in this book

Structure of the book

Chapter 2 argues that public investment in sport has always been characterized by a dual purpose – to extend social rights of citizenship and to use sport to address a wide range of policy issues (with sport's presumed externalities being the most consistent and strongest rationale). However, until recently the ability of sport to address such wider policy issues was taken for granted, largely on the basis of a view of sport as a relatively cheap and simple solution to social problems, with its mythopoeic status ensuring a relative absence of monitoring and evaluation – sport works. However, the emergence of New Labour's Third Way concerns with civic renewal, social inclusion, active citizenship and social capital placed sport on a broader policy agenda. This was reinforced by an emphasis on joined-up government and a policy imperative that all areas of public investment contribute to strategic policy goals. However, this was also accompanied by notions of evidence-based policy-making and outcome-oriented welfare effectiveness. In such circumstances the relatively untested claims of sport's wider roles came under much closer scrutiny and robust research to inform evidence-based policy-making was in short supply.

Chapter 3 is about methodology and politics rather than research methods. It explores some basic issues confronting us as we seek to understand current research on the nature and extent of the wider social role of sport. It outlines the logic of the assumptions about sport, the claimed personal and social impacts and provides a context for understanding current research findings and their potential strengths and limitations. It illustrates some of the reasons for the relatively weak cumulative research base to inform evidence-based policy-making. It also explores the political, bureaucratic and professional interests involved in policy formulation and the fact that research is only one, small, element of this process. Drawing on the work of Pawson and Weiss a theory-based approach to evaluation is outlined.

The next five chapters explore aspects of these issues in specific areas of sports policy. Chapter 4 outlines sport's presumed contribution to social and community regeneration, an issue at the heart of New Labour's social inclusion agenda. It argues that the precise nature of *social capital* and the processes underpinning its formation are undertheorized in this policy debate and explores the perspectives of Bourdieu, Coleman and Putnam (who dominates the policy debate). It examines the current, limited, research on sport, sports clubs and social capital, which seems to indicate a limited role for sports clubs in the social regeneration agenda.

Chapter 5 examines the concept of sport-in-development and the approaches referred to as *sport plus* and *plus sport*. This is based on fieldwork (and ongoing research) and provides some of the intellectual and emotional inspiration for the book. Although this is an area characterized by unrealistically ambitious claims made by agencies such as the United Nations, it is also the area in which many are working in highly innovative ways to explore the real potential of sport to address wider social issues. The chapter argues that in these circumstances sporting organizations (rather than 'sport') have the potential to play an important role in civil society. The chapter uses two case studies – the Mathare Youth Sport Association (Nairobi) and Go Sisters (Lusaka) – to illustrate the *sport plus* approach to the development of aspects of civil society and the use of sport to address issues of HIV/AIDS. The chapter also illustrates the contribution that a theory-based approach to monitoring and evaluation can make to organizational and personal development.

Chapter 6 examines the various perspectives on the presumed relationship between sports participation and (improved) educational performance. In some ways this is a generic chapter, as the issues raised relate most clearly to the presumed key sports-related *intermediate impacts* (e.g. cognitive abilities; self-efficacy; physical self-worth; self-esteem; self-confidence; social capital). In addition to examining the extent to which 'sport' has such impacts, the bigger question concerns the extent to which any of these are related to the desired outcome of improved educational performance. It also illustrates many of the methodological issues faced by other areas – wide variations in the definition of terms (e.g. participation; educational achievement); limitations of self-reporting and cross-sectional research; difficult issues of self-selection and direction of cause; lack of controls for significant variables. The difficulties faced by researchers in providing robust evidence is reflected in the increasing popularity of the 'at least it does not do any harm' position.

Chapter 7 examines issues relating to sport and crime reduction (and deals with many of the mechanisms and intermediate impacts explored in Chapter 6). This is one of the most persistent rationales for investment in sport and the chapter explores various theories of the causes of crime and the extent to which there is evidence that sport can provide some solutions. The chapter illustrates an increasing recognition that there is a need to understand the various types of programmes and mechanisms which work for particular groups, with the growth of *sports plus* programmes indicating a growing recognition of the limitations of sports-only approaches.

Chapter 8 is slightly different from the others as it deals with economic issues – sport and urban regeneration, the economic impact of sporting events, the nature and size of the sports economy and the economic benefits of increased physical activity. However, it deals with the same broad themes about the nature of the processes, mechanisms and relationships between sport and economic outcomes, for example, the nature of the economic 'multiplier' and the problems involved in defining precisely the sports economy. However, this chapter also best illustrates our second theme – the relationship between interests, power and research evidence. Given the economic and political interests involved in many of these areas (e.g. bidding for large-scale sports events; expensive regeneration projects) there is a clear tension between power and knowledge in the shaping of policy, with cost benefit competing with *political benefit*.

Chapter 9 reflects on the nature of the evidence reviewed in earlier chapters and returns to some of the themes explored in Chapter 3 – the nature of evidence-based policy-making; the relationship between research and policy; the widespread concern about information on *sufficient conditions*. In this regard the realist proposal to shift analysis from families of programmes (e.g. sport and crime) to *families of mechanisms* in order to explore and understand better middle-range mechanisms fits well with the proposal that researchers need to work with policy-makers and practitioners to explore their *programme theories*. In this context a range of policy-oriented researchers propose that we adopt a more eclectic approach to the 'world of evidence' (Faulkner *et al.*, 2006). The chapter ends with a 'not proven' verdict and a plea for more considered and realistic claims about the potential of sport to contribute to often complex, and not fully understood, social problems.

End of the warm up

My experience of more than a quarter of a century of contract research – seeking to combine academic rigour (and increasing experience) with the understandable demands of the commissioning agencies for relatively unambiguous 'evidence' of the effectiveness of their investments to placate *their* masters – has convinced me that there is a need to think more clearly, analytically and less emotionally about 'sport' and its potential. This might be difficult for the sports evangelists, for those who have invested much in their professional repertoires, for those wanting apparently cheap and simple answers (if not solutions), for generalist civil servants with little understanding of 'sport' (but a desire to 'do something') and those operating in a still relatively marginal policy area with demanding, if often ill-informed, masters. If sports policy and practice are to mature and their interventions to become less ambitious and more effective, there is a need to 'de-mythologize' or 'de-centre' sport. In a sense *sport* is a collective noun which hides much more than it reveals – perhaps this simplifying function is part of its political attraction. There are almost endless variations of sport processes, mechanisms, participants and experiences – individual, partner or team sports; motor or perceptually dominated sports; those which require physical or mental dexterity; task versus ego orientation and so on. If research is to inform policy, then it is essential to seek to explore the question of *sufficient conditions* – which sports, in which conditions, have what effects for which participants? Of course, as we will see, we are still left with even more fundamental issues about the relationship between any *sports effects* and their 'contribution' to the solution of wider social and economic problems.

Weiss suggests that nobody in high office reads social science journals (far less books) and Pawson argues that as one ascends the intervention hierarchy the capacity to absorb complex information dwindles by the bullet point – so that rules out some potential readers! However, although some of the key target audiences will not read this, I hope that those who might talk to them will – the students, practitioners and researchers who might come across it (and hopefully agree with some of what they read) can eventually engage in the necessary 'conversations'.

2 From sport for all to sport for good

The active citizen is a responsible citizen

The history of public policy for sport in the United Kingdom (and elsewhere) has been characterized by an essential duality. Government involvement and investment have been characterized by the dual purposes of extending social rights of citizenship while also emphasizing a range of wider social benefits presumed to be associated with participation in sport. Of course such duality is a common characteristic of most social policies, where the extension of social rights has mostly been accompanied by social obligations and duties (Roche, 1992). Writing about cultural policy, Bianchini (1992) suggests that 'citizenship' represents an attempt not simply to extend social rights, but also to bridge the potentially socially disruptive gap between the individual and the community and between the exercise of individual rights and the common good. Harrison (1973), writing about state intervention and moral reform in nineteenth-century England, points to the inherent tension between social and moral reform. Although social reform requires the lessening of constraints on individual liberty, moral reform requires the building up of constraints. Citizenship implies responsibilities and duties as well as rights.

Consequently, much of the nineteenth-century government interest in sport (and other aspects of leisure, such as libraries, museums, parks) combines genuine concerns to improve the quality of life and health of the new urban working class with attempts to create a new civic culture and, by implication, 'citizens' (Bailey, 1978). Consequently, participation in socially sanctioned leisure activities was not simply about individual welfare and rights – the act and process of participation were central to the idea of the citizen. Participation was both an expression and an affirmation of citizenship and, by implication, a deeper social consensus: the responsible citizen is the participating citizen, with non-participation frequently viewed as a potential threat to social stability. In such institutions as the English public schools and movements like Muscular Christianity, sport was regarded as 'character building', developing virtues or moral personality traits such as discipline, honesty, integrity, generosity and trustworthiness (President's Council on Physical Fitness and Sports, 2006). Further, the supposed efficacy of sport was strengthened by being regarded as a 'neutral' social space where all citizens, or sport people, met as equals and in an environment regarded as 'unambiguously wholesome and healthy in both a physical and moral sense' (Smith and Waddington, 2004: 281).

It could be argued that such policies are based on sport's 'mythopoeic' status. Mythopoeic concepts tend to be ones whose demarcation criteria are not specific and, as will be suggested throughout the book, this can be applied to the way that an overgeneralized notion of 'sport' is frequently used in policy debates. Such concepts are based on popular and idealistic ideas which are produced largely outside sociological analysis and which 'isolate[s] a particular relationship between variables to the exclusion of others and without a sound basis for doing so' (Glasner, 1977: 2–3). Such myths contain elements of truth, but elements which become reified and distorted and 'represent' rather than reflect reality, standing for supposed, but largely unexamined, impacts and processes. The strength of such myths lies in their 'ability to evoke vague and generalised images' (Glasner, 1977: 1). The mythopoeic nature of sport can partly be illustrated by the fact that it is a rich source for a wide variety of metaphors: playing the game, level playing fields, it's not cricket, first past the post, getting to first base, throwing in the towel, being on a winning team.

From management by objectives to objective-led management

However, despite nineteenth-century beliefs about the contribution of sport to improved health and the construction of civic cultures, systematic central government interest in sport dates largely from the 1960s. As in the nineteenth century, government's interest reflected a concern with the potentially negative effects of rapid economic, social and cultural change. The understanding of the context which seemed to require government intervention is illustrated by the first annual report of the Advisory Sports Council (1966: 1), which stated that:

> We have entered a new era of dramatic evolution in our material progress … more and more people are acquiring leisure and the means to enjoy it … consequently we are faced with the need for better, more abundant and sophisticated facilities for our leisure activities.

This was a reflection of a more general concern to promote public planning, provision and management for sport to cater for the demands of the new 'leisure age' (Sillitoe, 1969; Blackie *et al.*, 1979; Veal, 1982). The general organizational infrastructure for leisure policy was reorganized and extended, with an executive Sports Council being established in 1971 to support the voluntary sector and to encourage local authorities to provide for increasing demand 'in the interests of social welfare and the enjoyment of leisure among the public at large' (Sports Council Royal Charter, 1971:1). Underlying these developments was a vague social-democratic consensus about the extension of welfare services to provide for a widening range of social rights of citizenship, although as Roche (1992) points out, this was not subject to widespread political, or even theoretical, debate (for an analysis of similar developments in the Netherlands see van der Poel, 1993; Germany see Nahrstedt, 1993; France see Hantrais, 1989).

Within this context, identified inequalities in participation in sport led to the designation of certain groups as being 'recreationally disadvantaged'. If all aspects of social citizenship were to become a reality, public provision must provide equal opportunities for all. This led to the formulation of policies of 'recreational welfare' (Coalter *et al.*, 1988). Rather than increase supply in response to what was initially assumed to be the inevitable rise in demand, policy became concerned to democratize areas of public leisure. The language of policy quickly shifted from a concern with expressed demand to an attempt to address the issues of 'need' (Rapoport and Rapoport, 1975; Mennell, 1979). In Britain the 1975 White Paper, *Sport and Recreation* defined recreational facilities as 'part of the general fabric of the social services'. Policies of positive discrimination were developed, under the vague slogan of Sport for All (McIntosh and Charlton, 1985) with the identification of 'target groups' and associated special concessionary and promotional strategies aimed at reducing constraints and encouraging participation (for accounts of similar developments in France see Hantrais, 1984).

However, the ambiguity and duality of sports policy were also present. The 1975 White Paper also promoted the idea of recreation *as* welfare (Department of the Environment, 1975: 2), stating that,

> by reducing boredom and urban frustration participation in active recreation contributes to the reduction of hooliganism and delinquency among young people ... The need to provide for people to make the best of their leisure time must be seen in this context.

As Henry (2001) points out, such policy developments occurred during a period of emerging economic crisis, with the Labour government seeking a loan from the International Monetary Fund, devaluing the pound and reducing public expenditure, thus ending the period of welfare expansion. Against the background of economic decline, rising unemployment and problems of inner-city decay, there was a quickening of the pace of governmental use of sport in urban policy. For example, in 1976 the Urban Programme was extended to include environmental and recreational provision; in 1977 the Department of the Environment launched the *Leisure and the Quality of Life Experiments* (1977a) and published a study entitled *Recreation and Deprivation in the Inner City* (Department of the Environment, 1977b). Such experiments and publications did not represent a coherent government policy for sport (that was the responsibility of the Sports Council). Rather, it has been argued that the apparent political neutrality and popularity of sport, and its presumed ability to provide 'an economy of remedies' (Donnison and Chapman, 1965), made it a more attractive option than addressing fundamental structural change (Coalter *et al.*, 1988; Henry, 2001). Therefore the vocabulary of motives shifted to recreation *as* welfare with increasing recourse to what economists refer to as 'externalities' and 'merit good' arguments (Gratton and Taylor, 1985) – i.e. that participation in sport may be an individual social right of citizenship, but such participation also leads to collective benefits such as improved health and reduced crime. Henry (2001) illustrates a general shift in central government funding away from local government leisure and recreation services to funding via the Urban Programme and a concentration on the inner city and increased targeting of particular social groups and deprived areas. Related to this was an increasing willingness to provide substantial dedicated funds to the Sports Council for specific 'social' programmes, despite its supposedly quasi-autonomous status (Henry, 2001). The most striking example of this occurred under the new Conservative government of Margaret Thatcher, following the urban riots of 1981. The Sports Council allocated £3 million over three years for a demonstration project entitled Action Sport (Rigg, 1986). This can be regarded as the forerunner of many subsequent sports development projects. The problem-oriented nature of this was indicated in the Sports Council Annual Report 1981/2 which stated that the purpose of Action Sport was 'to demonstrate the part that could be played by sport and physical recreation within deprived urban areas'. The intention was to 'select ready-made leaders from among the unemployed … because of the urgency, in view of the social problems, of putting leaders on the street' (quoted in Rigg, 1986: 12). The overall aim of Action Sport was to demonstrate that leadership can develop positive attitudes to sport and recreation and increase participation. I will explore some of the lesson from Action Sport in Chapter 4, but here it is worth noting Deane's (1998: 153) comment that many of the schemes

> suffered … credibility problems with local community representatives. Local community representatives perceived the schemes as being a short-term attempt by central government to show that they were doing something for the young unemployed … [and] saw the Action Sport schemes as a complete waste of resources.

Nevertheless, although the rhetoric of recreation *as* welfare was ideologically potent, it remained politically weak and relatively marginal to core public policy developments, and the Sports Council's largest single financial commitment (45 percent of the total) was to elite sport (Coalter *et al.*, 1988). More importantly, few attempts were made to examine systematically the effectiveness of recreation *as* welfare policies, with monitoring usually being restricted largely to measuring participation and the nature of participants (Rigg, 1986).

Further, a more general attack was made on public provision for sport and recreation as Margaret Thatcher's neoliberal government subjected the nature and content of social citizenship to fundamental moral, economic and political questioning. The neoliberal moral critique of social citizenship was one of passivity – that, in practice, it consisted solely of rights, with few associated *responsibilities* and duties (Roche, 1992). This 'nanny state' had led to passivity and a decline in the willingness, or ability, of welfare recipients to take responsibility for their own consumption and welfare. The *economic* critique was that local governments were financially profligate and, in order to reduce public sector borrowing deficits, there was a need to control local government spending. The *political* critique was of local government per se: because of what was seen as bureaucratic inefficiency and lack of accountability and responsiveness to consumer needs, local government's role as a direct provider should be abolished or reduced greatly (Coalter, 1998). Despite reflecting different historical trajectories and national circumstances, broadly similar shifts in policy can be identified in the Netherlands (van der Poel, 1993; Lengkeek, 1993), Germany (Nahrstedt, 1993), France (Poujol, 1993) and Australia (Sport and Recreation Victoria, 1994).

Although this critique was aimed at all forms of public provision, there were specific attacks on sport and recreation services at both national and local levels. Despite the formal rhetoric of welfare and 'sport for all', policies for sport occupied 'an uneasy place between ideologies of the market and ideologies of welfare', with policies being 'modified by, or subordinated to, more fundamental political philosophies and economic realities' (Coalter *et al.*, 1988: 188). In terms of local sports provision it was claimed that universal subsidies were inefficient, ineffective and a form of regressive taxation (Audit Commission, 1989). They were perceived to generate artificially high levels of demand among groups who could afford to take responsibility for their own consumption and they had demonstrably failed to attract the disadvantaged groups for whom they were intended. For example, commenting on the fact that the proportion of professional people who participate in sport regularly is about twice that of unskilled manual labourers, the Audit Commission (1989: 10) said that, 'across the board subsidies have a perverse effect from a redistributional perspective. Many poorer people are, through their rates, paying to subsidise the pastimes of the rich.'

More tellingly, given our concerns with the supposed wider social impacts of sports participation, the Audit Commission (1989: 7) strongly criticized the widespread lack of monitoring and evaluation:

> Many authorities do not have a clear idea of what their role in sport and recreation should be ... only a minority ... can demonstrate their achievements in terms of numbers of people participating or increases in participation ... even those which place great emphasis on social objectives have only qualitative evidence to demonstrate their achievements.

Such analyses led to the more general policy of Compulsory Competitive Tendering (CCT) being applied to local authority sport and recreation services. This required them to compete to retain the management of their facilities (on the presumption that this would lead to increased economic efficiency and a greater customer focus), while retaining control of strategic policy and methods of implementation (pricing, programming) (Coalter, 1995). Despite the lack of clarity as to the precise role of public provision for sport as a component of social citizenship, reaction to the extension of CCT to sport and recreation services was almost uniformly negative. Bramham *et al.* (1993) argued that welfare rights were being replaced by consumer rights (see also Aitchison, 1992; Clarke, 1992; Ravenscroft and Tolley, 1993). Ravenscroft (1993: 42) argued that public leisure provision (largely sport and recreation services) had ceased to be a constituent part of a liberal democratic model of freedom and had become 'a *central feature* [emphasis added] of a deeply divisive process of constructing a new citizenship, one in which the politics of choice has been replaced by the politics of means'.

However, such responses largely ignored the relative failure of local authority sport and recreation services to cater for disadvantaged groups. Second, the 'defence of welfare' position was based on oversimplified assumptions about the nature of constraints on participation in sport and cultural activities. Although it must be acknowledged that entrance charges are one component of the sport participation decision, research suggests that they have a relatively small influence – cultural capital may be more important than financial capital (Coalter, 1993; Gratton and Taylor, 1995). From an economics perspective Gratton and Taylor (1985) suggest that the failure of supply-side subsidies to attract lower income groups in proportion to their number in the population indicates a basic 'marketing failure', i.e. many of those who do not use publicly provided facilities are not 'constrained' or 'excluded' – they simply do not wish to use them. For example, in England in 2002, in the four weeks before interview, 58 percent of higher professionals took part in at least one activity (excluding walking), compared to 29 percent of those in routine occupations (Sport England, 2005). Such persistent differentials raise important issues for later policies of 'sport and social inclusion', whose success depends on achieving a basic necessary condition of increased participation in sport by many socially marginal and consistently 'under-participating' groups.

The introduction of CCT, with the associated need to produce detailed contract specifications to provide the basis for monitoring performance, also marked a broad shift from the rather vague approach of management by objectives ('catering for the sporting needs for the community'; 'contributing to the community's quality of life') to objective-led management. This was welcomed by the Sports Council (1990: 1), saying that 'CCT presents local authorities with the opportunity to precisely define what service they are seeking to provide for their communities'. However, a large-scale evaluation of this aspect of CCT concluded that there was a widespread failure to formulate quantifiable, non-financial performance measures, largely because of a lack of previous monitoring information and absence of sports strategies to provide a framework for such targets (Coalter, 1995). More critically, Walsh (1991) suggested that competition had illustrated the lack of adequate management information and information services. Bovaird (1992) suggested that the new-found emphasis on objective-led management was largely symbolic, reflecting a need to establish a legitimating myth that leisure departments have a sense of direction and an explicable rationale for their actions! Nevertheless, throughout the 1990s, performance measurement became an increasingly important issue – culminating in New Labour's concerns with evidence-based policy-making and outcome measurement (see below).

Sports policy: a lottery?

Although the replacement of Margaret Thatcher by John Major in 1990 did not lead to a substantial change in the broader neoliberal policies, it led to a more proactive approach to sport, an area of strong personal interest to Major and one which articulated closely with his more traditional view of Conservatism. His ability to pursue this interest was facilitated by what Henry (2001: 92) refers to as a 'masterstroke in terms of leisure policy' – the establishment of the National Lottery in 1994 – which 'allowed the Conservative government to both decrease tax-driven subsidy and to increase financial support for sport, the arts and heritage'. This ensured large sums of money becoming available (by 1999 over £1 billion had been allocated to sport), although Henry (2001) argues that because access to Lottery funding was based on a bidding process and some degree of matched funding, it clearly did not address issues of needs-driven welfare spending.

Major published the first strategy for sport since 1975: *Sport: Raising the Game* (Department of National Heritage, 1995). Policy was formulated within a traditional, one-nation, Conservative discourse, emphasizing sport's role in reinforcing heritage, nationhood and national pride (Henry, 2001). In his introduction, Major stated that, 'sport is a central part of Britain's National Heritage ... a binding force between generations and across borders ... one of the defining characteristics of nationhood and local pride'. This was reflected in a focus on 'traditional sports' in school and elite sport. However, such sports were not only important because of their contribution to nationhood and pride, but also because of their character-building effects (Department of National Heritage, 1995: 2) because 'competitive sport teaches valuable lessons which last for life. Every game delivers both a winner and a loser. Sports men [sic] must learn to be both.'

Despite such collective and individual sporting outcomes, the document downplayed the equity issues implied by the, now discarded, slogan of 'sport for all' and effectively ignored the central role of local government in promoting social citizenship and mass participation. Issues of nationhood and national pride underpinned the major element of the initiative – elite sport – with Major arguing that 'sport at the highest level engages the wider community' (Department of National Heritage, 1995: 2). To combat what was perceived as the relative decline in Britain's international sporting performance it was proposed to establish a Lottery-funded British Academy of Sport on the Australian model (Green, 2004). Despite Major's electoral defeat in 1997, the emphasis on school sport and elite development was adopted by the New Labour government of Tony Blair. However, because of a desire to find a new or 'Third Way' to address social and economic problems, sport was to achieve a new, more clearly articulated, prominence in social policy.

New Labour and 'active citizenship'

The election of a New Labour government in the UK in 1997 placed sport more centrally on the broader social policy agenda, largely because of the presumed externalities, or benefits, associated with participation. Further, the nature of its contribution was stated more precisely and systematically than had ever been done before. For example, *Policy Action Group 10* (DCMS, 1999: 23) stated that 'sport can contribute to neighbourhood renewal by improving communities' performance on four key indicators – health, crime, employment and education'. Even more precisely and ambitiously, the Scottish Office (1999: 22) stated that:

> Arts, sport and leisure activities … have a role to play in countering social exclusion. They can help to increase the self-esteem of individuals; build community spirit; increase social interaction; improve health and fitness; create employment and give young people a purposeful activity, reducing the temptation to anti-social behaviour.

Although this may look like a more precise statement of the recreation *as* welfare policies of the 1970s and 1980s, the underpinning socio-political philosophy of New Labour ensured that such policies moved beyond their previous rather ad hoc and often rhetorical status. The presumed link between sport and 'active citizenship' was to be made much more explicit.

The increased emphasis on the potential of sport is explained by the nature of New Labour's agenda. The desire was to create a 'Third Way' between the perceived failures of previous Labour governments' policies of state control, state provision and anti-individualism and the Thatcherite neoliberal, free-market policies and extreme individualism. The Third Way – between the state and the market – is a relatively amorphous term which draws on a number of sources: the communitarian ideas of Etzioni (1993), Putnam's (1993, 2000) concepts of social capital, Hutton's (1995) notions of a 'stakeholder' society and, most prominently, the writings of Giddens (1998). The Third Way represents an attempt to modernize and reform all aspects of government, to strengthen civil society, to address issues of 'social exclusion' and to encourage 'active citizenship'. For example, in 1999 Tony Blair (quoted in Keaney and Gavelin, n.d.: 2) asserted that part of New Labour's mission was 'to create a modern civic society for today's world, to renew the bonds of community that bind us together'. Room (1995) argues that, whereas previous welfare policies were distributional, based on a largely economic concept of 'poverty', the new concerns of policies to combat social exclusion were relational – identifying the issues in terms of inadequate social participation, lack of social integration and lack of power. In this regard Giddens (1998: 104) states that social exclusion is 'not about gradations of inequality, but about mechanisms that act to detach groups of people from the social mainstream'. This perspective resulted in an increased policy emphasis on social processes, relationships and the organizational capacities of communities (Forrest and Kearns, 1999).

In policy terms the formal definition of social exclusion was provided by the Social Exclusion Unit (1998) as being a shorthand label for a combination of linked problems of unemployment, poor skills, low income, poor housing, high crime environment, bad health and family breakdown. As the above policy statements from Policy Action Group 10 and the Scottish Executive illustrate, it was increasingly assumed that sport had a significant contribution to make to the solution of several aspects of social exclusion.

However, policies addressing issues of social exclusion are not simply about social (or sporting) participation and the strengthening of communities. There is also a parallel emphasis on accountability and responsibility (Le Grand, 1998), summed up in the concept of 'active citizenship'. Although Giddens's (1998: 66) Third Way values include such social democratic values as protection of the vulnerable, freedom and equality, they also assert a belief that there are 'no rights without responsibilities'. Consequently, the emphasis on community and social inclusion is accompanied by an emphasis on 'active citizenship' and personal responsibility – to work or seek to work, to provide for family, to behave responsibly, to take responsibility for personal health, to contribute to the solution of community problems and so on. The emphasis on both personal and civic responsibility is illustrated by the then Home Secretary David Blunkett's (2001) desire to find a way to empower people in their communities in order to enable them to provide answers to contemporary social problems.

Such thinking recasts central assumptions about the nature and role of welfare provision and its purpose. It marks a shift from a traditional notion of 'passive welfare', in which citizens consumed benefits and services as of right, to one of 'active citizenship' in which these benefits are rewards, or at least viewed in terms of their ability to assist people to become active and responsible citizens. This shift in attitudes to welfare is symbolized in the renaming of Unemployment Benefit (a right) as Job Seeker's Allowance (the exercise of personal responsibility). White (1998) has argued that most social inclusion policies are 'employment-centred', aimed at increasing the employability of the socially excluded, providing employment opportunities and encouraging civic responsibility (Levitas, 1996). Holtham (1998) argues that New Labour's commitment not to raise tax or government spending meant that efforts had to be confined to helping the relatively small proportion of the population who were most at risk of being 'excluded', but who also accounted for a very high proportion of the most visible social problems, such as crime. The solution was not simply bigger handouts, but helping them to find work. Collins and Kay (2003: 22) quote a Department of Social Security (1998) document, stating that the government's aim is to rebuild the welfare state around work and conclude that underpinning such policies is 'the belief that work will provide the income, status and self-esteem and thereby make recipients into active citizens, exercising their political and consumer rights' – again, participation in sport might be both an affirmation of citizenship and (more importantly) a means of helping people to find employment and a more complete citizenship.

The historically asserted potential of sport's ability to address wider social issues was restated and reinforced by a broader change in social policy. In New Labour's agenda all institutions of civil society, and certainly those in receipt of public funding, are regarded as having the potential to contribute to the agenda of social inclusion and active citizenship – reflecting a key New Labour mantra about the reduction of departmentalism and the encouragement of 'joined up government'.

In this regard Kearns (2004: 4) suggests that one of the appeals of the concept of social exclusion was that 'it provides a potential route to achieving coherence across government programmes, so that all parties see that their efforts are contributing to an overriding objective'. Kearns (2004) suggests that the related concept of social capital has a similar attraction. Broadly speaking, the concept of social capital is taken to refer to various social and moral relations that bind communities together. Communities deemed to be 'high' in social capital are ones with strong community networks and civic infrastructure, an active citizenry, a strong sense of local identity and solidarity and norms of trust and mutual support. These issues will be examined in more detail in Chapter 4, but here it is sufficient to note that the attraction of this concept is that evidence seems to suggest that communities high in social capital tend to have a number of positive aspects: lower crime rates, better health and lower rates of child abuse. As issues relating to social inclusion and social capital are clearly not the property, or goal, of any single government department, such concepts provide central government with a cross-departmental outcome measure that can be viewed as strategic and holistic. Second, social capital is a phenomenon that individual government departments can adopt as an objective, enabling all to 'sing from the same hymn sheet' (Kearns, 2004). In such circumstances all institutions of civil society have the potential to contribute to this broader social inclusion, active citizenship and social capital agenda. For example, the concepts of active citizenship and social capital clearly inform Scottish Office (1999: 5) claims that 'people who participate in sports and arts activities are more likely to play an active role in the community in other ways'.

In a similar vein, Policy Action Group 10's (DCMS, 1999: 5) action plan for sport and the arts stated:

> Participation in the arts and sport has a beneficial social impact. Arts and sport are inclusive and can contribute to neighbourhood renewal. They can build confidence and encourage strong community groups. However, these benefits are frequently overlooked both by some providers of arts and sports facilities and programmes and by those involved in area regeneration programmes.

Consequently, such political and funding circumstances served to revive and reinforce sport's traditional claims about its ability to provide an 'economy of remedies' (Donnison and Chapman, 1965) to a variety of social problems. Although a convincing case could be made that such policies were simply more coherent statements of approaches developed in the early 1980s (Rigg, 1986; Houlihan and White, 2003), sport's ability to articulate with core Third Way concepts provided a much greater degree of legitimation and apparent integration. Houlihan and White (2002: 2) suggest that sport development 'is normally at the margin of the government's field of vision' being 'located in a sector of government activity that is crowded with services that are both relatively resource rich and politically heavy' (e.g. education, health, foreign policy, social services). While this is clearly so, the predominance of 'cross-cutting' policy concepts such as social inclusion and social capital provided sport with a historical opportunity to suggest that it had the ability to at least complement others' efforts and make some contribution to overarching policy objectives. In fact, given the dominance of this agenda, it has been impossible for government departments, non-departmental public bodies (e.g. Sports Councils) and those in receipt of public funding to ignore it – funding became increasingly dependent on an organization's ability to illustrate (at least theoretically) their contribution to the social inclusion agenda.

Within sports policy it is claimed that this agenda marks a shift from the traditional welfare approach of developing sport *in* the community, to seeking to develop communities *through* sport (Coalter *et al.*, 2000; Houlihan and White, 2002). In New Labour's social inclusion agenda the test of effectiveness shifted from the equity-oriented 'sport for all', to what Richard Caborn, Minister of Sport, referred to as 'sport for good', as sport is called upon more systematically to provide an economy of remedies to a variety of social problems. The extent of this shift is indicated by Caborn's statement to the 2003 conference of the Central Council for Physical Recreation (the UK convention of governing bodies of sport), that 'we will not accept simplistic assertions that sport is good as sufficient reason to back sport'. Of course, this political attitude to sport is not new. In 1983 Denis Howell, the first Labour Minister of Sport, stated that 'if sport doesn't have a social role … it would be irrelevant. If sport is servicing the people of the country … it must take account of the changing nature of the social challenges which we all have to face' (quoted in Coalter *et al.*, 1988: 70). However, in Howell's era, sport's contribution was much more ad hoc and not related systematically to a broader integrating vision of the type provided by the social inclusion, social capital and 'joined up government' agendas.

However, increased emphasis on an instrumental, externally driven, approach to sports policy has not been confined to the UK. For example, Bloom *et al.* (2005) have undertaken a major review of the socio-economic benefits of sports participation for Sport Canada. The extensive review examined the effect of sports participation on health, skills development, social cohesion and economic performance, recommending a holistic approach to sport policy-making by linking it to wider areas of social policy. In Australia Driscoll and Wood (1999) undertook a project for Sport and Recreation Victoria examining the role and importance of sports clubs and 'sporting capital' to rural communities' experiencing substantial social and economic change. In Australia, where elite sports funding has dominated the agenda for decades, the Australian Sports Commission (2006: 3) felt the need to produce a consultative document, *The Case for Sport in Australia*, because 'the importance of sport as a means to achieve wider social, health economic and environmental outcomes has been increasingly recognised by the Australian Government and others over recent years'.

In the United States of America, Crompton (2000: 65–6) has argued for the need to 're-position' leisure services by identifying their public benefits, because

> Providing resources to a leisure department so a minority of residents can have enjoyable experiences is likely to be a low priority when measured

against the critical economic, health, safety and welfare issues with which most legislative bodies are confronted.

In fact the presumed potential of sport to address a range of issues has been embraced by the United Nations. For example, in November 2003 the General Assembly of the United Nations adopted a resolution affirming its commitment to sport as a means to promote education, health, development and peace. It also agreed to include sport and physical education as a tool to contribute towards achieving the internationally agreed development goals, including those contained in the United Nations Millennium Declaration. Under the collective term of 'sport-in-development' UN agencies such as UNICEF have actively explored the use of sport to achieve some of the eight millennium goals, including the promotion of universal primary education, promoting gender equality and empowering women, combating HIV/AIDS and addressing issues of environmental sustainability – even contributing to world peace (see Chapter 5).

However, accompanying this new, more systematic, emphasis on the social role of sport there has been an increased, general, concern with evidence of effectiveness. In the UK New Labour has placed an emphasis on 'evidenced-based policy-making', value for money, 'welfare effectiveness' and outcome evaluation of various forms of public investment. I will examine the implication of these issues in detail in Chapter 3. However, here it is worth examining briefly the often unarticulated logic underpinning the widespread claims being made about sport's contribution to a variety of policy agendas (many of which are the subject of detailed examination in subsequent chapters in this book).

How does sport achieve the results?

The presumption that sport can help to address the multifaceted aspects of social exclusion (e.g. reduce crime, increase employability, improve health) and contribute to community development and social cohesion implies that participation in sport can produce outcomes which strengthen and improve certain weak, or negative, aspects of processes, structures and relationships, or change negative behaviours thought to characterize deprived urban areas. Several writers have listed the structural and processual aspects of sport that are presumed to be able to produce a range of benefits, ranging from the psychological via the socio-psychological to the social (Svoboda, 1994; Keller *et al.*, 1998; Wankel and Sefton, 1994; Reid *et al.*, 1994; Collins *et al.*, 1999; Coalter *et al.*, 2000). In summary, the claimed potential benefits of participation in sport are:

- physical fitness and improved health;
- improved mental health and psychological well being, leading to the reduction of anxiety and stress;
- personality development via improved self-concept, physical and global self-esteem/confidence, self-confidence and increased locus of control;

- socio-psychological benefits such as empathy, integrity, tolerance, cooperation, trustworthiness and the development of social skills;
- broader sociological impacts such as increased community identity, social coherence and integration (collectively referred to as social capital).

As Figure 2.1 illustrates, the presumed social significance of these, mostly individual, positive outcomes is that, via resultant changes in attitudes and behaviour, they are assumed to lead to wider impacts (see also Coalter, 2002, 2006).

What might be termed as 'traditional sports development' was concerned largely with providing sufficient opportunities to achieve certain *sporting outcomes* and *impacts* – increased and more equitable participation and the development of sporting skills. From this 'sport for all' perspective, participation was usually the only measure of effectiveness (and even this basic information was rarely collected at project level) (Coalter *et al.*, 2000; Collins *et al.*, 1999). Such equity objectives are central to the new social inclusion agenda – if 'sporting inclusion' is to be achieved, the various underprivileged and at-risk groups need to participate in sport (Collins and Kay, 2003). However, as we are concerned largely with the nature and quality of evidence about the various impacts and outcomes supposedly associated with participation in sport, it is worth noting that, even at the most basic level, our understanding of the motivations underpinning sport is rather limited and rarely goes beyond correlations (see e.g. Sallis *et al.*, 2000; Foster *et al.*, 2005). The conclusion of a major systematic review of research on the psychological and

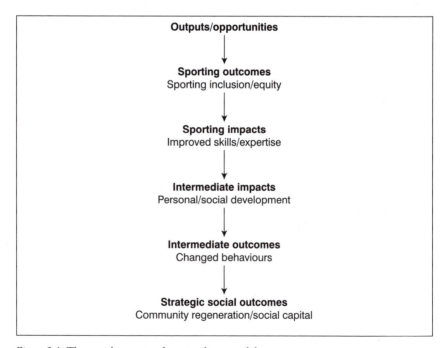

Figure 2.1 The social impacts of sport: a logic model

ecological factors relating to sports participation (Foster *et al.*, 2005: 2) was that there was 'insufficient high quality research evidence about the reasons why adults and young people do and do not participate'. More generally, other systematic reviews (e.g. Kahn *et al.*, 2002; Blamey and Mutrie, 2004) conclude that there is insufficient evidence to assess the effectiveness of a variety of interventions aimed at increasing physical activity.

However, participation is only a basic *necessary condition* for the achievement of the higher level social inclusion objectives, which shift the test of effectiveness to the *outcomes* associated with sports provision and participation As Figure 2.1 illustrates, the assumption is that participation will lead to *intermediate (individual) impacts* (e.g. improved fitness, increased sense of well being, improved self-efficacy and (maybe) self-esteem, the development of social skills). The presumed logic is that such impacts are then likely to lead to *intermediate outcomes* (i.e. changes in behaviour): decreased drug use, decreased anti-social behaviour, increased healthy lifestyle, improved educational performance, increased employability. In fact, following White's (1998) argument that most Third Way policies are 'employment-centred' (see also Levitas, 1996) the presumption seems to be that sport can improve participants' employability by contributing to such factors as their improved heath, increased self-confidence, improved social (and maybe administrative and technical) skills. Again, participation in sport might be both an affirmation of, and means via which to obtain, citizenship. More vaguely, the accumulation of such behaviours, plus the more general impact of an improved and active local sports infrastructure (clubs, organizations) will produce *strategic social outcomes* such as increased social capital, community cohesion and social regeneration.

Some or all of these presumed outcomes have always been implicit in the ideology of sport and in policy rationales. However, they have rarely been articulated systematically, and even less frequently monitored and evaluated. For example, in an analysis of 180 items on sport and social exclusion, Collins *et al.* (1999: 3) found only 11 studies had 'anything approaching rigorous evaluations and some of these did not give specific data for excluded groups or communities'. In a review of 120 programmes for at-risk youth in the USA, Witt and Crompton (1996a) found that 30 percent undertook no evaluation and only 4 percent undertook pre/post evaluation of participation-related changes. Of course, this is not a problem restricted to sports research, as Oakley *et al.* (2005: 12) report that in one major social science review only 2.5 percent (78) of the 3,180 references located for five reviews could be classified as methodologically sound evaluations of interventions providing clear outcome data. An even smaller proportion (1.2 percent) was 'sound' evaluations of effective interventions. Consequently, Bloom *et al.* (2005: preface), examining the socio-economic benefits of sport participation in Canada, concluded that

> there is relatively little empirical knowledge about the way sport participation benefits Canadians through its impact on health, education, social cohesion and the economy. As a result, policy-makers lack the evidence required to

make informed policy decisions and to connect sport issues to other policy priorities.

As is implied by the logic outlined in Figure 2.1, there are many methodological difficulties in measuring such presumed impacts and outcomes. Even where intermediate impacts can be measured (and attributed to participation in sport), the relationship of these to intermediate outcomes (i.e. changed behaviour) presents substantial difficulties. For example, Taylor (1999) suggests that the major problem in identifying and measuring the effects of sports participation on crime is that this influence (if it is effective) is essentially indirect, working through a number of intermediate processes, such as improved fitness, self-efficacy, self-esteem and locus of control and the development of social and personal skills. Consequently, in most cases it is misleading to argue that 'sport' reduces crime, or leads to improved educational performance. Such issues are compounded by the difficulties in controlling for intervening and confounding variables which will also influence attitudes and behaviour, the difficulties of undertaking longitudinal analysis and the precise definition and measurement of desired outcomes. At its most basic the majority of sports development programmes do not have the resources or expertise to undertake such evaluations and, because of short-term funding, rarely last long enough to have a realistic chance of achieving measurable and lasting change (Collins *et al.*, 1999).

However, Coalter *et al.* (2000) argue that the absence of systematic evaluation can also be explained partly by the apparent theoretical strength, coherence and widespread acceptance of the description of sports' potentially (for some inevitable) positive contributions – the combination of the mythopoeic nature of sport and a policy desire for relatively cheap and apparently convincing solutions leads to the potentially positive benefits of sport being regarded as almost inevitable outcomes of participation. As Long and Sanderson (2001) illustrate, such a belief in the possibilities of sport is maintained in the absence of robust confirming evidence – a mixture of belief and theory, professional and personal repertoires, political and organizational self-interest and ad hominem arguments permits the assumption of such outcomes. About 20 years ago Glyptis (1989: 153), commenting on local authority sports schemes for the unemployed, wrote that 'virtually all provision has been based on the basis of assumed need and presumed benefit ... in the field of sport and the unemployed there is a danger that assumptions have already been enshrined as conventional wisdom'.

For whatever reasons, in the new environment of evidence-based policy-making and an emphasis on effective investment in welfare, sport seems to lack systematic evidence for many of its claimed externalities. For example, in 2002 the Department of Culture Media and Sport and the Strategy Unit of the Cabinet Office (2002) published *Game Plan*, a broad ranging evaluation of some of the claims made for sport. Game Plan claimed to find robust evidence only for sport and physical recreation's contribution to fitness and health, concluding that the range of other claims were 'not proven' (e.g. crime reduction; economic impact of mega events; improved educational outcomes) and stated that 'the evidence base needs to be strengthened to enable policy makers to construct and target effective interventions' (DCMS and Strategy Unit, 2002: 79).

This analysis was also shared in less dramatic terms by the DCMS and Home Office (2006: 14) report *Bringing Communities together through Sport and Culture*, which concluded that 'too much work using sport [is] still focused on output rather than outcome', with the Office of the Deputy Prime Minister (2004: 36), in a report exploring issues of sport and neighbourhood renewal, suggesting that 'links between sport and regeneration are not clearly expressed or understood, [and there is a] ... frequent failure to evaluate or monitor outcomes from sporting activities properly'.

However, in addition to a perceived absence of robust evidence about various physical, physiological, psychological and sociological outcomes supposedly associated with sports participation, there is also a widespread lack of even more valuable evidence relating to *sufficient conditions*: the type of sports and the conditions under which the potential to achieve the desired outcomes are maximized. Svoboda (1994) argues that presumed positive outcomes are 'only a possibility' and a direct linear effect between simple participation and effect cannot be assumed. Coalter *et al.* (2000: 85) in a wide-ranging review of the social and economic impacts of sport concluded that there was 'a widespread lack of empirical research on outcomes, and more importantly, *the mechanisms and processes* via which they are achieved (especially in "real life" situations)'.

Patriksson (1995: 128) outlines this concern by stating:

> The point is that sport has the potential both to improve and inhibit an individual's personal growth. The futility of arguing whether sport is good or bad has been observed by several authors. Sport, like most activities, is not a priori good or bad, but has the potential of producing both positive and negative outcomes. Questions like 'what conditions are necessary for sport to have beneficial outcomes?' must be asked more often.

It could be argued that while politicians desire descriptive (and simple) evidence of outcomes, policy-makers and practitioners require an understanding of sufficient conditions – the *processes* or mechanisms via which the potential of sport can be maximized – in order to increase their ability to design and manage programmes to increase their potential effectiveness. We turn to issues of evidence and process in Chapter 3.

Standing up and being counted

Historically, public investment in sport has been characterized by a dual purpose: to extend social rights of citizenship and to use sport to address a wide range of social issues. As Harrison (1973) argues, whereas social reform requires increased freedoms, moral reform requires new constraints – in public policies for sport, as in other areas of social policy, rights and responsibilities are always present. However, until the last decade, the ability of sport to address such wider social issues was largely taken for granted. Various combinations of a general absence of a culture of performance definition and evaluation, the mythopoeic status of sport, the apparent theoretical strength of claims about sport's benefits, a view of sport as a relatively cheap and simple solution to social problems and sport's general marginal policy status (Houlihan and White, 2002) resulted in a widespread failure to monitor and evaluate sporting investments (which were always small in comparison to mainstream policy areas).

However, the advent of New Labour, with its Third Way concerns with civic renewal, social inclusion, active citizenship and social capital, placed sport (and other forms of voluntary and civic activity) on a broader policy agenda. This was reinforced by an emphasis on joined-up government and a desire for all areas of public investment to contribute to strategic policy goals. This was also accompanied by notions of evidence-based policy-making and outcome-oriented welfare effectiveness. In such circumstances the relatively untested claims of sport's wider social role came under much closer scrutiny. It is to these issues that we now turn.

3 Sport and social impacts

Do we need new rules?

Evidence-based policy-making

As outlined in Chapter 2, the new importance of sport in social policy has been accompanied by an emphasis on measurement, evaluation and effectiveness. The broad shift from the vague and imprecise management by objectives (e.g. 'catering for the sporting needs of the community') to objective-led management (defining measurable targets) that had begun with CCT has been reinforced. Further, with CCT being replaced by Best Value, the emphasis shifted from output-led to outcome-based evaluation. Emphasis was placed on *welfare effectiveness* and, most importantly, the contribution that all services make to so-called *cross-cutting agendas* – health, crime, social and economic regeneration and education.

Solesbury (2001: 7) suggests that New Labour had a pragmatic, non-ideological stance and in terms of policy the watchword was 'what matters is what works'. To ensure welfare efficiency and effectiveness and to maximize the chances of achieving desired outcomes, policy interventions should be based on evidence drawn from relevant successful interventions. For example, the White Paper, *Modernising Government* (Cabinet Office, 1999: 16) stated:

> This Government expects more of policy makers. More new ideas, more willingness to question inherited ways of doing things, better use of evidence and research in policy making and better focus on policies that will deliver long term goals.

This new emphasis is encapsulated in the phrase *evidence-based policy-making* and led to a number of organizations being established to accumulate and disseminate evidence about the efficacy of practice – in health there is the National Institute for Clinical Excellence (NICE) and the NHS Centre for Reviews and Dissemination; in education the Centre for Evidence-informed Education Policy and Practice (EPPI Centre) and the Association of Directors of Social Services has established a research in practice initiative (Solesbury, 2001). In sports policy several research reviews were commissioned by government and public organizations to examine the evidence for sport's claimed wider impacts and to identify 'good practice' models as a basis for policy: *Sport and Social Exclusion* (Collins et al., 1999); *Policy*

Action Team 10: Report to the Social Exclusion Unit – Arts and Sport (DCMS, 1999); *The Role of Sport in Regenerating Deprived Urban Areas* (Coalter et al., 2000 for the Scottish Executive); *Game Plan* (DCMS and Strategy Unit, 2002); *The Benefits of Sport* (Coalter, 2005, for sportscotland) and the establishment of an on-line research-based Value of Sport Monitor by Sport England and UK Sport (www.sportengland.org). Although this new emphasis appears to have been strongest in the UK, similar reviews were published in Canada (Bloom et al., 2005) and Australia (Australian Sports Commission, 2006).

The intent of the sports-related reviews was to inform an evidence-based approach, in which accumulated research evidence would inform sports policy, provision and practice in a range of areas. However, as discussed in Chapter 2, the overall conclusion of these reviews was that there was a general lack of robust research-based evidence on the outcomes of sports participation, leading Bloom *et al.* (2005: preface) to conclude that, 'as a result, policy-makers lack the evidence required to make informed policy decisions and to connect sport issues to other policy priorities'.

Others went further and suggested that not only do we lack systematic measurement of outcomes, but also an understanding of '*the mechanisms and processes* via which they are achieved (especially in "real life" situations)' (Coalter *et al.*, 2000: 85; see also Patriksson, 1995). In Weiss's (1997) vivid phrase, much (sports) policy and practice has been, and continues to be, not 'aim, steady, fire', but 'fire, steady, aim'! (See Figure 3.1 for the contrast between the theory and practice of evidence-based policy-making (especially in sport).)

But if it works, how does it work?

However, Pawson suggests that, even if these reviews of research had produced systematic and methodologically robust evidence of a range of positive outcomes, this would not have solved the issue relating to evidence-based policy and practice because 'evidence, whether new or old, never speaks for itself. Accordingly, there is debate about the best strategy of marshalling bygone research results into the policy process' (Pawson, 2001a: 2). Pawson (2001a) identifies two main

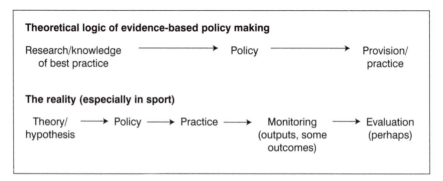

Figure 3.1 Contrast between theory and practice

approaches to marshalling evidence to inform policy – meta-analysis and narrative review – but suggests that they both have significant limitations for informing policy and practice. Although most of the reviews undertaken to inform sports policy are narrative reviews, it is worth briefly outlining Pawson's analysis of both approaches, as it serves to illustrate the demands which evidence-based policy-making has made on researchers, the dilemmas posed and the nature of the often unexamined assumptions made about evaluating policy interventions. This also provides the basis for exploring Pawson's (2001b, 2006) alternative – realist synthesis – a perspective that has important implications for understanding the strengths and limitations of much of the research reviewed in this book.

Meta-analysis

Numerical meta-analysis (or systematic reviews, or research synthesis) seeks to provide a 'summary of summaries' (Pawson, 2001a: 7) of research on a *family of programmes* targeted on a specific issue (e.g. the contribution of sport to cognitive development or educational achievement; the contribution of sport to the reduction of cardiovascular disease; the role of sport in crime reduction). This is achieved by compiling a database of existing research (usually based on specified and rigorous methodological criteria (e.g. randomized control trials), classifying each project on the basis of mode of delivery, examining each for some numerical measure of impact (the net effect of the intervention, such as increased educational scores) and undertaking an overall comparison by calculating the 'typical' impact of such programmes (the mean effect). In areas of relevance to sports policy this has been used most widely in medical/scientific areas such as fitness and physical and mental health, but it has also been used in the area of research into sport and cognitive development or educational performance (Etnier *et al.*, 1997). Such approaches seek to identify the 'stubborn empirical generalisation' so beloved by politicians – e.g. school sport causes improved educational performance – and thereby identify the 'best buy' in policy terms (Pawson, 2001a: 6).

The emphasis is on numerical measures of outcomes (Pawson, 2001a), e.g. correlations between participation in sport and reduced crime; between sports participation and educational achievement. In this approach methodology tends to be the key arbiter. For example, Etnier *et al.* (1997), reviewing the evidence relating to the relationship between physical activity and educational performance, found that the largest measured relationships are obtained from the weakest research designs and the weakest relationships are found in the most robust research designs. Jackson *et al.* (2005) in a systematic review entitled *Interventions Implemented through Sporting Organisations for Increasing Participation in Sport*, used highly restrictive selection criteria, including randomized and cluster controlled trials, quasi-randomized trials and controlled before-and-after studies. They could find no relevant studies and concluded:

> There is an absence of high quality evidence to support interventions designed and delivered by sporting organisations to increase participation in

sport. Interventions funded and conducted in this area must be linked to a rigorous evaluation strategy in order to examine overall effectiveness, socio-demographic differentials in participation and cost-effectiveness of these strategies.

(Jackson *et al.*, 2005: 2)

Of course these comments could apply to most areas of social research and not just to sports research. For example, Oakley *et al.* (2005: 12) refer to the results of more general systematic reviews in social science which 'confirmed those of health research in showing that better designed studies were generally less likely to demonstrate effectiveness. In other words poor study design and over-optimistic results tended to be linked.' Nevertheless, such findings are partly a function of the methodological criteria applied and the associated definitions of robust evidence and illustrate the tension between the need for rigour and the need for practical guidance for policy and practice.

Because of the emphasis on methodological rigour and measured outcomes, vitally important issues of process and context are largely ignored. In fact, Pawson (2006) argues that the approach, based on a medical model, is concerned solely with the effects of the *treatment* (e.g. participation in sport) and ignores various other potentially relevant factors, or seeks to include studies which have controlled for them (e.g. via random allocation; control groups). The result is that such an approach implies that programmes (or treatments) have powers – *sport* reduces crime; *sport* leads to increased educational performance. Consequently, significant issues are downplayed or effectively ignored. For example, Blamey and Mutrie (2004: 748), reviewing research on physical activity promotion, conclude that 'trying to combine results from interventions and evaluations that have used varying methods is difficult and can sometimes mask the reasons why projects have been successful or not'. Others regret that the application of rigorous methodological criteria leads to the inevitable ignoring of the wider 'world of evidence' (Faulkner *et al.*, 2006: 120), such as the cultural context of programmes, programme diversity and, most importantly, processes and mechanisms and participants' reactions (Oakley *et al.*, 2005).

As Pawson (2001a) argues, the problem is that it is quite possible for a programme to work well with one type of subject, but not with another. For example, sports programmes may have different impacts on the behaviour of petty thieves and habitual criminals, or those who favour team and competitive environments compared to those who prefer non-competitive, individual activities, or those most susceptible to sport's values.

It is worth noting that such concerns have also been expressed by medical researchers (where systematic reviews are widely used). For example, Roth and Parry (1997: 370, quoted in Faulkner *et al.*, 2006: 118) argue that such an approach tends to concentrate on a 'circumscribed set of questions and issues related to outcomes rather than process and to efficacy rather than effectiveness', by which they mean that what works in a clinical trial setting might not be what works (or is needed) in typical clinical practice setting. In similar terms, Blamey and Mutrie (2004: 742) suggest that, in relation to increasing levels of physical activity, the concentration on the efficacy and effectiveness of interventions has led to 'limited knowledge of how such programmes can be generalised to wider populations, settings and organisations'.

In other words, different processes and differential effects are lost in aggregation and the reduction of analysis to mean effects. For example, Fox (1992: 35) reviewing the impact of primary school PE programmes on children's self-esteem, while reporting a generally positive effect, states 'unfortunately, mechanisms for these changes have been difficult to isolate'. He quotes Sonstroem (1984) who argues 'at this time it is not known why or in what manner exercise programmes affect self-esteem, or which people are responsive' (Fox, 1992: 35). More generally, Papacharisis *et al.* (2005: 247) sum up the issues by stating that 'there is nothing about ... sport itself that is magical ... It is the experience of sport that may facilitate the result.'

As we will see in subsequent chapters, there is an emerging recognition that, rather than simply measuring outcomes (itself a very difficult task), what is required is a better understanding of process – which sports work for which subjects in which conditions (Patriksson, 1995; Coalter *et al.*, 2000)? These remain some of the key unanswered questions in many areas of sports research.

Narrative reviews

Pawson's (2001a) second approach – narrative reviews (or descriptive analytical method) – seeks to address the issue of process and has been the approach adopted in recent sports-related reviews (Collins *et al.*, 1999; Coalter *et al.*, 2001; Australian Sports Commission, 2006). Like meta-analysis, the aim is to examine a family of programmes in the hope of finding those particular approaches which are most successful. Pawson (2001a: 18) suggests that this approach has 'a slightly more pronounced explanatory agenda, being more likely to try to identify *why* interventions were successful. The approach is often to identify examples of "best practice", or "exemplary programmes for an honourable mention".'

This leads to attempts 'to extract enough of the "process" of each programme covered so that the "outcome" is rendered intelligible' (Pawson, 2001a: 14). Of course, this best practice approach has a long history in sports policy. It has been reflected in the policy of demonstration projects long favoured by Sports Councils in the UK, in which short-term investment is used to illustrate the value of certain approaches, which can then be adopted by local authority providers. The narrative review attempts to describe enough of the process of delivery to permit an understanding of the outcomes and how they were achieved. A key aspect of this approach is that programmes – e.g. sports provision for young people at risk – are not regarded as something with causal powers. Rather, the narrative review seeks to adopt 'a configurational approach to causality' (Pawson, 2001a: 16) in which the outcomes are regarded as resulting from a particular set or combination of factors, and that these will almost certainly vary between apparently similar programmes. This has been recognized in commentaries about sports research (although rarely reflected in policy rhetoric). For example, Svoboda (1994: 15) suggests that positive outcomes from sports participation are 'only a possibility' and a direct linear effect between simple participation and effect cannot be assumed. He argues that such factors as supervision, leadership or management will affect outcomes, as well as the nature and type of sporting activity (for similar positions see also Sugden and Yiannakis, 1982; Sports Council Research Unit NW, 1990; Nichols and Taylor, 1996; Witt and Crompton, 1996a).

However, Pawson (2001a) notes a series of limitations with narrative reviews. First, the process of information extraction is necessarily selective and, as social interventions and associated processes are descriptively inexhaustible, few research reports, research reviews or academic articles (the main source of information) will contain all relevant information. In other words, this approach is almost wholly dependent on published material and the decisions of authors, editors and the funders of research about the significance of issues for inclusion. In this regard Thornton and Lea (2000) refer to a general 'publication bias' and Oakley *et al.* (2005: 12) report that because of 'reporting deficiencies ... applicability and generalisability were limited by scant information'. Biddle *et al.* (2004: 689), in a review of school-based interventions to increase physical activity among young people, state that 'the extant literature did little to improve understanding of what kinds of programmes or what aspects of programmes bring about health gains or valued outcomes'.

Second, in most areas of social intervention learning from failure is as important as learning from success. However, it is rare for negative results to be published. The potential significance of this is emphasized by Sibley and Etnier (2003: 253), who in examining the relationship between physical activity and cognition in children conclude that 'studies with null results are often not published ... which typically leads to a positively biased effect size being found for published studies'. More generally, there may be a reluctance to publish negative results on the part of public agencies operating in vulnerable and dependent areas and under pressure to deliver short-term outcomes – such as sport (Houlihan and White, 2002).

Third, most narrative reviews seek to identify 'exemplary programmes' (good practice) on the basis of 'proximal similarity' (Shadish *et al.*, 1991). This involves identifying the various attributes which appear to make a programme successful (e.g. locally recruited leaders; non-competitive sports; voluntary and often casual attendance; positive relationships between leaders and participants; and so on) in order to provide the basis for the design of similar programmes. However, Pawson (2001a) argues that this approach is rarely possible, as switching a programme to another location will entail possibly significant changes in infrastructure, practitioners and the nature and receptiveness of target participants. We will return to this question of outcomes, evidence and policy in the last section of this chapter. Such issues, of course, have significant implications for the various narrative reviews and material reviewed in later chapters in this book.

Before turning to Pawson's proposed solution, it is worth considering some of these issues in relation to sport.

Sport's wider social role: ill-defined interventions with hard-to-follow outcomes?

Pawson (2004) has argued that a wide range of social policy interventions can be characterized as 'ill-defined interventions with hard-to-follow outcomes'. This could also serve as the broad conclusion to be derived from the various UK-based sports-related reviews, which concluded that the definitions of desired outcomes were very vague and extremely ambitious (often encompassing most aspects of the social inclusion agenda). One possible explanation for this is provided by Weiss (1993), who emphasizes the essentially political nature of much policy formulation, resource bidding and programme development. Weiss (1993: 96) argues that,

> Because of the political processes of persuasion and negotiation that are required to get a program enacted, inflated promises are made in the guise of program goals. Furthermore, the goals often lack the clarity and intellectual coherence that evaluation criteria should have ... Holders of diverse values and different interests have to be won over, and in the process a host of realistic and unrealistic goal commitments are made.

This is in part aided by the mythopoeic and metaphorical nature of discussions about sport (see Chapter 2). Such attitudes, and the apparent theoretical strength and coherence of claims about sport's positive contributions, in part explain the widespread failure to undertake systematic evaluation of presumed outcomes – theory permitted the assumption of outcomes. The narrative reviews' general conclusion is that the policy-relevant research base is underdeveloped, with few robust and detailed examples of 'best practice' on which to base policy and, more importantly, practice. A typical finding is that of West and Crompton (2001) who, in a review of 21 North American outdoor recreation programmes aimed at reducing recidivism, found a widespread absence of clear statements of rationale and associated theory about the presumed relationships between participation, changed attitudes and changed behaviour (see also Collins *et al.*, 1999; Witt and Crompton, 1996a).

Most of the reviews found that, although externalities have been a major rationale underpinning sports policies, their definition has been vague (e.g. a wide range of actual and potential behaviours are encapsulated by the notion of 'anti-social behaviour', or young people 'at risk'), with limited monitoring and little rigorous evaluation. Where monitoring had been undertaken it was often restricted to descriptive *output* measures – classes provided, coaches trained, numbers of participants attracted. More generally, in relation to projects to promote physical activity, Blamey and Mutrie (2004: 750) conclude that 'the vast majority of physical activity service provision has gone unmeasured in terms of behaviour change and health impact'. Although some of the narrative reviews provide descriptive case studies, their utility is limited because of restricted nature of the outcome measures used and a widespread lack of real detail on process. Of course, the absence of monitoring and evaluation is also explained by more pragmatic factors, such as limited funding and the short-term nature of many of the projects. In such circumstances the available resources and time are committed to setting up the project, with projects often too short-term to have measurable effects (Collins *et al.*, 1999), or there was a lack of monitoring and evaluation expertise (or enthusiasm) among staff.

However, claims for sport's impacts are wide-ranging and operate at a variety of different levels – physiological, psychological, socio-psychological, behavioural, social and societal. Each of these areas of research is characterized by different methodological traditions and criteria for the validity and reliability of evidence. Therefore it is worth briefly considering some general methodological issues relating to the definition and measurement of sport's presumed effects and the subsequent lack of robust research to provide the basis for the identification of 'exemplary programmes' (detailed consideration will be provided in relation to each area in the relevant chapters).

Is it logical?

Some of the general methodological issues related to providing the evidence for sport's impacts can be illustrated via Figure 3.2, which provides a broad outline of the theoretical logic underpinning the assumption that participating in sport leads to certain outcomes.

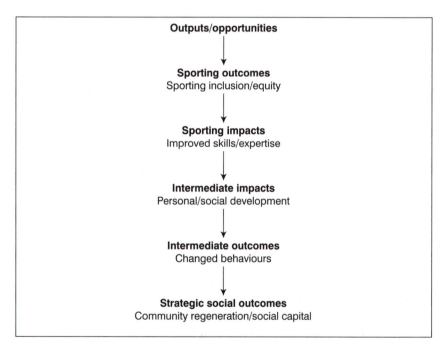

Figure 3.2 The individual and social impacts of sport: a logic model

The first thing to notice about Figure 3.2 is that, as we move from the top to the bottom, the presumed effects become more indirect, difficult to define and measure and increasingly difficult to attribute solely to sport. Measuring *sporting outcomes* – the effectiveness of a programme in attracting relevant target groups – is straightforward in terms of methods (and is usually where the so-called evaluation of traditional sports development programmes stopped). Nevertheless, it is surprising how frequently this is not done (Coalter *et al.*, 2000; Collins *et al.*, 1999). Even when these data are collected they are often deficient in a number of ways. For example, in a series of case studies, Coalter *et al.* (2000) found:

(i) The recording of attendances (visits), rather than people (visitors), leads to a non-calculable overestimate of the number of participants from relevant communities.

(ii) There was no record of frequency of attendance, with no data about the level and intensity of participation, nor the commitment of participants – all factors which influence the impact of participation on such outcomes as fitness, health, attitudes, diversion from drugs and reduction in social isolation. More generally, in relation to programmes to promote increased physical activity Blamey and Mutrie (2004) conclude that there is a lack of information about dose, intensity and duration of interventions.

(iii) There was a widespread lack of longitudinal monitoring to assess adherence to programmes, or the extent to which any short-term measured changes in attitude or behaviour are sustained over time.

As Figure 3.2 illustrates, the assumption is that participation in sport will lead to certain *sporting outcomes*, such as improved fitness and the development of certain skills and felt competences. In turn the logic assumes that these changes will result in broader, more generalizable, intermediate *impacts*, such as increased self-efficacy, self-confidence, sense of well-being, improved self-esteem and social skills (see Chapter 6 for more detailed analysis). The general theory underpinning such programmes is that these intermediate impacts are likely to lead to *intermediate outcomes* (i.e. changes in behaviour), such as decreased drug use, decreased anti-social behaviour, increased healthy lifestyle or improved educational performance. The accumulation of such behaviours, plus the more general impact of improved sporting infrastructure (clubs, teams, volunteers), will produce *strategic social outcomes* such as increased social capital, community cohesion and social regeneration (see Chapter 4). However, as with any social processes, such impacts and, especially, outcomes are 'only a possibility' (Svoboda, 1994: 15) and the search for the 'stubborn empirical generalisation' remains illusive. It cannot be assumed that any, or all, participants will automatically obtain the presumed benefits in all circumstances, or that changes in attitudes and perceptions will necessarily lead to sustained changes in behaviour. Such impacts and outcomes remain only a possibility for a variety of reasons.

(i) Participation in sport is just one of many things that people do. Therefore its impact will depend on the relative salience of the experience compared to other influences. For example, Hastad *et al.* (1984) found that the extent of sports participation had little effect on deviancy, with more important influences being the nature of deviant associates, peer status and personal values.

(ii) The definition and nature of 'participation' is crucial and is rarely articulated in either policy statements or programme aims. The impact of participation in a sports programme will be influenced by such factors as the frequency and intensity of participation and the degree of participants' adherence over time. Although these factors are obviously important for fitness and health benefits, they also have clear implications for the development of values, attitudes, skills and behaviour.

(iii) The nature and extent of any effects will depend on the nature of the experience, i.e. the process. Sport is not a homogeneous, standardized product or experience. This diversity is illustrated by the acceptance by all UK Sports Councils of the all-encompassing definition of sport contained in the Council of Europe's European Sports Charter (quoted in Sport England, 2004: 3):

Sport means all forms of physical activity which, through casual or organised participation, aim at expressing or improving physical fitness and mental well-being, forming relationships or obtaining results in competitions at all levels.

There are individual, partner and team sports; contact and non-contact sports; motor-driven or perceptually dominated sports; sports which place differing emphases on strategy and physical skills and sports can be both competitive and non-competitive. Consequently, in terms of producing sporting outcomes, intermediate impacts and intermediate outcomes, it is best to regard sports as a series of different *social relationships* and *social processes*, in which it is assumed that certain types of learning, or socialization, may occur (Svoboda, 1994; Coakley, 2003). From this perspective, following Patriksson (1995) and Pawson (2001a), the key analytical issues relate to which sports and sports *processes* produce which *outcomes* for which *participants* and in which *circumstances?*

(iv) It is usually difficult to disentangle the effects of participation in sport from parallel social influences and developmental and maturational processes. Care needs to be taken in measuring *intermediate impacts* and assuming that these are 'sports-effects' in some straightforward way. Consequently, there are difficult issues relating to intervening and confounding variables. For example, it is possible that maturational processes, increasing social commitments, or wider social pressures may explain a change in young people's attitudes. A related issue is that sports programmes aimed at crime reduction are increasingly working in collaboration with other agencies (e.g.

youth or education services). In such circumstances it is almost impossible to isolate specific sports-effects.

(v) Even if participation in particular types of sports assists in the development of certain types of competence, confidence, efficacy and attitudes for certain types of people, this cannot simply be taken to imply that these will be transferred to *intermediate outcomes* (changed behaviour). For example, Taylor (1999) argues that the major problem in identifying and measuring the effects of sports participation on crime is that this influence is indirect, working through a number of intermediate impacts or processes, such as improved fitness, self-esteem, self-efficacy and locus of control and the development of social and personal skills. Consequently, in most cases it is misleading to argue that *sport* reduces crime, or leads to improved educational performance. Rather, the contention is that sports may in certain circumstances lead to the development of certain dispositions which may, in certain circumstances, lead to a reduction of anti-social behaviour or improved educational performance among certain individuals.

(vi) As participation in sport is mostly a matter of choice, the difficult issue of self-selection is usually present. It is possible that sport may attract particular types of people who are susceptible to sport's impacts, with those deemed to be most in need of the experiences (either from a personal or community perspective) being the least likely to participate. For example, Keller *et al.* (1998) argue that the process involved is not simply a matter of values learned in sport being transferred, but suggest that individuals need to be receptive to the positive attitudes and values on offer, with the norms and values acquired in different areas of life being mutually reinforced. In other words, some people will have a propensity to accept the supposedly positive values and attitudes deemed to be inherent in sport and others will not. The issue of self-selection (and simple reinforcement) is a central dilemma in research on the nature of relationships between sports participation and educational performance, where there is a major methodological issue relating to the direction of cause. For example, are those who are educationally successful also those who are attracted to sport or does participation in sport lead to improved educational performance? Widespread deficiencies in research design mean that this is still a relatively open question (see Chapter 6).

Such difficult methodological issues do *not* provide an argument against the potential efficacy of sport, simply that it will have differential impacts on different participants and that these are rather difficult to measure. As we will see, the issue of *how* and *in what circumstances* sports programmes work is a matter of conjecture and debate in many areas, such as the precise nature of its contribution to physical self-worth, self-efficacy and self-esteem and their relationship to such things as cognitive development, educational performance and crime reduction. However, these issues return us to Pawson's (2006) proposed third approach to addressing the central issues of evidence-based policy-making.

It's not what you do, but the way that you do it

Much policy discourse relating to sporting and sport-related outcomes ignores the vitally important distinction between *necessary conditions* (i.e. participation in (any) sport) and *sufficient conditions* (the conditions under which the potential outcomes are achieved). Clearly, participation in sport (however defined) is a *necessary condition* to obtain any of the potential benefits – a not inconsiderable problem as many of the persistently low participation groups are among those included in the new social inclusion agenda.

Solely outcome-based evaluations are unable to *explain* either success or failure – the 'how and why?' questions. Despite the policy rhetoric, sport (however defined) does not have causal powers. We have already noted Pawson's (2001a) argument for a configurational approach to causality, in which outcomes can only be understood as a result of the interaction of a particular combination of circumstances – a particularly important issue given the heterogeneity of sports, sports' experiences and the various target groups included under the rubric of the 'socially excluded'. In other words, there is a need to stop generalizing about such a heterogeneous, summative, concept as sport and examine issues relating to types of sport and how they are delivered and experienced (Patriksson, 1998).

However, although the narrative review methodology acknowledges such issues, Pawson (2001a) argues that there is a major limitation related to the limited nature of published data on programme processes. Indeed, Pawson (2006: 27) suggests that, as programmes are open and active interventions dealing with 'active subjects', there are real limitations on our capacity to fully grasp the complexity of the social processes involved. Further, in terms of policy prescription, he argues that it is rarely possible to replicate programmes because of the context-specific nature of a range of factors (e.g. infrastructure, practitioners, the nature and receptiveness of participants).

Tacon (2005) summarizes the hierarchy of approaches by referring to Scriven's (1994) categorization as follows:

- black box evaluations in which the researcher concentrates on a programme's outcomes, but does not analyse its contents;
- grey box evaluations which explore the contents, but do not fully reveal the principles of operation;
- white box evaluations which address effects and the inner workings, connections and operations of programme components. The white box is Pawson and Tilley's (2000) realistic evaluation, or Pawson's (2006) realist synthesis.

Pawson's (2001b, 2006) *realist synthesis* is closely allied to the assumptions informing narrative reviews, but seeks to address the widespread issue of insufficient information and limitations on generalizability. The realist synthesis is 'not an evaluation technique, but a framework' (Pawson, 2001b: 3). Like narrative reviews it assumes a *generative approach* to causation, with outcomes being a function of the relationships and interactions between the programme content and processes and the participants' responses and choices. Consequently this approach entails examining available information to answer Patriksson's (1998) question about 'what conditions are necessary for sport to have beneficial outcomes?'

Of course, the implication that outcomes are essentially contingent (i.e. not guaranteed) raises difficulties for policy-making and investment strategies. However, a partial solution is provided by the approach to *generalization*, because 'the policy community is not offered a "best buy" … but a tailored, "transferable theory" – (this programme theory works in these respects, for these subjects, in these kinds of situations)' (Pawson, 2001b: 4). This approach shifts the focus from families of programmes (sports projects) to *families of mechanisms*, with the key issue being the assumed programme *mechanisms* which underpin policy-makers' and providers' investment decisions and presumably vaguely inform the design and delivery of the programme. The key idea of theory-based evaluation is that policy-makers' and programme providers' beliefs and assumptions underpinning any intervention can be expressed in terms of a 'programme theory' – a sequence of causes and presumed effects (Weiss, 1997). Not only does this approach seek to describe actual mechanisms, but it 'aims to surface the theoretical underpinnings of the program in advance and use the theories to help structure the evaluation' (Weiss, 1997: 510).

> Theory-based evaluation … allows … an in-depth understanding of a working of the program or activity – the 'program theory' or 'program logic'. In particular it need not assume simple linear cause-and-effect relationships … . By mapping out the determining or causal factors judged important for success, and how they might interact, it can then be decided which steps should be monitored as the progress develops, to see how well they are in fact borne out. This allows the critical success factors to be identified.
>
> (World Bank, 2004: 10)

For example, the various arguments that participation in sport can lead to a reduction in the propensity to commit crime seem to be based on a varying mixture of assumptions about sport's ability to address certain (largely male) adolescent development needs for adventure, excitement, autonomy and identity formation and provide a context for young people at risk to mix with more positive adult and peer role models. In doing so it produces a series of sport-related intermediate impacts, such as improved cognitive and social skills, reductions in impulsiveness and risk-taking behaviour, improved self-esteem and self-confidence, increased locus of control and self-discipline and improvements in education and employment prospects. It works most effectively via voluntary participation in relatively small groups, in less competitive and task-oriented environments, with quality leadership providing a number of 'protective factors' (e.g. adult support and affirmation). In certain circumstances a 'sport plus' approach might be necessary, with the various additional, complementary, programmes dealing more systematically with core personal development issues. Leaving aside for the moment the key question about the extent to which any of these lead to reduced criminality (see Chapter 7), the realist's issue for investigation is the extent to which particular types of sports provision contain such components and processes and the extent to which these work with certain subjects (e.g. types of offender) in particular circumstances. It is worth noting that such concerns about programme mechanisms do not relate simply to the more traditional social uses of sporting intervention: crime reduction, educational achievement, social cohesion. As we will see, concerns about mechanisms are also evident in areas such as the presumed economic impact of sporting events and the nature of assumptions underpinning the use of economic multipliers (Chapter 8).

This need for a theory-driven approach to assessing the effectiveness of interventions has been highlighted by some sports researchers (Coalter et al., 2000; Coalter, 2002; Nichols and Crow, 2004; Tacon, 2005, 2007). Although it has not been systematically or widely developed, it is implicit in the evaluation of much research examined in this book, either via the attempt to identify the various components of programmes, or by an admission that there is a need to go beyond correlations and develop a more sophisticated understanding of processes and interaction of components.

From a policy perspective, the significance of an approach based on programme theories is that it requires sports policy-makers, providers and managers to articulate much more clearly and precisely the nature of their assumptions about sports programmes. They need to consider how participation in their specific sports programmes (i.e. not 'sport') is presumed to lead to specific intermediate impacts and then to broader intermediate outcomes (although in terms of programme theories, the easier questions relate to intermediate impacts, i.e. individuals' changed attitudes and competences). Interestingly, Weiss (1997) also raises the distinct possibility that different actors in the process of policy formulation and programme delivery may have different theories about how their shared desired impacts and outcomes are to be achieved (for an example of this see Long and Sanderson, 2001). In such circumstances she argues that a theory-based approach has the potential to enable policy-makers, administrators and practitioners to 'work through their differences and agree on a common set of assumptions about what they are doing and why ... [so that] they can increase the force of the intervention' (Weiss, 1977: 517).

Do we know what game we are playing?

We have already noted that the definition of desired outcomes is often extremely vague and lacking in intellectual coherence (Weiss, 1993; Coalter et al., 2000; Collins et al., 1999; West and Crompton, 2001). This lack of precision means that significant programme content and design issues are rarely addressed and it poses major problems for any attempted evaluation of effectiveness, usually precluding comparison between projects. However, this is a problem which is not restricted to sport. For example, Bonner (2003), in attempting a realist evaluation of a Learning Communities Project, found that 'the projects struggled to state their aims or that their objectives were over-ambitious and unlikely to be reflected in outcome measurement' (quoted in Tacon, 2005: 24). Rossi *et al.* (2004: 134–5) argue that:

> Sometimes the political contexts within which programs originate do not permit extensive planning but even when that is not the case, conventional practices for designing programs pay little attention to the underlying theory. The human service professions operate with repertoires of established services and types of intervention associated with their respective speciality areas. As a result, program design is often a matter of configuring a variation of familiar 'off the shelf' services into a package that seems appropriate for a social problem without a close analysis of the match between those services and the specific nature of the problem. [However] a program's rationale and conceptualisation … are just as subject to critical scrutiny within an evaluation as any other important aspect of the program.

In this regard it should be noted that the realist synthesis approach requires information about both successful and unsuccessful interventions that appear to be based on similar assumptions and forms of provision. However, because of various combinations of academic conventions and political and policy pressures, details of failed programmes are rarely published, and even more rarely are the causes for failure analysed. Provocatively, Weiss (1997: 506) suggests that 'because so many programs have failed to show success, much program theory is undoubtedly wrong'!

A clear understanding of desired impacts and outcomes and the associated processes of participation should inform provision and enable an approach based on managing for outcomes – i.e. understanding how to design and deliver programmes in order to maximize the possibility of the achievement of the assumed impacts. This requires the adoption of an approach based on a *theory of change* (Granger, 1998), or programme theory (Weiss, 1997). The notion of a theory of change relates to such (usually unexamined) questions as:

- Why do we assume that participation in sport (or, more precisely, a particular type of sport) can have certain impacts on certain types of participants and communities?
- What are the properties and processes of participation in a specific sports programme that lead to such outcomes?
- Can we define clearly the theory of the relationship between participation in the specific sports programme and a range of intermediate impacts (e.g. increased self-efficacy; increased physical self-worth; increased self-esteem; increased self-confidence)?
- A much more difficult question relates to a theoretical understanding of how, and to what extent, such achieved changes will result in changed behaviours (reduced criminal behaviour; improved educational performance; reduction or cessation of drug use).

This last point relates to the crucial question about the extent to which programmes are designed and delivered on the basis of an understanding of the complex causes and nature of the problems which they seek to address (Rossi *et al.*, 2004): anti-social behaviour, crime, educational under-achievement, low self-esteem, lack of community cohesion. These issues need to be addressed, because such understanding is essential to the selection of relevant forms of provision – certain sports and forms of provision may be better than others for achieving relevant intermediate impacts with particular subgroups (see Chapters 6 and 7).

This theory-based, programme mechanism, approach is allied closely to the use of logic models which serve to demonstrate the nature and logical order of the assumptions concerning conditions for programme effectiveness and provide a frame of reference for evaluations of the programme (US Dept of Health and Human Services, 1999). However, a logic model approach can also strengthen claims for some degree of causality. An approach which systematically outlines the programme theory and mechanisms (where possible, based on prior research), ensures that the programme is delivered consistently as intended and monitors and evaluates as much of the programme as possible, will provide some basis for estimating both actual and potential programme impacts and outcomes which, for a range of reasons, may be very difficult to measure. Weiss (1997) suggests that theory-based evaluation seeks to specify the mechanisms by which change is achieved and not just the activities or characteristics which are associated with change. She hints at the wider methodological potential, by stating that such an approach 'can track the unfolding of events, step-by-step, and thus make causal attributions on the basis of demonstrated links. If this were so, evaluation would not need randomized control groups to justify its claims about causality' (Weiss 1997: 154).

In terms of the new emphasis on evidence and effectiveness, such an approach provides the basis for *process monitoring* and evaluation, rather than the much more limited outcome measurement. Space precludes a full exposition of the nature of process monitoring, but its importance is indicated by Mukoma and Flisher's (2004: 356) contention that 'programmes are seldom delivered exactly as designed and planned ... without detailed process evaluation we can only infer that perhaps the implementation did not occur as expected'. Or, as Pawson (2006: 31) puts it, 'all interventions are conditioned by the action of layer upon layer of contextual influences ... such contingencies represent the greatest challenges to evidence-based policy'.

Further, if process monitoring is participatory, it develops a greater ownership and understanding of the theoretical basis of the programme by those delivering it, leading to more integrated and coherent programmes. It also permits a more grounded analysis of the dynamics of local realities and resources (some of these issues will be dealt with in more detail in Chapter 5 on sport-in-development).

It is clear that the above issues are of vital practical importance to sports policy, provision, programme design and management. The conclusion from many of the areas considered in the rest of this book is that there is a need for better understanding of the processes of sports participation which lead, or do not lead, to desired policy outcomes. These issues relate not simply to attempts to advance academic knowledge, but also to improve practice and, perhaps most importantly of all, to understand the strengths and limitations of the claims that can be made for 'sport'.

As this book is centrally concerned with the issues raised by the increased rhetoric of evidence-based policy-making, we finally turn to a brief consideration of the role of researchers, the nature of evidence and their relationship to policy-making.

A rational exercise that takes place in a political context

Although there are strong academic, policy and management arguments for more rigorous approaches to monitoring and evaluation, there are also important questions relating to the degree of rigour and evidence required to inform policy – what is the relationship between an academic desire for methodological rigour and theoretically informed interventions and the more pragmatic, and political, world of policy? For example, Matarasso (1998: 5) refers to the problems associated with measuring the social impacts of public libraries and admits that they make such work unsatisfactory from a theoretical research perspective. However, he argues for the value of this limited data by suggesting that

> the decision-making processes of public administration, like the civil courts, depend on the balance of probabilities rather than the elimination of reasonable doubt ... in so far as research of this kind can inform policy, the evidence of social impact is at least as sound as that which informs most other areas of public service.

However, political scientists have gone beyond this 'weak evidence' perspective to suggest that there is a danger in the naïve assumption that 'by providing "the facts" evaluation assists decision-makers to make wise choices about future courses of action' (Weiss, 1993: 94). In this regard Solesbury (2001) warns against the danger of academic researchers confusing research with evidence and believing that only academic research counts in policy and decision-making. Echoing Weiss's (1993: 94) comment that 'evaluation is a rational exercise that takes place in a political context', Solesbury (2001: 9) argues that

> public policy is developed and delivered through the use of power ... There sometimes seems to be a tension between power and knowledge in the shaping of policy ... Emphasising the role of power and authority at the expense of knowledge and expertise in public affairs seems cynical; emphasising the latter at the expense of the former seems naïve.

Weiss (1993) points out that the programmes which researchers seek to evaluate are not neutral experiments, but are the products of political decisions and, in sport as in many other areas, are often the product of complex negotiations and partnerships (often as important as the programmes that they deliver). Perhaps this explains John Maynard Keynes's view that 'there is nothing a government hates more than to be well-informed; for it makes the process of arriving at decisions much more complicated and difficult' (quoted in Solesbury, 2001: 7). As we have already noted, such political considerations and compromises can lead to 'inflated promises [with] goals lacking the clarity and intellectual coherence that evaluation criteria should have' (Weiss, 1993: 96). In such circumstances evaluation evidence of (vague) programme outcomes has to compete for attention with other factors that carry weight in the political process – which will include the political and professional investment in previous policy decisions and the political and economic costs of changing policy (the dreaded U-turn). In these circumstances Weiss (1997: 98) suggests that political-benefit analysis may be more important than cost-benefit analysis and that

> If an evaluator also assessed a program's effectiveness in meeting political ends – such as showing that the administration is 'doing something' or that the program is placating interest groups or enhancing the influence of a particular department – he [sic] might learn more about the measures of success that decision-makers value.

Within this context Weiss (1993: 96, 98) explains something that consistently disconcerts researchers and raises even more complex issues about 'evidence':

> Programs can and do survive evaluations that show dismal failure to achieve goals... . A considerable amount of ineffectiveness may be tolerated if a program fits well with prevailing values, if it satisfies voters, or if it pays off political debts.

In addition to more general institutional political factors, there are also issues relating to the values, attitudes and interests of various established professional groups. Reflecting Rossi *et al.*'s (2004) identification of the importance of professionals' repertoires of established services and preferred types of intervention, Solesbury (2001: 8) asserts that

> in practice evidence is more plural than research ... [and] most professions also have shared norms, values, ideas in good currency, sometimes articulated and made explicit, often tacit. With ideas in good currency, provenance may be quite unknown. Their power lies, dangerously, in their conventionality; 'everybody knows that ...'.

It could be argued that the mythopoeic, metaphorical, status of sport is often reflected in a range of such professional, political and common-sense repertoires (or 'tacit knowledge'): everybody 'knows' that sport has positive benefits. The potential importance of such repertoires is illustrated by Weiss and Bucuvalas's (1980a) work among senior decision-makers in health services in the USA. They found that decision-makers used a series of frames of reference to assess both the 'truth' and the 'utility' of social science research. Although the quality of the research was a major concern, as was the congruence of findings with users' values and policy position, Weiss and Bucuvalas (1980a: 304) found that 'even more pervasive is the sense of conformity with what they already know – or believe they know'. Perhaps such perspectives serve to explain the increasing employment of consultants in many areas of policy research (including sport), as they are perceived to be more pragmatic and user-friendly than academic researchers, who are often viewed as inflexible and naïve about client needs.

Weiss and Bucuvalas (1980a: 305) suggest that the concept of the 'use' of social science research 'is an exceedingly ambiguous concept'. For example, Solesbury (2001) argues that New Labour's emphasis on evidence-based policy-making was not simply about welfare effectiveness, but also reflected a desire to challenge established repertoires and to strengthen its power and influence in such conservative institutions as the civil service. In this regard Weiss and Bucuvalas (1980a) found that their respondents made a distinction between their personal repertoires and the utility of research to challenge *institutional* policy and practice. This also raises the issue of research being filtered through a range of repertoires in the same policy area, or even a single organization – from programme managers and sports development officers keen to sustain the programme and their jobs, to senior policy-makers concerned to assess value for money and relative effectiveness, or to protect organizational positions and budgets.

With regard to the many ways to use research, it could also be argued that part of the increased emphasis on evidence of the long-assumed social benefits of sport has as much to do with the perceived low policy status of sport as it has to do with a desire to improve the effectiveness of welfare interventions. For example, Houlihan and White (2002) argue that sports development has mostly been subordinate to much more powerful policy communities (e.g. health and education) and, in general, it has been a policy-taker not policy-maker. Consequently, it could be argued that the social inclusion agenda is a mixed blessing, simply reinforcing this status – a shift away from the social democratic vision of 'sport for all' to a much more systematic and pragmatic emphasis on 'sport for good', starkly illustrated by Richard Caborn's (2003) assertion that 'we will not accept simplistic assertions that sport is good as sufficient reason to back sport'. The increased emphasis on evidence of effectiveness can also be viewed as part of the struggle to establish legitimacy in the eyes of established fields, dominated by high-status professionals and an accumulated body of systematic and 'scientific' knowledge, expressing scepticism about sport's claims. Interestingly, it is not always the case that policy areas with longer standing and higher status than sport, with a developed evidence-base, base practice on evidence. For example,

> Much primary care clinical activity, including the way care is organised, is unsupported by any substantial body of evidence. The primary care 'evidence gap' is not a single entity – it encompasses evidence gaps about implementation, effectiveness and applicability, as well as gaps in basic scientific knowledge.
>
> (Department of Health, 1999: 3)

Nevertheless, it is clear that sport's policy status increasingly depends on its ability to prove its cross-cutting value (or deliver the more easily measured elite sporting success). In such circumstances the requirement of realist synthesis (or knowledge in general) to learn from failure as well as success poses substantial dilemmas for a vulnerable policy area, under pressure to deliver short-term outcomes in a relatively short window of opportunity. In this regard Weiss (1993: 95) cautions that 'organisational vulnerability can become the dominant factor in determining what actions to take and the need to build and maintain support can overwhelm the imperatives to achieve program goals'.

These various considerations raise the question of the possible processes by which robust and sound research can influence the thinking of policymakers, bearing in mind that it may have to confront professional repertoires, political interests and established, but often vulnerable, vested interests. Most social scientists are wary of an

> 'instrumental/engineering approach' in which the parameters of the inquiry process are set narrowly. The aim is to solve the problem and both the problem and what constitutes a solution are defined by practitioners ... the inquiry and the knowledge sponsored by the model tend to be specific and concrete, rather than general and theoretical in character.
>
> (Hammersley, 1995: 126)

Such an approach accepts (and therefore affirms and legitimizes) the decision-makers' parameters of action, the loosely articulated premises underlying programmes (e.g. that sport can lead to improved educational performance), concentrates solely on the defined experimental variables and thereby implies that other elements outside the programme parameters are unimportant. In addition, the above analyses imply that even this type of research might have little effect, unless it has broader political, professional and public relations utility. More importantly, it would seem to be based on a mistaken view of how research enters the policy process.

Weiss and Bucuvalas (1980a) argue that there are very few 'big bang' moments in social policy, when a piece of research – a killer fact – overturns years of accumulated policies and practices. Because of the political, bureaucratic and interest-ridden nature of organizational decision-making processes, there are few examples of direct and immediate influence of research on decisions. Solesbury (2001) suggests that the results of research reach policy-makers and practitioners in diverse ways, but the diffusion of research into practice, especially in non-clinical and under-professionalized areas (such as sport), is a rather hit and miss affair. Weiss and Bucuvalas (1980b; quoted in Pawson and Tilley, 1997: 13) suggest that there is a long, gradual, cumulative process of 'knowledge creep', and describe the general pattern as:

> Diffuse and undirected infiltration of research ideas into [decision-makers'] understanding of the world ... [there are] few deliberate and targeted uses

of findings from individual studies. Rather they absorbed the concepts and generalisations from many studies over extended periods of time and they integrated research ideas ... into their interpretation of events ... [there was a] gradual sensitisation to the perspectives of social science.

This pattern leads them to suggest that a way forward is the adoption of an 'enlightenment' approach (Janowitz, 1972) which entails seeking to change policy-makers' understanding of both the strengths and limitations of social science research methodology and the wide range of possible uses of such research. Of course, as illustrated above, this will also require social scientists to understand better the world of the policy-makers. The enlightenment approach to engagement with policy-makers seeks to 'enrich and deepen understanding of the complexity of problems and the unintended consequences of actions' (Aaron, 1978: 166; quoted in Weiss and Bucuvalas, 1980a: 309).

Such an analysis returns us to theory-based evaluation, as both Weiss (1997) and Pawson (2006) propose that research and evaluation need to move away from simple outcome-based approaches, and not just because of their explanatory limitations. They argue that theory-based evaluation provides a potential basis for a partnership between researchers and policy-makers as it provides explanations, 'stories' of means and ends, and requires policy-makers and programme designers to explore the logic of their ideas and 'think harder and deeper about the programs they design' (Weiss, 1997: 517) and, very importantly, the nature of realistic outcomes.

In the area of sports policy such an approach would require politicians and policy-makers to move beyond the simplistic affirmations about 'sport-for-good' and articulate more clearly the nature of their assumptions about sports programmes: what type of participation is presumed to lead to what type of outcomes for what type of participant in what circumstances? More radically, to what extent can single service interventions realistically 'contribute' to the solution of complex, multidimensional, social problems? Of course, such an approach contains dangers, as it will inevitably lead to a clarification of the limitations of some of the claims for sport and challenge established repertoires and interest groups. For example, McDonald and Tungatt (1992: 33) argue that if sport is to be used to address broader issues of social inclusion, then sport may have to change because 'there is a danger that aims and objectives may incorporate many of the values that traditional sports provision stood for'.

As we will see in some of the chapters in this book, questions about process and the nature, organization and delivery of 'sport' are central to an understanding of the claimed outcomes (and a major element missing from much of the research on the social impacts of sport). Part of the mixed blessing of sport's involvement in cross-cutting policy agendas is that sport itself can no longer be taken as a given.

Final comment

This chapter has been about methodology rather than research methods, about ways of conceptualizing 'sport-for-good' programmes, rather than about how to collect information about them (some of these issues will be dealt with in subsequent chapters). It has sought to outline some basic issues confronting us as we seek to understand current research on the nature and extent of the wider social role of sport. It has outlined the logic of the assumptions about sport and the claimed personal and social impacts, highlighted the significant problems faced by researchers in many areas and provided a context for understanding current research findings and their potential strengths and limitations, Although not all of the issues raised apply equally to all areas of sports research, many aspects of research into the broader impacts of sport are at an early stage of development and, because of a wide diversity of definitions, programmes and research approaches, there is a weak cumulative research base. This has raised significant questions about the nature of research required, the rationale for such research – improving theory, understanding, policy, practice or status – and how it can be used to influence policy and practice. We will return to some of these issues in the final chapter of the book, but now we turn to an examination of many of these issues in detail in relation to a range of specific policy areas.

4 Sport and social regeneration

A capital prospect

The Third Way and active citizenship

As outlined in Chapter 2, the increased policy and political emphasis on sport in the United Kingdom can be explained by aspects of New Labour's agenda, its attempts to find a 'Third Way' between the state and the market and the centrality of concepts such as social inclusion, civic society and community and social regeneration. Whereas previous policies for addressing poverty were distributional, the concerns of policies to combat social exclusion are relational – a concern with inadequate social participation, lack of social integration and lack of power (Room, 1995). Giddens (1998: 104), the key theorist of the Third Way, states that social exclusion is 'not about gradations of inequality, but about mechanisms that act to detach groups of people from the social mainstream'. Forrest and Kearns (1999) argue that this perspective has resulted in an increased emphasis on social processes, relationships and the organisational capacities of communities. A core objective of the Third Way is to strengthen civil society, with Tony Blair (1999) stating that part of New Labour's mission was 'to create a modern civic society for today's world, to renew the bonds of community that bind us together' (quoted in Keaney and Gavelin, n.d.: 1)

However, policies of social inclusion and social renewal are not solely about simple social or sports participation and the strengthening of communities. There is also a parallel emphasis on accountability and responsibility (Le Grand, quoted in Halpern and Mikosz, 1998), summed up in the concepts of 'active citizenship' and 'no rights without responsibilities' (Giddens, 1998: 66). Consequently, the emphasis on community and social inclusion is accompanied by an emphasis on personal responsibility – to work or seek to work, to provide for family, to behave responsibly, to take responsibility for personal health, to contribute to the solution of community problems and so on. This emphasis on both personal and civic responsibility is illustrated by the then Home Secretary David Blunkett's (2001) desire to find a way to empower people in their communities – to assist them to become 'active citizens' – in order to provide their own answers to contemporary social problems.

Sport and active citizenship

Within this context the role of sport (and other aspects of leisure) has been emphasized. In England, Policy Action Group 10's action plan for sport and the arts stated that:

> Participation in the arts and sport has a beneficial social impact. Arts and sport are inclusive and can contribute to neighbourhood renewal. They can build confidence and encourage strong community groups. However, these benefits are frequently overlooked both by some providers of arts and sports facilities and programmes and by those involved in area regeneration programmes.
>
> (DCMS, 1999: 5)

The presumed link between sports participation and active citizenship is made even more explicit in the Scottish Office's (1999: 22) contention that 'people who participate in sports and arts activities are more likely to play an active role in the community in other ways'.

However, such statements illustrate a central ambiguity in the assumptions underpinning such policies: the direction of cause. In general, those most likely to participate in sport are from the higher socio-economic groups and have stayed in education after the minimum school-leaving age (Coalter *et al.*, 1995; Delaney and Keaney, 2005). This suggests that major aspects of 'social inclusion' come before and not as a result of participation in a single activity, such as sport. More generally, Warde and Tampubolon (2001: 11), using data from the 1999 British Household Panel Survey, illustrate that the likelihood of associational membership (which is central to this new agenda) is significantly increased by 'being male, being white, having more education, being of a higher social class [and] having greater personal income'. In a study of volunteering in Europe Gaskin and Smith (1995) note that, except in Sweden, there was a correlation between income and rates of volunteering. Consequently, the ability of certain activities and voluntary organizations to attract the 'socially excluded' may be more limited than is implied by policy rhetoric (a point strongly made about sport some time ago by McDonald and Tungatt, 1992). More generally, Skidmore *et al.* (2006: ix and xi), in research into the role of community participation in building networks, conclude that 'those already well connected tend to get better connected … community participation tends to be dominated by a small group of insiders who are disproportionately involved in a large number of governance activities'.

Once again it is possible to argue that policy has been formulated on misinterpretation of some evidence (*correlations* between sport and social participation), theoretical speculation (or wishful thinking) and the absence of robust research-based evidence. In part this has been recognized, with the DCMS and Home Office (2006: 14) report *Bringing Communities together through Sport and Culture*, concluding that, 'too much work using sport [is] still focused on output rather than outcome'. More fundamentally the Office of the Deputy Prime

Minister (2004: 36) suggested that 'links between sport and regeneration are not clearly expressed or understood'.

Another issue to consider is the regular failure of generalized discussions about sport and social regeneration to address issues of gender. Not only is female participation in sport much lower than male in all age groups, but women tend to participate in a narrower range of usually individualistic activities, which can often be combined with childcare – swimming, walking, keep-fit (Sport England, 2005; Coalter, 1999). Further, in terms of more general volunteering, men are much more likely to undertake voluntary work related to sport and recreation, with women more prominent in areas such as health, education and social services (although this varies between countries) (Delaney and Keaney, 2005; Lowndes, 2000). Consequently, the limited inclusivity of sport, especially among women in socially and economically deprived areas, raises significant questions for the nature and extent of sport's supposed role in strategies of social regeneration. I will return to issues of associational and sports club membership below, but first it is necessary to review the key summative concept that underpins much of this debate: social capital.

Social capital and social policy

The diffuse and contested concept of social capital is central to the social regeneration/social inclusion agenda. Its centrality to recent policy development is indicated by the range of UK government departments that have produced reviews of its nature, distribution and policy relevance (e.g. Performance and Innovation Unit, 2002; Office of National Statistics, 2001). Further afield, the Canadian Policy Research Initiative (2005) undertook a series of projects exploring the utility of social capital as a tool of public policy. Tony Blair's introduction to the Social Exclusion Unit's (2000: 5) consultation paper on neighbourhood renewal states that one of four imperatives is 'to revive and empower the community'. In this context, the document argues that reduced social capital is 'a key factor in decline' and that 'social stability and a community's ability to help itself' are built upon the 'vital resources of "social capital"' (Social Exclusion Unit, 2000: 24).

Although few sports policy documents explore the concept at length, these more general concerns are reflected in a broad shift from developing sport *in* communities to developing communities *through* sport (Coalter *et al.*, 2000; Houlihan and White, 2002). For example, Game Plan (DCMS and Strategy Unit, 2002: 60) refers to the use of sport in the community and elite success 'to build social capital'; the Central Council for Physical Recreation (CCPR) lobbied government for investment in sports clubs by asserting their contribution to the development of social capital (Nichols, 2003) and the concept clearly informs new community-oriented initiatives such as Sport England's (1999) *Active Communities* and *Bringing Communities together through Sport and Culture* and an increased emphasis on the social value of sports volunteering. However, the use of the concept of social capital in such documents is consistently vague, with no systematic attempt to articulate clearly its precise meaning and sport's role in its development.

Despite this, the policy attraction of even vague concepts of social capital is twofold. First, evidence seems to suggest that there is a correlation between communities high in social capital and a number of desired policy outcomes: lower crime rates, better health and lower rates of child abuse (Putnam, 2000). Second, Kearns (2004: 22–3) suggests that the (vague) concept of social capital contributes to New Labour's desire to reform central government by reducing departmentalism and encouraging 'joined-up government' – individual government departments can adopt it as an objective, enabling all to 'sing from the same hymn sheet'. Such policies enable and require sport to claim its contribution.

Whose social capital?

The concept of social capital is not new, with its roots in the classic concerns of sociology and political science with aspects of social cohesion and associational life (Portes, 1998; Field, 2003; Johnston and Percy-Smith, 2003; Farr, 2004). Although its meanings and relevance are disputed, a useful general definition of social capital is that it refers to social networks based on social and group norms which enable people to trust and cooperate with each other and via which individuals or groups can obtain certain types of advantage. Although Putnam's (2000) version is predominant in social policy in the UK, the broader academic debate concerns two additional theorists – Bourdieu and Coleman – although there are significant differences in their use of the term (related to their assumptions about the nature of society and social relationships).

First, Pierre Bourdieu's (1997b) concerns relate to the processes underpinning the reproduction of unequal access to resources, class-related patterns of educational achievement and the unequal distribution of power. Bourdieu is more widely known for his concept of *cultural capital*: forms of knowledge, skill, understanding and education rooted in the family 'habitus' which can be used to achieve success within a class-based educational system and serve to reinforce the social superiority of one group over another. Bourdieu (1986) viewed sport as a vehicle for expressing and reaffirming class differences – via class-restricted sports, or similar sports participated in at different locations with different social conventions (private tennis/golf clubs versus municipal courts/courses). He argued that the class distribution of various sports can be understood as a 'representation' of the wider social world and social classes' perception and appreciation of such factors as costs (economic, cultural and physical) and immediate or deferred physical and symbolic benefits linked to the positional value of each sport. This leads him to propose an instrumental view of sports and the associated 'social profits':

> One only needs to be aware that the class variations in sporting activities are due ... to variations in perception and appreciation of the immediate and deferred profits that they are supposed to bring ... in order to understand in its

broad outlines the distribution of these activities among the classes and class fractions. Everything takes place as if the probability of taking up the different sports depended, within the limits defined by economic (and cultural) capital and spare time, on perception and assessment of the intrinsic and extrinsic profits of each sport in terms of the dispositions of the habitus ...

(Bourdieu, 1986: 212)

Such a view of sport is clearly related to Bourdieu's (1997a: 51) less developed concept of social capital, defined as 'the aggregate of the actual or potential resources which are linked to a durable network of more or less institutionalised relationships of mutual acquaintance and recognition'.

Bourdieu's concept of social capital is related to both economic and cultural capital and is a means for maximizing the 'economic and social yield of academic qualifications' (Johnston and Percy-Smith, 2003: 323). Field (2003: 17) argues that, because of his central concern with the reproduction of various forms of inequality, Bourdieu views social capital as 'the exclusive property of elites, designed to secure their relative position'. As DeFilippis (2001: 801) puts it, 'people who realise capital through their networks of social capital do so precisely because others are excluded'. Most commentators agree that Bourdieu's treatment of social capital is instrumental, with individuals intentionally building such relationships for their own benefits (Portes and Landolt, 2000). In this regard it is interesting that one of Bourdieu's indicators of social capital is membership of golf clubs, especially their role in facilitating business networking and exchange – a conscious investment strategy, with the profits of membership of key (private) associations not being available to all (Field, 2003)

Bourdieu's conceptualization of social capital, largely ignored in sports policy discourse, has clear implications for general discussions of sport and social inclusion. Despite his rather structural approach to the issues, his analysis sensitizes us to the need to understand class-based 'perceptions and appreciations' underpinning the selection of sports and membership of associations. It sensitizes us to the importance of class and exclusion in the analysis of the functioning of some sports clubs and the dangers inherent in ignoring cultural boundaries that often divide communities via seeking to impose formulaic, mythopoeic, solutions on misconceived problems (Blackshaw and Long, 2005).

The second major modern theorist of social capital was Coleman (1988–9, 1994). Unlike Bourdieu, he did not view social capital as a positional good, the property or asset of certain social classes, but as a more ubiquitous resource. For Coleman social capital refers to mostly neutral aspects of social structure and social relationships which facilitate actions (Portes, 1998; Field, 2003), although like Bourdieu he stresses the conscious actions of individuals in the development and use of social capital. Coleman's main concerns relate to his interest in the community-based processes surrounding the development of human capital (education and employment skills and expertise) – something frequently emphasized in policy statements about the potential role of sport in social inclusion strategies. In this context social capital is:

the set of resources that inhere in family relations and in community social organisation and that are useful for the cognitive or social development of a child or young person. These resources differ for different persons and constitute an important advantage for children and adolescents in the development of their human capital.

(Coleman, 1994: 300)

Field (2003: 21) argues that because Coleman draws on individualistic rational choice theory, 'social capital was a means of explaining how people manage to cooperate, with it representing social processes resulting from the free choice of individuals to further their self-interest. Johnston and Percy-Smith (2003) illustrate that Coleman identified three aspects of relations of social capital: (i) obligations, expectations and trustworthiness of structures; (ii) information channels and (iii) norms and effective sanctions, which facilitate 'closure' of such networks and ensure that obligations are met and 'free-loaders' are expelled. The importance of sanctions and norms lies in the expectation of reciprocity and the fact that 'investment' is made not for altruistic purposes, but in the strong expectation that it will pay future dividends (see Leonard, 2004, for empirical evidence of this). Consequently, Coleman's concept of social capital has a strong element of closure, stability and social control. For example, Portes (1998: 10) notes that Coleman laments the decline of the 'close or dense ties' associated with 'primordial' institutions based on the family, and emphasizes the need to 'substitute obsolete forms of social control based on primordial ties with rationally devised material and status incentives'. In this regard, and in considering the presumed potential role of sports clubs, it is worth noting that Field (2003) suggests that this is accompanied by a distrust of 'constructed' forms of organization.

The final version of social capital is provided by Putnam (2000), who has dominated social policy debates. This places much less emphasis on kinship relations, closure, instrumentalism and more or less conscious choice. From this perspective social capital is viewed as an essentially neutral resource which is a property of collectives – communities, cities, regions. For Putnam (2000: 18–19), 'the core idea of social capital is that social networks have value ... [it refers to] connections between individuals – social networks and the norms of reciprocity and trustworthiness that arise from them'.

From Putnam's perspective social capital can be regarded as a public good, which serves to bind communities together. Communities with high levels of social capital are viewed as being characterized by three main components: strong social networks and civic infrastructure; strong social norms (i.e. informal and formal rules about personal and social behaviour and associated sanctions); and mutual trust and reciprocity among members of a community. Whereas Bourdieu and Coleman view social capital in terms of individuals and various types of social groups, Putnam's appeal to policy-makers is that he is more clearly interested in the role of organized voluntary associations. Putnam (2000) views the civic engagement, associational life and volunteering associated with social capital as important because they improve the efficiency of communities and societies by facilitating coordinated actions, reducing transaction costs (e.g. high levels of trust mean less dependency on formal contractual agreements) and enabling communities to be more effective in pursuit of their collective interests. In other words, social capital is not just a public good, but is *for* the public good (Szreter, 1998).

Putnam (2000) distinguishes between two types of social capital: bonding and bridging. The former refers to networks based on strong social ties between similar people – people 'like us' – with relations, reciprocity and trust based on ties of familiarity and closeness. Putnam (2000: 23) refers to this as a type of 'sociological superglue', whose function is to enable people to 'get by' and which works to maintain a strong in-group loyalty and reinforce specific identities. Putnam (2000) acknowledges that this can represent a 'dark side' of social capital, acting to impose conformity and downward levelling, excluding outsiders and may even be the basis for anti-social activities (e.g. the Mafia, urban street gangs). Bridging capital refers to weaker social ties between different types of people – more colleagues than family and friends. This is less of a glue than 'a sociological WD40' (Putnam, 2000: 23) and facilitates 'getting ahead' via, for example, the diffusion of information and employment opportunities (a central concern of the work-oriented social inclusion agenda). We will return to this distinction below, but here it is sufficient to note that the 'dark side is sidelined ... and Putnam's underlying belief is that social capital underpins a more productive, supportive and trusting society to general benefit' (Blackshaw and Long, 2005: 242).

The policy attraction of Putnam's version of social capital relates largely to a set of apparent correlations: that communities high in measured social capital (e.g. associational life, civic engagement, high levels of trust) seem to have a number of highly desired policy goals such as lower crime rates, better health and lower rates of child abuse. However, Johnson and Percy-Smith (2003: 327) refer to a degree of circularity in these arguments, with 'social capital being defined in terms of a set of characteristics which are then "measured" and taken as evidence that social capital does indeed (or does not) exist'. Portes (1998: 19) suggests that:

> As a property of communities and nations rather than individuals, social capital is simultaneously a cause and effect. It leads to positive outcomes, such as economic development and less crime, and its existence is inferred from the same outcomes. Cities that are well governed and moving ahead economically do so because they have high social capital; poorer cities lack this civic virtue.

More fundamentally, Portes (1998: 19) warns that 'equating social capital with the resources acquired through it can easily lead to tautological statements' – in other words networks can be 'resource poor': a significant issue for many socially excluded communities and one to which we will return.

Despite such reservations, Putnam's more civic version of social capital has been the most influential in establishing the broad parameters of the New Labour agenda about community renewal. This is largely because of its apparent promise of providing a solution to core aspects of the social inclusion agenda, such as active citizenship and community-based solutions to social problems.

Social capital: it depends where you look

It could be argued that much of the policy-led debate about social capital is somewhat one-dimensional, as it tends to be derived from an analysis of the supposed inadequacies of 'socially excluded communities', rather than Putnam's analysis of the reasons for the supposed decline of social capital. Most policy approaches seem to use a community-specific deficit model in seeking to strengthen aspects of community by a range of social interventions (including sport). However, such policies frequently ignore the wider social and cultural changes which Putnam (2000) identifies as contributing to the erosion of social connectedness and community involvement: suburban sprawl, commuting and related time pressures, television, home-based entertainment and 'privatisation' and the replacement of the post-war 'civic generation' by the increasingly disengaged and materialist 'baby boomers' and generation-X-ers.

Interestingly, Putnam points to a number of sports-related factors, which survey evidence suggests are worldwide phenomena (Coalter, 1999; van Bottenburg *et al.*, 2005; Zuzanek *et al.*, 2005): a decline in participation in traditional teams sports, the 'individualization' of sporting activity via increased emphasis on activities such as fitness suites, walking activities, a general decline in sports participation among young people (although not the older generation). However, despite the 'bowling alone' in the title of his seminal book, Putnam (2000: 111) states that 'virtually alone among major sports, only bowling has come close to holding its own in recent years. Bowling is the most popular competitive sport in America.' Further, it is more inclusive than most other sports in terms of age and social class, with more Americans bowling than ever before. In case readers regard bowling as a trivial example Putnam (2000: 113) reminds them that 'ninety-one million Americans bowled at some point during 1996, *more than 25 per cent more than voted in the 1998 Congressional elections*' (emphasis in original).

However, for Putnam the important issue is the changed nature of, and processes involved in, such participation, with a substantial decline in *organized* league bowling and the growth of commodified recreational bowling. The importance of this for Putnam (2000: 113) is that 'league bowling, by requiring regular participation with a diverse set of acquaintances, did represent a form of sustained social capital that is not matched by an occasional pickup game'. The fact that such changes in the nature of sport are widespread, reflecting more fundamental social, economic and cultural factors, raises important questions as to the extent to which the changing nature of sport is cause or effect and the extent to which single activities or organizations can be used to reinvigorate Putnam's version of social capital (Szreter, 1988).

More generally, some have questioned the extent to which such an analysis applies to Britain. For example, Hall's (1999: 457) review of levels of social capital in Britain, using aggregate measures of associational membership and generalized trust, concluded that 'the balance of the evidence seems to indicate ... that aggregate levels of social capital have not declined to an appreciable extent in Britain over the post-war years'. However, part of Hall's more general explanation for the relative stability of aggregate levels of social capital – improved levels of education and the growth of the middle class – may indicate the roots of the more narrow focus of policies of social inclusion (Holtham, 1998). This is supported by Warde *et al.* (2003: 518–19), who argue that 'while the volume of social capital is not declining, it is becoming increasingly class specific [with] ... a member of the service class [being] 2.7 times more likely than an unskilled manual worker to be a joiner'. Like Hall, Warde *et al.*, in an echo of Bourdieu, conclude that any benefits of social capital are increasingly going to professional and managerial workers (disproportionately male) relative to other social class groups. Consequently, the argument that there has been no *overall decline* in social capital is largely irrelevant to the social inclusion agenda, although it is possible that survey data, based largely on formal associational membership, provides a limited measure of a concept which is essentially about the *quality* of relationships and the resources accessed though them (Szreter, 1998). Nevertheless, the key issue for policy-makers is not about a *general* decline in social capital, but its presumed weakness or absence among specific, marginal groups often living in easily identifiable areas and who account for a high proportion of visible social problems, especially crime (Holtham, 1998).

Within this context there have been two broad sports policy responses: first, to seek to increase social/sports participation via area-based targeted programmes in socially deprived areas and, second, to emphasize the contribution which sports volunteering can make to 'active citizenship'. The targeted programmes include Sport England's (2001: 3) Sport Action Zones which were viewed as 'an opportunity for Sport England to build on its relationship with the "social exclusion" and "regeneration" agendas'. These usually contained a vague amalgam of aims including increased participation, improved health and crime-reduction. It is worth remembering Putnam's reservations about the limitations of simple sports participation – bowling alone – and the importance of both the context and process of such participation to the development of 'social capital'. It is for this reason that we will concentrate on the potential contribution of sports volunteering and membership of sports clubs to the development of social capital.

Sports volunteers: the real active citizens?

Reflecting the new emphasis on civic participation and active citizenship (and clearly drawing heavily on Putnam), Sport England and the Local Government Association (1999: 8) argued that:

> Voluntary and community activity is fundamental to the development of a democratic, socially inclusive society. Voluntary and community groups ... enable individuals to contribute to public life and the development of their

communities ... In so doing they engage the skills, interests, beliefs and values of individuals and groups.

The apparent potential of sport to facilitate forms of social participation is illustrated by the Home Office's citizenship survey in England (Attwood *et al.*, 2003). This found that, in the previous 12 months, 33 percent of the adult population was involved in groups, clubs or organizations for taking part in sport and exercise, or going to watch sport. They identified this as the largest single category of the rather loosely defined 'social participation', with hobbies, recreation, arts and social clubs second, with 24 percent participation. The key policy message seems to be that the potentially positive benefits of sport are not only to be obtained via active participation – involvement in the organization and provision of opportunities for sport provides opportunities for the exercise of civic responsibility and (akin to Coleman) the development of transferable skills and increased employability.

The scale of volunteering in sport makes these arguments appear plausible. For example, it is estimated that in Finland there are 60 sports volunteers per 1,000 population, with an equivalent figure for Sweden and Denmark of over 50, Germany over 40 and 26 in both France and the UK (Le Roux *et al.*, 2000), with voluntary sports organizations being the largest sector of Norwegian civil society (Seippel, 2006). More detailed analysis in the UK illustrates the impressive scale and importance of the voluntary sector in sport. For example, Nichols (2003) estimated that there were about 150,000 voluntary sports clubs in the UK, with about one-third of these being in existence for 50 years or more. Further, he estimated that between 12 and 14 percent of the population were members of such clubs (although no definition of 'sports clubs' is provided). Sport England (2003) estimated that there are approximately 1.5 million sports volunteers, accounting for more than one-quarter of all volunteering. This is more than three times the best estimate of the total number of people in paid employment in sports-related activities. Further, it is estimated that the hours worked by volunteers in sport amount to about 1.2 billion per year (80 percent of this in formal organizations), equivalent to 720,000 full-time equivalent jobs and worth £14 billion. Consequently, sports volunteers reduce the real costs of both provision and participation in sport and their work can be regarded as having a high social and economic value.

In this context Nichols (2003), on behalf of the CCPR, asserts that voluntary sports clubs make a substantial contribution to social capital. However, there is no conceptual discussion of the term and it is simply asserted that clubs provide a structure and opportunity for active citizenship and social interaction. While the latter assertion is clearly true, the former requires much more discussion and evidence than is produced in the report. In part Nichols (2003) supports this assertion by emphasizing the longevity of sports clubs – in his sample, 46 percent had been in existence for 30 or more years, with 34 percent for 50 or more years. However, Warde *et al.* (2003), via a longitudinal analysis of the British Household Panel Survey (1991–5), raise questions about the *stability of membership* of such clubs – a factor central to both Coleman's and Putnam's versions of social capital.

After trade unions and religious groups, sports clubs had the highest proportion who were members throughout the period covered by the survey; sports clubs had the largest proportion of the sample who were members in any one year of the survey (18.5 percent compared to 17.7 percent for trade unions); in the overall time-series sports clubs had also the highest proportion who were members in at least one year – 32.1 per cent compared to 28.1 per cent for trade unions and 26.4 for social clubs. Clearly, although many sports clubs have a stable core membership over time, this could be regarded as a relatively low proportion of total membership. This raises important questions about the nature and stability of the social capital generated by such clubs and the extent to which it is differentially distributed between different types of club members (this is discussed below).

Generalizations about such a heterogeneous area as the voluntary sector in sport are clearly not possible. For example, in a study of the voluntary sector in Europe, Gaskin and Smith (1995) identified a range of motivations for, and meanings attributed to, volunteering. They argue that volunteering ranges from those who are motivated by civic/democratic/moral values (akin to Putnam) to the more Coleman-like pragmatic approach to wanting to learn new skills. They also suggest that the nature, extent and meaning of voluntarism reflect complex relationships with political and religious cultures, the historic role of state and the nature and status of civic society. For example, there is a weak link between democratic participation and volunteering in the former communist countries of Eastern Europe. Sport England (2003) identified a broad continuum of motivations and types of sports clubs, ranging from the altruistic ('giving something back') to traditional sports clubs which were based simply on the mutual production and consumption of shared enthusiasms by similarly minded people. The 'limited' horizons of many such clubs were illustrated by one interviewee:

> At the end of the day we are a competitive swimming club. We are not a community or social group. We are not here to look after [the disadvantaged], although we will help where we can, we are not in a position to arrange transport; we are not in a position to reduce their fees. We will train people that want to train, but we cannot be used as a social service organisation.
>
> (Sport England, 2003: 21)

Such issues mean that we need to consider carefully claims about sports clubs' contribution to social inclusion and the development of certain types of social capital among particular types of membership.

Sports clubs and social capital

In addition to developing forms of what might be termed 'sporting capital' (networks giving access to sports-related technical skills and knowledge), it is highly probable that some (perhaps many) sports clubs provide the context for the development of Bourdieu's exclusive form of 'investment' social capital and some may also provide opportunities for the development of aspects of human capital (e.g. transferable administrative and social skills) – a claim widely made in the policy literature, with no reference to Coleman. However, the more general current policy questions relate to the ability of sports clubs to develop Putnam's civic-oriented form of social capital among the socially excluded – those who do not participate in sport and/or are traditionally not members of voluntary organizations. To explore these issues we will examine Putnam's two types of social capital: bonding and bridging.

Before proceeding, it is essential to remember that Putnam (2000) views civic engagement and associated social capital as important not in and of themselves, but because they improve the efficiency of communities by facilitating coordinated actions and enabling communities to be more effective in pursuit of their interests. In this regard it is worth noting Portes and Landolt's (2000: 546) argument that social capital consists of the ability to marshal resources, not the resources themselves and, irrespective of the strength of social capital, there is a limit to 'what enforceable trust and bounded solidarity can accomplish ... especially in the absence of material resources'. Consequently, from a policy perspective, this should be the basis on which to evaluate the contribution made by sports clubs and sports volunteering.

Also it is worth noting Woolcock's (2001) extension of Putnam's conceptual framework with the notion of *linking social capital*. Whereas bonding and bridging social capital are concerned with types of 'horizontal' social relationships, linking social capital refers to vertical connections between different social strata, including those entirely outside the community (offering access to wider networks and the potential to leverage a broader range of resources). This seems to be the concept underlying the Social Exclusion Unit's (2000: 53) assertions about the potential contribution of volunteering to the rebuilding of social capital, that 'it often brings people into contact with those outside their normal circle, broadening horizons and raising expectations, and can link people into informal networks through which work is more easily found'. In fact Skidmore *et al.* (2006: p. viii) suggest that broader policies to promote community participation in governance are concerned mostly with linking capital, the theory being 'that being involved in the governance of services, participants build relationships with public institutions or officials which give their community access to valuable external resources like money, support or political leverage'.

These assertions have clear policy and analytical implications for the role of certain types of sports club and, for example, the significance of their relationships and negotiations with governing bodies of sport, various parts of local government and their memberships of committees. These issues raise empirical questions and, as we will see, access to such social capital (and maybe even bridging social capital) may be restricted to particular members of organizations. However, we now turn to consideration of Putnam's two types of social capital.

Bonding capital: playing with mates

We have already noted that for Putnam bonding social capital refers to networks based on strong social ties between similar people – people 'like us' – with relations, reciprocity and trust based on ties of familiarity and closeness. Certain aspects of this could be regarded as part of the historic role of sports clubs: like-minded people (often from similar age ranges, educational backgrounds, sex, social class, race and religion) coming together to produce and consume a common interest – a particular sport. Interestingly, given Sport England's desire to encourage larger, multi-sports clubs, Horch (1998: 53), referring to the changing nature of German sports clubs, suggests that 'voluntary associations function better the younger and smaller they are, the more locally restricted they are, the more homogeneous the member interests and capabilities are and the less specialised knowledge is required'.

However, commentators and policy-makers have emphasized the limitations of bonding capital, especially for contributing to the wider social inclusion and social regeneration agenda (Performance and Innovation Unit, 2002). For example, in increasingly pluralist and culturally heterogeneous societies, it is argued that there is a danger that such capital can lead to segregation and exclusionary behaviour. It is possible that, while such capital can assist in community bonding, it may lead to 'defensive communities' (Forrest and Kearns, 1999: 1), linking disadvantaged individuals together, but effectively excluding them from the wider society (and its resources and opportunities). Forrest and Kearns suggest that the social and spatial links to the world beyond the immediate neighbourhood are important, especially the extent to which the neighbourhood may be socially and spatially isolated. For example, echoing Portes and Landolt's (2000) concern about 'resource poor' networks, P6 (1997: 6) argues that certain types of government training schemes tend to reinforce 'the wrong kind of networks ... where they only meet other unemployed people much like themselves'. Consequently, Forrest and Kearns (1999: 22) argue that 'the quality and degree of interaction with the world beyond neighbourhoods' is important, suggesting that 'cohesion may not be inherently positive – it can be inward-looking and suspicious of outsiders'. Others have argued that strong bonding capital can be oppressive by enforcing conformity among members, which in turn can restrict routes out of poverty and exclusion (Kearns, 2004; Portes and Landolt, 2000). These are charges sometimes made against sports clubs, based on intense local and club loyalties and competitive attitudes to others: 'sporting social capital can both unite and segregate' at the same time (Dyerson, 2001: 26).

Clearly the nature and significance of this bonding capital and the role of sports clubs in its development will vary, especially between urban and rural areas and between homogeneous and heterogeneous communities. For example, Driscoll and Wood (1999) explore the role of Australian rural sport and recreation clubs in periods of social and economic change and their contribution to the development of social capital. They conclude that in rural areas sports clubs have the potential to perform wide-ranging socio-cultural functions, including leadership, participation, skill development, providing a community hub, health promotion, social networks, and community identity, although their definition of the term 'social capital' – 'a collective term for the ties that bind us' – is very vague, with limited analytical utility.

Third Way policy-makers have tended to view Putnam's theories of civic engagement and generalized trust as being important because they enable communities to be more effective in pursuit of their broader interests. Consequently, questions remain about the extent to which information-poor and resource-poor networks in deprived areas of high unemployment can achieve this. While bonding capital may play a role in local social regeneration – for example, as an essential first step towards rebuilding confidence and cohesion – many policy-makers regard *bridging capital* as being more significant.

Bridging capital: bowling with acquaintances

Bridging capital refers to weaker social ties between different types of people – acquaintances rather than family and friends – and facilitates 'getting ahead' (Putnam, 2000). Such looser and more diverse networks are viewed as facilitating the diffusion of information and employment opportunities (a central concern of the social inclusion agenda). The attraction of this type of social capital for policy-makers is made clear by the Performance and Information Unit (2002: 43) who suggest that 'organisations that involve more *diverse memberships*, including contact with people of different nationalities or ethnicities, stimulate significantly higher levels of generalised trust'. Stolle (1998: 521), in an analysis of the relationship between trust and involvement in voluntary associations in Germany and Sweden, found that, 'joining a group with strong in-group trust [bonding capital] over time is negatively associated with generalised trust [and] the more diverse, more engaged voluntary associations, those with weak ties ... accommodate more trusting people'.

However, a study in Rotterdam illustrates some important questions about the ability of sport clubs to develop certain types of bridging capital, especially between indigenous and immigrant groups. Boonstra *et al.* (2005) concluded that, although the native Dutch wanted to meet people outside their 'own group', immigrants from Turkey and Morocco were more motivated to participate in sport with members of their own cultural group. Further, although cultural mixing was relatively easy with young people, the onset of puberty led to a more pronounced concern with identity formation and a desire for 'mono-ethnic sport'. They suggest that inter-ethnic and cultural tensions were imported into sport (mostly soccer) and were even magnified in sports-related aggression. Consequently, some clubs requested to play in different competitions outside the city, thus avoiding teams with different cultural backgrounds. In addition, in order to attempt to reduce such tensions, some clubs have limited the number of members of non-Dutch ethnic backgrounds. The study concludes that on the basis of this evidence there are two possible policy responses: to limit policy-makers' expectations of sport or, much more difficult, to intervene in sport to force mixed surroundings.

Although it is essential to be very careful about generalizing from this study of ethnic relations in one city with a particular history of race relations, it is clear that the potential to develop bridging social capital will vary widely depending on the nature, size, location and membership of clubs and the communities within which they are based. Although writing about a culture of extreme political and cultural polarization (Belfast), Leonard (2004: 927) raises important policy issues, arguing that

> moving from bonding capital to bridging capital is beset with contradictions. In order to set in motion the framework for bridging capital to emerge, the conditions that led to the development of bonding social capital need to be undermined.

For example, strong bonding social capital (in Rotterdam and Belfast) may reflect a wider distrust of political and public institutions, or experiences of discrimination, racism or sectarianism and in both cases be expressed and reinforced via sports organizations. Importantly, Leonard (2004: 941) suggests that communities apparently characterized by strong bonding social capital are not necessarily homogeneous and that transitions to bridging capital are likely to benefit individuals rather than communities: 'providing inclusive bridging capital is no easy task and may be achieved at the expense of groups once able to call on bonding social capital'.

One perspective on this is provided by Skidmore *et al.* (2006) who suggest, as we have already noted, that attempts to promote community participation frequently lead those who are already well connected to get better connected. In this regard, they provide a review of evidence of the processes via which this often occurs. Given the relative lack of research evidence on such processes in sports clubs, they are worth listing, as policy-makers consider the use of sports clubs as policy instruments (Skidmore *et al.*, 2006: x).

- Preferential attachment: the more governance structures you are involved in, the more attractive a potential participant you become to others because of the information or influence you bring with you.
- The rich get richer: having some linking social capital makes it easier for you to create more. You acquire knowledge and skills about how the system works, earn a reputation for being a 'good' participant and make contacts with people who are involved in other governance activities.
- Closure: Reflecting the analyses of Bourdieu and Coleman, the value of *linking social capital* often comes from preventing others from accessing it. It suits public sector partners to work with some community representatives rather than others, and it suits those representatives to be the community voices that public sector partners privilege in decision-making.
- Self-exclusion: potential participants may choose to exclude themselves from governance because they decide it is not for them; they think that their interests may be better served by shifting the 'game' into other, less formal

arenas where the rules work more in their favour; being denied the chance to participate becomes a rallying point around which alternative forms of collective action develop.

- Community dependency: this refers to familiar processes in many sports clubs in which certain people routinely take on a disproportionate burden of governance activities and create a vicious circle, which both increases the burden and dampens the enthusiasm of others for alleviating it. Non-participants expect not to participate because they assume others already will be taking part; participants expect to participate because they assume that, if they do not, others will not be willing to step in.
- Institutional dependency: institutions get in the habit of recruiting existing participants who are a known quantity and can be trusted to understand and work within the constraints of a demanding culture of delivery, rather than invest scarce time and resources in attracting new blood who will take time to settle in and may not ever develop the 'right kind' of working relationship.

These mechanisms, processes and approaches have clear implications for a research agenda to explore the processes of types of social capital formation and their distribution within various types of local sports clubs. However, although there is a relative dearth of such 'middle range' investigations, there have been some tentative macro, survey-based, studies which have explored correlations between levels of sports participation and certain indices of social capital. We now turn to a consideration of these.

Sports clubs and social capital: survey evidence

The two main studies which we will consider adopt Putnam's broad 'civic engagement' approach to the definition and measurement of social capital. They use large-scale survey data to explore the extent to which there are correlations between sports participation, sports club membership and various factors taken to be indicators of the existence of civic expressions of social capital (e.g. voting patterns; generalized trust; trust in political institutions).

Delaney and Keaney (2005), using data from the 2002 European Social Survey, found that members of sports groups were more likely than non-members to engage in civil behaviours (defined rather loosely as having contacted an official, signed a petition or voted in the last 12 months). They also found national-level correlations between higher levels of general sports participation and high levels of social and institutional trust (trusting people in general; trust in parliament), with club membership being a slightly more powerful predictor of such attitudes. With regard to relationships between individual club membership and indices of social capital, they also found positive, but much weaker, correlations than those at a national level. In attempting to address the issue of self-selection they controlled for age, income, gender, membership of other associations, years in full-time education and found a 'small but statistically significant effect of sports club membership on political engagement and trust in civil institutions' (Delaney and Keaney, 2005: 27). However, they found no relationship between simple participation in sport and a key component of social capital: trust in other people. Their conclusion is significant and reflects the more general concerns outlined above (Skidmore *et al.*, 2006; Warde and Tampubolon, 2001): 'the correlations between participation in sport and social trust may be more down to the type of people who participate in sport than participation itself' (Delaney and Keaney, 2005: 27). They also refer to similar findings about membership of cultural organizations, leading them to speculate that 'it may be associational membership in general rather than sports membership in particular which displays positive correlations' (Delaney and Keaney, 2005: 23). This leads them to conclude that, in terms of the social inclusion agenda, sports programmes would need to be complemented by other measures to stimulate social regeneration (a finding which parallels 'sport plus' analyses in other chapters).

Seippel (2006), using data from a random sample of the Norwegian population (aged 16–85; sample size 1,695), explores the extent to which participation in organized sport relates to generalized trust and the extent to which social capital derived from voluntary sports organizations has implications for general interest in politics, voting in elections, satisfaction with democracy and trust in politicians. It is worth noting that Seippel (2006: 171) considers these variables 'not as social capital (i.e. social relations), but as social phenomena that might be influenced … by variations in types and amount of social capital'. Seippel seeks to move beyond limited correlations and tentatively explore the nature of the *mechanisms* which might produce social capital. It is hypothesized that three social mechanisms might produce these effects. First, social relations as social capital may provide and facilitate *information* for individuals. Second, this is more likely to occur in 'connected' sports organizations (i.e. members have ties to members of other associations) than 'isolated' organizations focused solely on their sport. Although this is not explored, this clearly refers to both bridging and linking social capital. Third, Seippel, echoing Sport England and the Local Government Association (1999) and Skidmore *et al.* (2006), speculates that the more active members, involved in organizational work, will have access to more social capital and information. Finally, there is the possibility of reinforcement of identity and recognition via the reciprocity presumed to be central to such social relations.

The relatively weak relationship between club membership and generalized trust found by Delaney and Keaney is partially confirmed by Seippel. Although being a member of a sports organization had a positive effect, this was weaker than for membership of other voluntary organizations, with sport-isolated organizations containing less social capital than connected sports organizations. However, and contrary to expectation, the extent to which people were active in sports organizations added little more to the levels of generalized trust than simply being an ordinary member. In terms of general political interest and voting, membership of a sporting organization seems to have a significant, but marginal, effect and explains little of the variance regarding such attitudes as satisfaction with democracy or politicians' trustworthiness. This leads Seippel (2006: 178) to conclude that 'sports organisations contain a certain amount of social capital, but less than other voluntary organisations'. However, the very high level of membership of voluntary organizations and general trust in people and institutions in Norway may have reduced the measurable impact of sports organizations per se (Delaney and Keaney, 2005).

Significantly, both Delaney and Keany (2005) and Seippel (2006) acknowledge the potential importance of self-selection. In Delaney and Keaney's sample the well-established effects of gender, education, ethnicity, income and class were evident (although their influence varied between sports); in Seippel's sample, participants tended to be young and male (although education was not significant). Related to this, Delaney and Keaney's more general analysis concludes that, in the UK, while general levels of trust are not in decline, like sports participation, it is becoming increasingly unequally distributed.

Both Delaney and Keaney and Seippel admit the exploratory and tentative nature of their analyses and agree that there is a need to go beyond such aggregate correlations and explore the various social mechanisms within various types of sports clubs which might give rise to various aspects of social capital. In this regard the perspectives of Bourdieu and Coleman may be as useful as Putnam's for understanding the processes of social capital formation (if any) in sports clubs. However, club-level research evidence is limited and that which does exist seems to indicate a rather limited role for sports clubs in developing Putnam's more civic versions of social capital. For example, Ibsen (1999: A256) in an analysis of sports clubs in Denmark concluded that clubs' activities were 'not aimed at solving current problems in the community ... members' attachment to the association is little connected with the area where they are recruited'. In a student study of sports clubs in south London, Andrew (2004) found that only 4 percent were involved in local non-sport groups and only 30 percent were involved in local issues (with a tendency for these to be from professional and managerial groups).

Clubs' rules OK?

Despite the policy rhetoric and desire to find a place within the social inclusion agenda, many in sport also express concern about the implications of a new, more directive, agenda for sports clubs. For example, it is argued that the voluntary sports sector makes a crucial contribution to the sport and health policy goals simply by sustaining current levels of sports participation. Sport England (2004: 14) defend this vital role by suggesting that requiring sports clubs to adopt different agendas contains substantial risks and arguing that 'any external assistance offered needs to emphasise that it is designed to help them achieve their aims'.

Such dilemmas are partly explained by the vision of volunteering underpinning the assertion that 'voluntary and community activity is fundamental to the development of a democratic, socially inclusive society' (Sport England and the Local Government Association, 1999: 8). This appears to be based in part on a vision of altruistic welfare organizations (e.g. Help the Aged) in which people do things for more vulnerable and needy sections of the community, without any anticipation of reward (rather similar to Putnam's perspective). However, Sport England (2003) and others (Ibsen, 1999; Horch, 1998) suggest that most sports clubs do not conform to this model, but are more akin to a form of mutual production and consumption. Horch (1998: 47), in an analysis of German sports clubs, argues that certain widespread processes may serve to undermine the positive aspects of sport clubs. In particular, he highlights the danger that the search for funding may 'burden the sport club with general socio-political responsibilities and standards that have nothing to do with the original interests of the members, such as health promotion and the integration of foreigners'. Such responses parallel Field's (2003: 118) statement of wider concerns that 'the essence of social capital is that it consists of activities and relationships freely engaged in by individuals, which only suffer if government stepped in'.

Field (2003: 119) also quotes Fukuyama (2001: 18) as warning that excessive state intervention 'can have a serious negative impact on social capital' and refers to Coleman's doubts about the ability of constructed forms of organization to provide the required normative cohesion and network closure central to the effective working of social capital. This view that volunteerism and associated social capital consist of freely chosen activities and relationships also informs a further concern about the difficulties in developing sports volunteering as part of a social inclusion agenda. For example, McDonald and Tungatt (1992), reporting on research on sports development projects such as Action Sport in the 1980s, conclude that although many unemployed people attended the sports leadership courses, many did not have the desire or confidence to lead. Further, many were reluctant to commit to attend regularly to assist with frequent sessions, making forward planning difficult. McDonald and Tungatt (1992: 16) concluded that 'the typical reaction is that inner urban life has enough stresses of its own without further responsibilities'. Such analyses are supported by Skidmore et al.'s (2006) concerns about 'preferential attachment' and 'community dependency' and Delaney and Keaney's (2005) conclusion that sports programmes need to be complemented by other measures to stimulate social regeneration.

McDonald and Tungatt (1992) are alert to the perception of initiatives as being top–down impositions (see also Forrest and Kearns, 1999) and suggest that the best way to build confidence and social skills is for sports leaders 'to work closely alongside existing and embryonic, community groups ... acting as a catalyst'. Perhaps most radically, McDonald and Tungatt (1992: 33) argue that if sport is to be used to address broader issues of inclusion and the development of social capital, then sport may have to change, as 'there is a danger that aims and objectives may incorporate many of the values that traditional sports provision stood for' (see also Blackshaw and Long, 2005). Such analyses imply that there is a potential conflict between developing sport *in* communities and developing communities *through* sport and that perhaps these involve very different social processes and mechanisms (Coalter and Allison, 1996; Delaney and Keaney, 2005).

Can we capitalize on sport?

Many of the policy intentions in this area can be characterized, in Pawson's (2004) phrase, as 'ill-defined interventions with hard-to-follow outcomes'. Much of the policy-led debate about the contribution of sport and sports clubs to social regeneration or civic renewal via the development of social capital has been conceptually vague and largely descriptive. There has been a failure to articulate systematically what is meant by social capital and to distinguish between the social relations taken to be characteristic of forms of social capital and the presumed positive outcomes (the key issue for the social inclusion agenda). The policy debate has been dominated by versions of Putnam's civic-oriented definitions of social capital, accompanied by assumptions or assertions that such relations are characteristic of sport and sports clubs – part of community networks/civic infrastructure; producing a sense of local identity; generating solidarity and equality among members and operating on relationships based on trust, support and reciprocity. Further, in the context of the social inclusion and regeneration agenda, such social capital is viewed not simply as a public good, but is *for* the public good, with the presumption (or strong hope) that it will contribute to wider community effects – increased community cohesion, an increase in communities' ability to take coordinated actions, mobilize resources and pursue their interests (and not simply in sport).

Consequently there appear to be at least three key evidence-based policy questions. First, following Seippel, what type of social capital is produced by what size and type of sports club (e.g. isolated or connected; single or multi-sport; urban or rural) and in what types of community? Clearly clubs have differing relationships with 'communities', with geographical and social mobility frequently loosening previous social and cultural links with local communities. However, policy discourse rarely refers to the potential of the broader 'sports community' , in which participation in such processes as leagues, competitions, governing bodies, ground sharing and so on provides theoretical opportunities for the development of forms of both bridging and linking social capital. However, even where forms of social capital are produced, the relatively limited research indicates that, within clubs, both bridging and linking social capital are probably differentially distributed between (say) participants and administrators. This set of issues also relates to the key question of self-selection and the social skewing of sports participation, the extent to which sports clubs attract those who already possess various degrees of social capital and civic attitudes and the extent to which these individuals continue to benefit from this (Skidmore *et al.*, 2006).

The second key question, reflecting the core concerns of this book, relates to the nature of the processes involved in the formation and sustaining of different types of social capital, with Bourdieu, Coleman and Putnam offering differing approaches to this issue (and the presumed outcomes). Here there appears to be broad agreement among academics that policy-led attempts to construct social capital will probably fail, as social capital is based on activities, relationships and norms freely engaged in by individuals (with Bourdieu and Coleman emphasizing individual motivations and perceived benefits). Others suggest that attempts to use sports clubs to achieve such wider policy goals (e.g. via conditions associated with funding) can undermine their essential (mostly non-altruistic) purposes, qualities and stability.

Third, if social (rather than sporting) capital is generated, to what extent does it have wider community effects? Existing, admittedly limited, research implies that the more general causal impact of sports clubs in terms of Putnam's desired wider civic engagement (and social trust) may be limited. This is also related to Portes and Landolt's (2000) concept of 'resource poor' networks and the essential distinction between relations constituting social capital and the ability to access and use resources. However, it might be that policy-makers' negative interpretation of bonding social capital is misplaced. If sports clubs are capable of developing certain types of bonding capital (and this requires further investigation), then, in certain circumstances, this may be viewed as a positive, if limited, contribution to social regeneration – perhaps an essential first step for certain marginal and vulnerable groups (although as Leonard (2004) and Boonstra *et al.* (2005) clearly illustrate, attempts to move beyond this face substantial difficulties).

More generally, from both an academic and policy perspective, the analysis of club-level processes and relationships could usefully draw on the work of Bourdieu and Coleman. Although largely ignored in the sports policy literature, their writings have clear implications relating to members' motivations for joining particular types of clubs, the nature of the processes and perceived benefits of participation (Lillbacka, 2006) and the extent to which these are dependent on some form of closure (i.e. exclusion). In this regard it is worth noting Skidmore *et al.*'s (2006) assertion that, even in initiatives to promote social generation, the value of linking social capital often comes from preventing others from accessing it (closures effected both by organization members and public sector partners). Such analyses might serve to illustrate better the precise nature of sports clubs and processes of social capital formation and the potential, or limitations, in terms of a social regeneration agenda.

More fundamentally, perhaps the role of most sports clubs in broader social regeneration processes in advanced or post-industrial societies is marginal. For example, Szreter (1998) even questions whether membership of voluntary organizations per se (especially only one type of organization) is sufficient to engender social capital (and the associated information, opportunities and resources). Clearly, these are matters for serious consideration and theoretically informed research and perhaps provide an opportunity for closer collaboration between academic researchers and policy-makers in a self-proclaimed era of evidence-based policy-making.

5 Sport-in-development

Sport plus

A global role for sport?

In the previous three chapters we have looked at the seemingly important, if often intellectually incoherent, role being attributed to sport in the search for solutions to particular social problems and broader issues of social regeneration and community development in the UK (and to a lesser extent in countries such as Canada and Australia). However, even greater and much more ambitious claims are being made for sport on a global scale, as sport is increasingly regarded as an important component of development strategies. For example, at the World Sport's Forum in March 2000 Louise Fréchette, the UN Deputy Secretary-General, stated that:

> The power of sports is far more than symbolic. You are engines of economic growth. You are a force for gender equality. You can bring youth and others in from the margins, strengthening the social fabric. You can promote communication and help heal the divisions between peoples, communities and entire nations. You can set an example of fair play. Last but not least, you can advocate a strong and effective United Nations.

In 2002 at the Olympic Aid Roundtable Forum in Salt Lake City, Kofi Annan, Secretary-General of the United Nations, stated that:

> Sport can play a role in improving the lives of individuals, not only individuals, I might add, but whole communities. I am convinced that the time is right to build on that understanding, to encourage governments, development agencies and communities to think how sport can be included more systematically in the plans to help children, particularly those living in the midst of poverty, disease and conflict.

Following these statements, in November 2003 the General Assembly of the United Nations adopted a resolution affirming its commitment to sport as a means to promote education, health, development and peace and to include sport and physical education as a tool to contribute towards achieving the internationally agreed development goals. Building on UNESCO's definition of sport and physical education as a 'fundamental right for all' and the Convention on the Rights of the Child's designation of the right of the child to play (Swiss Agency for Development and Cooperation, 2005), the United Nations declared 2005 to be the Year of Sport and Physical Education. Consequently, 'the United Nations is turning to the world of sport for help in the work for peace and the effort to achieve the Millennium Development Goals' (United Nations, 2005a: p. v). These goals include universal primary education, promoting gender equality and empowering women, combating HIV/AIDS and addressing issues of environmental sustainability. The wide-ranging contribution expected of sport is stated clearly (United Nations, 2005b: p. v):

> The world of sport presents a natural partnership for the United Nations system. By its very nature sport is about participation. It is about inclusion and citizenship. Sport brings individuals and communities together, highlighting commonalities and bridging cultural or ethnic divides. Sport provides a forum to learn skills such as discipline, confidence and leadership and it teaches core principles such as tolerance, cooperation and respect. Sport teaches the value of effort and how to manage victory, as well as defeat. When these positive aspects of sport are emphasized, sport becomes a powerful vehicle through which the United Nations can work towards achieving its goals.

Such initiatives served to promote and legitimate a range of sports-based initiatives – under the collective term of *sport-for-development*, or *sport-in-development*. Of course, several bottom–up sport-in-development initiatives had existed prior to the recent UN interest. For example, the Mathare Youth Sport Association (MYSA) was established in Nairobi in 1987 (Hognestad and Tollisen, 2004) and the community development oriented Sports Coaches Outreach (SCORE) was established in South Africa in 1991. In fact, the high-profile achievements (and lobbying) of such organizations played a part in persuading the UN to embrace sport as a contributor to development processes. Further, government organizations such as the Norwegian Agency for Development Cooperation (NORAD) and the Norwegian Olympic Committee and Confederation of Sports (NIF) have been investing in sports programmes to seek to strengthen civil society since the early 1980s.

However, the concept of sport-in-development was given major impetus and greater coherence by the HIV/AIDS pandemic. In 2001 the Kicking AIDS Out! network was established, following an initiative by the Edusport Foundation (a Zambian Sports NGO founded in 1999) and NORAD. Members are committed to promoting the use of sport to build awareness about HIV/AIDS through educational games, activities and sport (this is explored in more detail in one of the case studies in this chapter). It has developed into a rather loose international network of organizations from Namibia, South Africa, Tanzania, Zambia and Zimbabwe and involves international partners such as the NIF, UK Sport, Commonwealth Games Association of Canada and Right to Play (Canada). The network organizations also have a core aim of strengthening aspects of civil society by promoting sustainability and personal and community development via the training of coaches, trainers and peer leaders. The rapid development of the sport-in-development network is indicated by the holding of the first International Conference on Sport and Development in Magglingen, Switzerland, in 2003. As a result of this, an internet platform (www.sportanddev.org) was established, seeking to develop a common working framework for the promotion of sport and development. The conference also issued the so-called Magglingen Declaration (www.sportanddev.org). In fact the Declaration is little more than a systematic restatement of the widespread, and mostly unsubstantiated, claims for the social role of sport: physical and mental health, improved educational performance, sociability, overcoming social barriers, teaching mutual respect and providing the basis for partnerships. However, in this area, even more than in others, the attempts to build multinational alliances and funding partnerships and address problems of enormous proportions lead to 'inflated promises [with] goals lacking the clarity and intellectual coherence that evaluation criteria should have' (Weiss, 1993: 96).

Sport plus or plus sport?

In this policy area we are also faced with widely ambitious, extremely difficult to define and measure claims for the social impacts of sport, accompanied by a widespread lack of robust research on the effectiveness of sport-in-development programmes (in part reflecting their relatively recent establishment). For example, Kruse (2006: 8), as part of an evaluation of the international Kicking Aids Out! network, reflecting the more general concerns outlined in Chapter 3, stated that:

> We have not come across any systematic analysis of how to understand the relationships between sport and development or an assessment of to what extent such a relationship exists – or in other words a discussion of the causal links between an increased emphasis on sport and a positive impact on HIV/AIDS. What is it with sport that could lead to such an impact – what and where are the linkages and can they be documented? ... The strong beliefs seem to be based on an intuitive certainty and experience that there is a positive link between sport and development.

Reflecting the previous assertion about the 'mythopoeic nature of sport (Chapter 2), Kruse (2006: 8) speculates that one of the reasons for the almost uncritical belief in the positive benefits of sport is that 'it is intriguingly vague and open for several interpretations'. Although organizations had overall objectives which provided vision and direction, Kruse (2006: 27) found that 'intermediate objectives are missing providing targets for how much and when results were expected' and 'indicators are used in the application for funds, but not for actual monitoring and reporting', with the absence of clear targets 'making it difficult to assess performance'.

Such issues are compounded because of the variety of sport-in-development projects and the diversity of aims. It is possible to divide sport-in-development projects into two broad approaches. Some can be described as *sport plus*, in which traditional sport development objectives of increased participation and the development of sporting skills are emphasized. However, this is rarely the sole rationale and very rarely the basis for external investment and subsequent evaluation. Almost without exception, the presumed instrumental role of sport is emphasized, with sport being used to address a number of broader social issues (e.g. gender equity; HIV/AIDS education). These outcomes are pursued via varying mixtures of organizational values, ethics and practices, symbolic games and more formal didactic approaches – but rarely simply through sport. In such circumstances sport is mostly a vitally important necessary, but not sufficient condition. The other approach can be described as *plus sport*, in which social, educational and health programmes are given primacy; and sport, especially its ability to bring together a large number of young people, is part of a much broader and more complex set of processes. Short-term outcomes (e.g. HIV/AIDS education and behaviour change) are more important than the longer term sustainable development of sport. Of course, there is a continuum of such programmes and differences are not always clear-cut. Nevertheless, this continuum has implications for the definition of outcomes and 'success' and timescales for evaluation.

From economic aid to civil society

In launching *Sport for Development and Peace*, the United Nations stated that although they had collaborated with a range of organizations in the commercial, public and voluntary sectors, 'what was missing, however, was a systematic approach to an important sector in civil society: sport' (United Nations, 2005c: 1).

Sport's institutional and organizational location in relatively weak civil societies is clearly as important as the games themselves. Hognestad (2005) places the new emphasis on sport and civil society within a broad policy shift from a reliance on economic aid to a more diffuse focus on the role of culture in development processes. He quotes the report from the World Commission on Culture and Development (1995), *Our Creative Diversity*, which defined development as an expansion of people's possibilities of choosing, while stressing the significance of bringing issues of culture to the mainstream of development thinking and practice – 'not to substitute more traditional priorities that will remain our bread and butter – but to complement and strengthen them' (quoted in Hognestad, 2005: 3). Hognestad (2005) illustrates that the Norwegian government's *Action Plan for the Eradication of Poverty in the South 2015* emphasizes the connections between poverty and cultural conditions and the significance of securing cultural rights as an important part of the fight against poverty.

Such policies, although dealing with substantially different contexts, have superficial conceptual similarities with New Labour's concerns with social regeneration and the reconstruction of civil society (Chapters 2 and 4). Somewhat sceptically, Van Rooy (1998) argues that the concept of civil society has become an 'analytical hatstand' on which donors can opportunistically hang a range of ideas around politics, organization and citizenship. Further, the precise nature of civil society in non-industrialized countries has been a subject of much debate (Pollard and Court, 2005), with some commentators raising questions about the widespread utility of such terminology. Others (Comaroff and Comaroff, 1999) suggest that the concept of civil society needs to be broader and include involuntary membership and kinship relations. Such concerns are clearly illustrated by a NORAD report (2002) on civil society and Mozambique which concluded:

> An estimated 60 per cent of the population lives according to traditional norms and structures with little notion of the state, formal laws and their rights. Governance is in the hands of indigenous/'non-state'/'non-system' leaders and structures that exist in many if not most areas, the leaders have legitimacy in that their position and their powers are accepted by the local communities and there is a degree of formality, structure and division of responsibilities. They have important functions in the distribution of resources (especially land), the resolution of conflicts, and in some cases even impose 'taxes'.

The issue of the nature of civil society is, of course, intimately related to issues of social capital (see Chapter 4). It is suggested that where the state is weak, or not interested, organizations in civil society and the degrees of trust and reciprocity they engender provide informal social insurance, can increase community participation and strengthen democracy, can facilitate various types of social development and economic growth and, via forms of *linking capital*, can change attitudes of both national and international organizations (World Bank, n.d.).

However, concern has been expressed about the possible consequences of external aid to such civil society organizations. As the debt-ridden crises of many African societies have led to a weakening of the state and institutions of civil society, there has been a proliferation of external non-governmental organizations (NGOs), giving them effective control of areas such as health, education and welfare provision (reinforced by the HIV/AIDS pandemic) (Armstrong and Giulianotti, 2004). Some have argued that the rapid growth in influence of locally non-accountable NGOs represents new forces of neo-colonialism; with their main leadership and strategies being formulated in the West, they are viewed as promoting new forms of dependency. Giulianotti (2004) has raised questions about the exporting of overly 'functionalist' views of sport by new 'sports evangelists' and questions the nature and extent of the dialogue between donors and recipients, the extent to which 'empowerment' is a clear goal and the precise nature and meaning of cross-cultural cooperation between donor and recipients. The area of sport-in-development is characterized by a variety of such NGOs – NIF, Right to Play, CARE, UK Sport, Australian Sports Commission, Commonwealth Games Association of Canada, UNICEF – and some of these concerns are certainly worth considering. However, this is a matter for empirical investigation rather than critical assertion. For example,

Najam (1999) identifies five roles which an NGO can adopt in the policy process (defined largely by its activities) and Keck and Sikkick (1998) outline a range of political tactics.

However, it would be naïve to assume pure altruism in all cases and the potential tensions are vividly illustrated by Munro (personal communication), the founder of MYSA, who stated that 'the best thing that happened to MYSA was that nobody was interested for the first five years'. The implication of this is that the lack of interest and aid permitted the establishment of locally based aims, objectives and principles and MYSA was eventually strong enough to negotiate funding on the basis of its own definition of its needs. However, this option is not open to all, as in this case it was achieved at a high personal financial cost and serves, in part, to emphasize the need to be aware of the concerns about the nature and rationale of donor/recipient relationships.

Others have expressed concerns about the possible 'neo-colonialist' nature of sport in many developing countries – concerns that certain traditional sports have been displaced and/or destroyed by the importation, or imposition, of 'western' sport and, more especially, its values (Eichberg, 2006). However, while admitting the need to be sensitive to processes of neo-colonialism, 'a western hegemony of institutions and structure' (Saavedra, 2007: 4) and the dangers of regarding sport in an abstracted 'de-historicised' and 'de-politicised' manner, some emphasize the extent to which sports (especially soccer) have, to various degrees, been reinterpreted, amended to reflect aspects of indigenous cultures and reflected in certain ways of watching and playing (Bale and Cronin, 2003; Armstrong and Giulianotti, 2004; Pelak, 2006). The main vehicle of many sport-in-development projects is soccer, largely because it is well-established and has a widespread appeal throughout most of Africa. Armstrong and Giulianotti (2004: 14) argue that, 'the strength of African football is to be found at grassroots level, where the game is unquestionably the dominant athletic pastime among children and young men'.

They suggest that, in the post-colonial era, football provides one avenue of symbolic mobility for those communities that are denied entry to more conventional forms of social advancement, such as education and employment (although as we will see, sports organizations can address such issues). In addition to its basic facility and equipment requirements and relatively low skill entry level (Hognestad and Tollisen, 2004), Armstrong and Giulianotti (2004) point to the well-established competition structure (e.g. the Nations Cup dates from 1957 and the African Champions Cup from 1964); the post-colonial use of football to develop national identities and to achieve wider cultural recognition and the increasing presence of African players in European professional teams (although there are major issues relating to exploitative contracts and abuse of young players). Finally, although Giulianotti and Armstrong (2004) suggest that football provides an avenue of symbolic mobility, they also point out that the development of soccer (and sport in general) has been greatly constrained by high unemployment, rising poverty levels, long hours spent in the informal economy and the rapid increase in HIV/AIDS.

Sport and gender relations

Such concerns and dilemmas are at their clearest in relation to women and the role of sport in development. Many of the Millennium Development Goals are clearly aimed at changing the position, status and power of women – ensuring universal primary education, promoting gender equality and empowering women and combating HIV/AIDS. Yet, as Saavedra (2005) notes (see also Pelak, 2006), much of the organization of, and participation in, sport has largely been a hegemonic masculine enterprise, which has reinforced gender distinctions and unequal power relations and in which female participants often put their femininity at risk. In such circumstances female involvement in sport is often regarded as a transgression of the 'natural' order. However, Saavedra (2005: 1) argues that:

> Despite this and actually because of this, many view female involvement in sport as a potential radical and transformative process for women and girls, and possibly for the world of sport and society in general. Sport as an embodied practice may liberate girls and women from constraining hegemonic feminine ideals, empower them within their communities, provide positive health and welfare outcomes, and ultimately transform gendered notions leading to a more egalitarian world and unleashing the productive, intellectual and social power of women. This then would contribute to overall development – economic, social and political.

Applying such an analysis to South Africa, Pelak (2006: 387), while acknowledging the continued male-dominated and patriarchal nature of sporting organisations, argues that, 'changes to local practices that incorporate women and girls are potentially empowering ... women footballers are not only challenging historic boundaries within soccer but also contributing to the broader socio-political transformation of South Africa'.

Saavedra (2005) points to three broad obstacles that need to be understood and dealt with in order to involve women in sport-in-development organizations and programmes. First, 'avoiding physical and social violence is a major safety factor concern and takes on particular meanings in relationship to sport' (Saavedra, 2005: 5). Simply travelling to and from sporting events exposes women to risk, with traditional authority and power relations also providing the possibility of abuse by coaches and trainers. Second, a rigid economic and social division of labour and a constant struggle to meet basic needs place severe constraints on women and girls, requiring creative, and often collective, solutions to allow space and time for sporting activity. Related to this is the fact that 'a woman or girl seen to dishonour her referent group or overstep gender boundaries may face physical and social punishment by family or retribution from elements within the community' (Saavedra, 2005: 5).

Finally, Saavedra (2005) highlights the complex issue of confronting gender and norms of sexuality and the extent to which sport-in-development organizations seek to address such issues. For example, the provision of gendered sports such as netball may enable girls and young women to improve their fitness and health, develop certain types of skill, competence and self-efficacy and take greater control and ownership over their bodies. However, it is possible that such sport may fail effectively to challenge directly wider socio-cultural and gendered norms. For example, playing traditionally male games such as soccer can provide a more direct challenge to male power and wider socio-cultural relations. In fact, as we will see, many of the sport-in-development organizations adopt a form of the latter approach.

Developing people, creating citizens

It is essential not to adopt easy generalizations about sport-in-development organizations and recognize that there may be significant differences in organization/ funder relationships, the balance between sport plus and plus sport and the role that they seek to play in 'civil society'. In fact, there is a wide variety of outcomes – including those relating to civil society (and social capital) – which must be considered and an overconcentration on traditional intermediate outcomes may be misguided.

We have noted the significance attributed to the role of sport (or perhaps more accurately sports organizations) in civil society and the assumed potential of organizations in civil society to increase participation and strengthen democratic impulses (always recognizing the exclusionary potential of such organizations). Many sport-in-development programmes are based on the production of *youth peer leaders* and the training of young people to coach and provide sport and life skill programmes. Many involve young men and women at various levels of planning, implementation and decision-making, providing important experience of control, empowerment and a sense of collective responsibility (via the much emphasized status of 'role models'). In other words, *people* (or 'responsible citizens') are a major outcome of many such organizations, one that is central to their sustainability and precedes the programmes whose impacts are often the subject of evaluation. It could be argued that it is these aspects of sport-in-development organizations which best illustrate the UN's (2005c: 1) reference to sport as 'an important sector in civil society'.

Such organizations often try to compensate for wider failures of national and local states, weak civic structures, disintegrating families, poorly developed labour markets, failing educational institutions, deeply rooted gender inequalities and poverty – all of an order, scale and depth unknown in developed economies. For example, Burnett (2001: 49) in discussing the issues involved in assessing the impacts of sport-in-development projects, refers to the pervasive influence of poverty:

> Poverty is however not simply a quantitative or economic phenomenon, but indicates a particular location and experience of being human. Kotze (1993: 3) refers to the all-embracing nature of poverty 'in the sense that it encompasses material, social, physical and intellectual insecurity'.

Munro (2005), the founder of the MYSA, argues that such circumstances generate a lack of self-belief which is reinforced by the lack of good role models, especially for boys whose fathers abandoned their family and who grow up surrounded by too many 'successful' failures whose small fame and fortunes depend on illegal activities. Munro (2005: 4) illustrates the importance placed on role models by asking rhetorically: 'role models for youth: is anything more important in development?' He argues that in most African countries the poor are the majority and youth constitute the majority of that poor majority and that 'among the many debilitating aspects of poverty is that the poor, and especially the youth, lack confidence and belief in themselves'. Consequently, 'after food, water, shelter, health and education, nothing is more important for future development than providing good role models for our youth' (Munro, 2005: 4).

In many traditional sports development programmes leaders and coaches are regarded simply as *inputs* – qualified sports development officers who use their professional expertise to develop programmes for local communities. However, the increasing emphasis on developing communities through sport has led to a greater emphasis on a 'bottom-up' approach (Deane, 1998; Witt and Crompton, 1996a; Coalter *et al.*, 2000), with local leadership being regarded as a vital factor in the success of many programmes. Such strategies are based on recognition that the involvement of local people increases the sense of ownership and credibility of sports programmes and also a desire to ensure longer term sustainability.

Such analyses place youth peer leaders, teachers and coaches at the centre of such organizations and programmes. In addition to being a vital resource for the sustainability of the organizations, their use is also based on education and learning theory. For example, it is argued that, because young people's attitudes are highly influenced by their peers' values and attitudes, peer educators are less likely to be viewed as 'preaching' authority figures and more likely to be regarded as people who know the experiences and concerns of young people (YouthNet, 2005; Kerrigan, 1999). Further, Payne *et al.* (2003) illustrate that, to be effective, role models must be 'embedded', based on the development of supportive, longer term trusting relationships. In line with social learning and self-efficacy theory (Bandura, 1962), evidence suggests that major factors underpinning the effectiveness of role models are the characteristics of the model and their *perceived similarity to the learner*. Learning is more likely to occur when the learners perceive that they are capable of carrying out the behaviour (self-efficacy expectancy), think that there is a high probability that the behaviour will result in a particular outcome (outcome expectancy) and if the outcome is desirable – all of which can be reinforced via peer education. In this regard, Kerrigan (1999), in discussing the role of peer educators in HIV/AIDS programmes, argues that the key to successful peer education lies in the fact that it makes possible a dialogue between equals and collective planning to adopt practices which are contextually and culturally relevant. Saavedra (2005) emphasizes the special importance of female role models in sport-in-development organizations – 60 percent of Kicking Aids Out! peer leaders are female (Nicholls, 2007). In activities which seek to confront traditional, exploitative and often abusive social relations there is a need for female role models. Many, if not all, sport-in-development programmes are based loosely on such, often not fully articulated, understandings.

Of course such an approach is highly dependent on the selection and training of appropriate peer educators, especially where the work is undertaken somewhat informally (YouthNet, 2005), and Kerrigan (1999) emphasizes the importance of appropriate, accurate and repeated training. However, although accepting the theoretical legitimacy of the peer educator approach, Kruse (2006) points to the lack of research on the nature and quality of such processes, arguing that there is a lack of information about the quality of the exchanges in particular contexts, the extent to which peer leaders and coaches are given sufficient training and the extent of supervision and support provided after initial training. In this regard Nicholls (2007: 1) argues that 'the necessary support for peer educators is not always available in the resource poor and donor-driven world of development through sport' – once again we are faced with questions of processes and mechanisms.

The case studies

We now turn to two case studies: the Mathare Youth Sport Association (MYSA) and Go Sisters. While these case studies serve to illustrate many of the issues specific to sport-in-development raised above, they also illustrate many issues dealt with in other chapters. In particular, they provide excellent examples of systematic approaches to the use of sport for broader social purposes which do not take presumed outcomes for granted, but seek to develop organizations and design programmes which maximize the possibility of achieving such outcomes (albeit bearing in mind Kruse's (2006) concerns about the current lack of systematic evidence and the broader concerns about resources).

Mathare Youth Sport Association (MYSA)

Background

Mathare, in north-east Nairobi, is one of the largest and poorest slums in Africa, with a population of about 500,000 people living in an area of 2 kilometres by 300 metres (1.2 miles by 0.2 miles). It is a maze of low, rusted iron-sheeting roofs with mud walls. Housing is wholly inadequate: most houses measure about 8 feet by 6 feet and hold up to 10 people. Few houses have running water, open gutters of sewage run throughout, the road infrastructure is extremely poor, refuse and litter dominate the area and the local authority provides few services (www.mysakenya. org; Brady and Kahn, 2002; Willis, 2000).

MYSA, which receives its core funding from the Stromme Foundation (Norway) plus varying donors, was started by Bob Munro (a Canadian UN environmental development officer) in 1987 as a small self-help project to organize sport (mostly soccer) and slum cleanup and environmental improvements. The concentration on soccer is explained by the extremely high levels of local interest, low skill entry levels and basic facility and equipment costs (an attempt to introduce basketball failed because of lack of facilities and the expense of basketballs). It is now the largest youth sports organization in Africa, with more than 1,000 teams and 17,000 members. MYSA's teams range from under 10 to 18 years of age, organized in 16 zones: the biggest league in Africa. MYSA also has two male semi-professional teams, Mathare United (Atkins, n.d.). These teams were established for two reasons. First, to provide the top of the development pyramid and provide motivation and role models for the junior players – in 2004 MYSA supplied eight players for Kenya's African Nation's Cup squad. Second, it was hoped to develop players and benefit from transfer fees which could be used to provide economic security for the broader MYSA programme. However, reflecting wider aspects of corruption in Kenyan society and sport, football agents in association with the Kenya Football Federation (KFF) undermined this strategy, by depriving MYSA of its legitimate share of two transfer fees, leading to an intervention by FIFA and a threat of sanctions on the KFF. This led to the eventual suspension of the KFF and a Kenyan government threat to deport Munro for bringing Kenya into disrepute! This incident raises significant issues about the role of such organizations, promoting ethical values in areas of civil society controlled by cliques which operate in a corrupt manner and the nature of the 'linking capital' which they (or senior members) develop with national and international organizations (e.g. FIFA). (For a systematic and detailed analysis of the corruption of the KFF see Munro, 2006.)

Producing citizens

MYSA initially attracted young males who played on waste ground in the slums with footballs made of recycled plastic bags and twine. The attraction of MYSA was threefold: (1) access to real footballs (not to be underestimated in conditions of such poverty); (2) organized and structured games, which simulated the professional game; (3) an ordered and protective environment, which was especially important for the many street children attracted to MYSA. However, it soon developed into a much more complex and ambitious sport-plus project, whose ultimate ambition is 'to help produce the leaders needed for building the new Kenya' (Munro, 2005: 5). Soccer is an entry point to a comprehensive, interdependent programme, in which all elements are mutually reinforcing in order to produce a form of social capital and the associated responsible citizens. This is illustrated by the 11 key elements of MYSA outlined by Munro (2005):

(i)   Give youth a sporting chance.
(ii)   Give girls a sporting chance and a chance to become equal partners in MYSA.
(iii) Link sport to community service.
(iv)   Youth are owners and decision-makers (with the average age of elected leaders and volunteer coaches being 15–16).

(v)   Best leaders earn their way to the top. They are elected from zonal league committees to Sports Council/Community Service Council and then to the MYSA Executive Council.

(vi) Learning by doing, with assistance but limited interference.

(vii) Help youth to help themselves by helping others: 'when you are poor cooperation and sharing are crucial for survival' (Munro, 2005: 3).

(viii) Help young leaders to stay in school. This is achieved via a points-based educational scholarship system.

(ix) Organizational and financial transparency.

(x)   Plan for organizational sustainability. MYSA has many decision-makers and clear lines of accountability. There is a 'retirement' policy to ensure that it remains a youth organization.

(xi) Plan for financial sustainability. A major part of this was the establishment of Mathare United, which it was hoped would generate income from matches and the sale of players. There are also plans to open a commercial coaching academy.

Clearly many of these 11 elements reflect components of the definitions of social capital (Chapter 4) as consisting of social networks based on social and group norms which enable people to trust and cooperate with each other and via which individuals or groups can obtain certain types of advantage. Further, this is clearly a form of *bonding social capital* as it is based on strong social ties of familiarity and closeness between people who share very similar social and economic circumstances – many members refer to MYSA as a 'family'. This is reinforced by the fact that all its 60 full- and part-time employees are recruited from MYSA members (who possess a deep sense of responsibility to act as positive role models). These basic elements are reinforced by an overarching philosophy of mutual self-help and a number of specific practices and activities which serve formally to reinforce certain values and attitudes.

'You do something, MYSA does something'

The sense of involvement, responsibility and values of active citizenship are reinforced by member involvement in decision-making at all levels, with a strong emphasis on mutual self-help – stated succinctly by Munro (2005: 2): 'You do something, MYSA does something. You do nothing, MYSA does nothing.' This ethic of reciprocity and trust (which also acts as a form of 'closure', reducing the problem of 'free-loaders') is especially important in a society where there is widespread corruption.

The ethical and philosophical issues of respect for self and others, responsibility and citizenship are embedded in all activities. For example, during soccer games a yellow card is awarded to anyone other than the captain who speaks to an official (a substitute player is permitted). The player then has to referee six junior matches to put him or herself in the place of a referee before being permitted to play again. In addition, a green card is awarded to the most sporting player and is a highly valued award, as it is accompanied by educational scholarship points. As part of its commitment to helping young leaders to stay in school, MYSA has about 400 annual Leadership Awards (it also provides small libraries and study rooms to compensate for the lack of study space in overcrowded dwellings). Although schooling is free up to the age of 14, many schools require pupils to wear uniforms (prohibitive for many living in poverty) and in the post-14 schools fees are required. The awards are paid to the school of the winner's choice and are used to pay for tuition, books and uniforms. Points towards these awards are also linked to volunteer and peer leadership and coaching work. This illustrates an aspect of social capital emphasized by most theorists, that the social relations/networks provide access to certain resources and advantages.

A more general commitment to community service is compulsory for all members of MYSA, including the semi-professionals in Mathare United. The aim of the work is to increase environmental awareness and entails a 'clean up', in which teams from the various zones clear drains, cut grass and remove litter. Although this work makes little overall impact on the overwhelming environmental problems of Mathare, the core value being emphasized here is that of collective responsibility: 'if you get something from the community you must put something back into the community' (Munro, 2005: 2). Of course, such work also raises MYSA's profile in the community (members wear their bright yellow t-shirts) and assists in the building of recognition and trust (especially among parents). The extent of programme integration and re-enforcement of values is emphasized by the fact that each completed clean-up project earns a soccer team three points towards its league standings. Success is clearly a combination of sporting talent and social responsibility.

A further example of integration and re-enforcement of the relationship between sporting ability and social responsibility is the criteria used for the selection of teams to travel to Norway to play in the Norway Cup. This is for teams between the ages of 10 and 19, has been in existence for over 30 years and claims to be the biggest international soccer tournament in the world. This is a highly valued opportunity to travel abroad and selection is not based solely on soccer ability, but also on general behaviour and contribution to the general work of MYSA.

Consequently, MYSA's importance goes well beyond the traditional functions of most sporting organizations. In effect, it operates in a number of areas in civil society, seeking to compensate for major failures of the local and national states' welfare provision, and is facilitated and given coherence by soccer and soccer-related programmes. Munro (2005: 5) sums up his view of MYSA's achievements as follows:

> MYSA's most important achievement by far is that it has produced thousands of new and good role models to encourage and inspire all the youth in Mathare and in other poor urban and rural communities throughout Kenya ... To avoid scaring the present political leaders ... I do not say this too often in Kenya: that the main aim of MYSA is to help produce the leaders needed for building the new Kenya ... within 20 years I honestly expect that a MYSA

'graduate' will become President. I also earned a lot of female admirers when I added: 'And she will do a good job'.

The reference to a female president brings us to MYSA's role in seeking to empower women.

Empowering women

Girls' football started in 1992 and the concentration on soccer can be regarded as an attempt to use a presumed male preserve to challenge gender stereotypes (a vital aspect of addressing issues of HIV/AIDS). With boys expressing scepticism about girls' ability to play the game, the provision of 'girls' sports' would risk simply re-enforcing deep-rooted stereotypes. However, the economic and social position of young women led to substantial recruitment difficulties. For example, 'out-of-school, girls work eight times as many hours in unpaid domestic work as out-of-school boys' (Brady and Kahn, 2002: 5). Consequently, programming had to be flexible enough to permit both the completion of domestic tasks and to address parental fear about safety after dark (Saavedra, 2005). A major goal for MYSA (and Go Sisters) was to use sport to reduce young women's social isolation by providing them with public spaces and opportunities to develop. As Brady and Kahn (2002: 1–2) state:

> Typically, the kinds of public spaces that are seen as legitimate venues for females – markets, health clinics, and so forth – are those that enable women to fulfil their domestic roles as homemakers and mothers ... 'public space' de facto becomes men's space.

Brady and Kahn (2002: 5) further emphasize the more general subordinate position of young women and the close relationships between subordination, poverty and sexual vulnerability.

> The disparities between girls and boys are further compounded in school, where a gender gap exists that widens with age ... at ages 15–19, fewer girls are enrolled in school ... girls are under pressure to be sexually active whether or not they are married. Because of their economic vulnerability, many young women exchange sex for money. Boys and girls between the ages of 15 and 24 have the highest rate of new HIV infections in the country, and girls in this age group are more than twice as likely to become infected as boys.

This analysis also underpins MYSA's extensive HIV/AIDS education programme, which is delivered by peer educators via group discussions, lectures and street theatre (drama/arts/puppetry). Munro (2005) suggests that pride and dignity associated with participation and success in all aspects of MYSA can provide the self-confidence to say 'no' – reinforced within MYSA by the systematic conscious addressing of gender issues with young males. Although little evidence exists about the effectiveness of such an approach, Brady and Kahn (2002) quote young women speaking positively about AIDS education and an ability to resist sexual advances – although, of course, the link between poverty and sexual exploitation remains widespread (see Mwaanga, 2003).

MYSA's more general commitment to gender equity is indicated by the establishment of a Girls' Task Force to examine issues of a gendered division of labour, a perception that boys were given priority in relation to facility access, reports of harassment and a decline in girls' enrolment. However, despite MYSA's success in recruiting young women, overcoming parental opposition, questioning gender stereotypes and integrating young women into the structure of the organization, they still face familiar problems in retaining adolescent girls. For example, boys outnumber girls in all age groups by about four to one. The largest numbers of girls (and boys) are in the youngest, under-12, age group. Because of this, MYSA has combined the two oldest age categories (under 16 and 18) into one group (Brady and Kahn, 2002). Despite these general difficulties, Brady and Kahn (2002: 1–2) state:

> We posit that participation in non-elite sports programs appropriate for girls of average physical ability and skills can meet the simultaneous needs of offering girls new venues in which to gather and breaking down restrictive gender norms ... Girls' participation can begin to change community norms about their roles and capacities. In this way, sports may be a catalyst for the transformation of social norms.

The second case study relates to a more limited and focused organization and programme, but one which has many components similar to MYSA.

Go Sisters

This Zambian programme, which seeks to empower girls and young women through sport, is part of the Education Through Sport (EduSport) organization, which was established in 1999 and is part of the Kicking Aids Out! network. It acts in partnership with various NGOs, religious groups, schools, sport associations and government institutions. EduSport, with 12 employees, seeks to use sport, recreation and other forms of physical activities to promote empowerment, general and HIV/AIDS education and health. Like MYSA, EduSport is based on the concept of Youth Peer Leaders (YPLs) in which young people are trained to coach and lead their peers in sport and life-skill training, thereby involving some of them in planning, implementation and decision-making. Go Sisters seeks to achieve its goals through the promotion and development of soccer. The centrality of sports development is indicated by the fact that the programme claims to have over 4,000 participants, about 50 soccer teams, has five teams participating in the women's football league (which it helped to establish) and in 2003 it contributed seven players to the national team. The main aims of Go Sisters are:

(i) To provide extra-family social, supportive, networks, a safe social space and reduce the social isolation of females.

A major goal is to provide safe and legitimate public spaces for females, not just to play soccer but also for 'after play life'. Most public spaces are dominated by males, with females usually having to go directly home because of domestic duties, or fears for their safety. As with MYSA, Go Sisters has had to confront the highly restrictive character of female domestic labour, the opposition and concerns of parents and the gendered nature of public space. For example, Mwaanga (2003: 11), a founder of EduSport, comments that:

> In low income urban Lusaka and most rural areas in Zambia, adolescence is a time in which the world expands for boys and contracts for girls and gender disparities in opportunity and expectations become pronounced. Many adolescent girls have narrowed social networks and few collective spaces in which they can gather and meet with peers, receive mentoring support and acquire important life skills.

To work in such conditions often requires various compromises, such as girls having to get up early in the morning to complete domestic tasks before going to school, to enable them to take part in after-school games. However, as girls become more successful and, for example, are able to travel abroad to take part in the prestigious Norway Cup, parental resistance frequently lessens. Further, because most activities take place in public spaces within the communities, they attract wider community interest and provide a very public expression and legitimation of positive female role models.

(ii) To provide girls and young women with experience of decision-making and perceptions of control and experience of empowerment.
(iii) To develop self-esteem and increase female expectations and ambitions.

The importance of this aspect of Go Sisters' work (and all sport-in-development projects) is emphasized by Mwaanga (2003) who quotes the argument of the American Association of University Women (1998) that the restriction of girls to home spaces and duties narrows their options for full participation in public life. This sets them on the path to marginalization as they are socialized not to participate in making decisions which affect their lives.

(iv) Reduce school drop-outs.

Like MYSA, Go Sisters places a high priority on keeping girls in school and it has a similar, if more limited, system of educational scholarships. Unlike MYSA's system based on an assessment of commitment and contribution to the organization, Go Sisters' approach is closer to traditional charity. Those regarded as being most in need are identified and funded by the Swedish International

Development Agency. Although local sponsors are also used, this is an unstable source of funding. Where it is not possible to get girls into school, Go Sisters' volunteers are involved in the provision of alternative 'community schools' – especially in rural areas, where many young children are unable to travel the relatively long distances to state schools. Another reason for this approach is that it is difficult to gain access to rural children (especially girls) if they are not in school.

(v) Provide sexual health information, especially relating to HIV/AIDS.

Go Sisters is part of the Kicking Aids Out! network and HIV/AIDS education is central to its work in a society where UNAIDS/WHO estimated that, in 2003, 16.5 percent of 15–49 year olds were living with HIV or AIDS. Of these, 57 percent were women. Nearly half of Zambia's population is under 15 years old and, according to UNAIDS/WHO estimates, 85,000 of these children were living with HIV or AIDS and over 600,000 children were AIDS orphans. Young women aged 15–19, who suffer inequality and abuse, are approximately six times more likely to be infected than males of the same age. There is a widespread belief among males that sex with a virgin is a cure for AIDS, leading to abuse and rape. Various aspects of traditional Zambian culture can also make women more vulnerable to HIV infection. Among these is 'sexual cleansing' – a ritual in which a deceased man's relatives have sex with his widow, in the belief that this will dispel evil forces (www.avert.org/aids-zambia). Traditionally in Zambia, as in many parts of the world, men play a dominant role in most relationships, while women and girls are generally expected to be submissive. With females also having restricted access to education and mass media, they often lack the confidence, skills and knowledge necessary to negotiate safe relationships with men and to make independent lifestyle choices. For example, data indicate that less than two-thirds of adults (of either sex) believe that a woman can refuse sex if she suspects that her husband has HIV (www.avert.org/aids-zambia).

Go Sisters seeks to address such issues via its organizational and programme commitment to empowerment, the development of self-esteem and self-confidence and a consistent attitude to gender relations and men's attitudes. However, unlike some programmes which seek to use sport as a 'fly-paper' to attract large numbers of young people to formal HIV/AIDS education classes, Go Sisters adopts a much more integrated and sophisticated approach. HIV/AIDS-related games are integrated into the sporting process via their use as warm-up and warm-down exercises. These games range from simple dancing and chanting of HIV/AIDS messages to more symbolic, subtle, games (as illustrated in Box 5.1).

Initially, the more abstract games such as Common Tag are introduced without explanation and the players then discuss and develop their meaning – this approach is regarded as much more effective than the simple provision and repetition of medical information, or moral prohibitions.

Box 5.1 Common Tag

(i) To help participants learn that condoms can protect them from HIV infection
(ii) To help participants develop dodging and running skills

The object of this game is for the players to be the last to get tagged. One player is picked to be the 'HIV'. She must try to physically tag the other players by touching them on any part of the body. A player can only be tagged if at that moment, he or she is not in possession of the ball. As there are a limited number of balls, the players must pass the ball to the player who is to be tagged. The ball acts as the protection against 'HIV'. When a player is tagged, they leave the game for a moment. They may go to the counselling corner to learn about the importance of counselling and testing. When everyone is tagged, a new game is started and all can rejoin.

Mwaanga (n.d.)

But are they hitting the mark?

Not surprisingly, there is little systematic evidence about the impacts of such programmes – they are relatively new, resources and expertise are limited and the environment is usually not conducive to undertaking robust research. However one small research study of two Zambian organizations who are members of the Kicking Aids Out! Network illustrates the complexity of undertaking evaluations of the effectiveness of such organisations. The study (Kruse, 2006) was based on a quasi-experimental design (40 participants and a control group of 40) to assess the effectiveness of a programme in increasing the knowledge of HIV/AIDS, changing attitudes to discrimination and developing life skills. Although stating that the results should be regarded as 'preliminary', Kruse (2006: 33) reports that 'there are only insignificant differences in level of knowledge about HIV/AIDS and in attitudes to stigma and discrimination' between the participants and the control group. This, of course, reflects the more general issue that all sports programmes operate in a broader social context, in which participants are subject to a range of other experiences and influences, making it very difficult to isolate the 'sports effects'. In this case most young people seemed to have knowledge about HIV/AIDS from other sources (school, media, posters, peer groups, churches, personal experience). However, Kruse (2006: 33) speculates that 'existing HIV/AIDS knowledge may be reinforced through KAO games and sports'. One presumes that this speculation is offered because of the additional finding that the sports participants had greater aggregate 'life skills' than the control group, defined as 'the ability to make independent decisions and say no in matters of sex and also the level of self-confidence'. Kruse (2006: 34) argues that:

The wide difference between the exposed who acquired the skill to make their own decisions and their unexposed counterparts could be attributed to the emphasis laid by the KAO programme on decision-making as a fundamental skill in the fight against HIV/AIDS.

However, this conclusion about life skills and changed behaviour – intermediate outcomes – appears to be based solely on answers to one question: 'Have you learned that you can make your own decision to say no?' Clearly, to seek to assess the effectiveness of a programme (or make statements about self-efficacy) on the basis of this single question is unsatisfactory, especially as it tells us nothing about the relationship between what has been learnt and subsequent behaviour.

An evaluation by Botcheva and Huffman (2004) of a different type of Zimbabwean soccer-based HIV/AIDS education programme produced opposite results. This can be regarded as a *plus-sport* approach as it was based on the concepts of role models and social learning using locally and nationally known soccer players to deliver a classroom-based curriculum (combined with warm-up games, role-plays, discussions, and brainstorming activities). The evaluation, using a treatment and a control, group, produced opposite findings to the Kruse study. Although the programme appeared to improve significantly student knowledge, attitudes and perceptions of social support related to HIV/AIDS, no changes in student self-efficacy and sense of control were observed.

However, there is also reason to suggest that, even if such programmes could be made more effective and evaluations more robust, such an approach fails to address the full complexity of issues of evaluation in relation to sport-in-development programmes. An example of this is provided by Mwaanga's (2003) small-scale piece of postgraduate research on EduSport, which illustrates the need for realistic outcome measurement, in this case grounded in the material circumstances of young women. He also illustrates the paradox of personal development and empowerment in conditions of extreme poverty and deprivation. In a qualitative study based on interviews with eight participants and three focus groups with 6–8 participants, Mwaanga (2003) illustrates the highly significant point that the level of participation was a key moderator of programme effectiveness. Not surprisingly, the YPLs were more likely to benefit than simple participants. They are the most committed, have gone through the various training programmes, have experience of decision-making and perceptions of control and status and are conscious of their positions as role models.

More fundamentally, Mwaanga (2003: 109) raises difficult questions about the meaning and purpose of empowerment in a context of extreme poverty. For example, 'the girls seemed to consider one's economic status as crucial in the empowerment process. The respondents reported how girls in their communities engaged in prostitution in order to ... fund their education.' Mwaanga's (2003: 109) somewhat contentious conclusion is that, although engaging in prostitution is risky in terms of contracting HIV, it 'still indicates empowered behaviour'. He bases this conclusion on Zimmerman's (1990) contention that empowered individuals will not always make choices which are socially desirable or beneficial in terms of health outcomes. Perhaps more accurately, the methodological individualism which underpins much thinking about sporting outcomes needs to be questioned and a recognition given to the fact that actions and choices take place within the material, economic and cultural realities within which the 'empowered' live. Or, as Weiss (1993: 105) puts it:

> We mount limited-focus programs to cope with broad-gauge problems. We devote limited resources to long-standing and stubborn problems. Above all we concentrate attention on changing the attitudes and behaviour of target groups without concomitant attention to the institutional structures and social arrangements that tend to keep them 'target groups'.

In the next section we return to one of the main themes of the book: how to define and measure the effectiveness of the wider impacts of sport. We will illustrate some issues posed by sport-in-development projects (although some of the comments relate to other sports-based initiatives).

Evaluation: accountability or development?

Most sport-in-development programmes are *sport plus*. They tend to be more complex organizations/programmes than many traditional sports-development programmes, not relying solely on 'sport' to achieve their desired intermediate impacts and outcomes. In addition, they are dealing with much more fundamental economic, cultural and health issues. Consequently, they raise significant questions about how we should approach their evaluation. Pollard and Court (2005) refer to growing pressure on international and national NGOs to improve the standard of their monitoring procedures, to become more accountable, justify roles, work more effectively and to retain their legitimacy. For example, the Business Plan for the UN International Year of Sport and Physical Education (UN, 2005a: 11) refers to the need for 'monitoring and evaluation of sport and development programs and … the selection of impact indicators that would show the benefits of sport and development programs in the field'. A UNICEF publication on monitoring and evaluation of such programmes (UNICEF, 2006: 4) states that 'there is a need to assemble proof, to go beyond what is mostly anecdotal evidence to monitor and evaluate the impact of sport in development programmes'. However, Pollard and Court (2005: 22) stress that the 'key question … is who is doing the judging'. In this regard it is not unusual for organizations to be resistant to monitoring and evaluation (M&E) – especially if it is viewed as disruptive of programme delivery in resource-poor organizations. This reaction is often based on a belief that M&E relate solely to *accountability*, providing largely quantitative evidence that programmes have been provided, have attracted the target type and number of participants and have achieved the outcomes desired by sponsors and partners (e.g. 'effective' HIV/AIDS education programmes, usually restricted to measured attitudinal change). For example, Shah et al. (2004: 21–2), writing on behalf of the CORE Initiative (Communities Responding to the HIV/AIDS Epidemic), argue that too often:

> Staff who collect monitoring data are not ... sure why they are collecting the information and pass it up to the chain of supervisors until it is eventually incorporated into a report for the donor. Monitoring data collected under these circumstances are not often analysed by field staff and are therefore infrequently used to make decisions about adapting the project's strategy or activities.

It is not suggested that accountability and measures of performance are *not* important – they are. Transparency and accountability are important not only to funders, but especially in societies where transparency might not be the norm. However, any such measures must reflect the particular circumstances of sport-in-development projects. For example, drawing on her work in South African townships, Burnett (2001: 43) emphasizes the need for 'a unique and context-sensitive research instrument' and the need 'to establish the "value-added" dimension of the impact on the community (represented by social networks, institutions and groups) and on the individual'. In other words, there is a need for a consideration of realistic and locally relevant outcome measurement, grounded in material circumstances (of course, this statement has much wider application, but is vitally important in the context of donor/client dependency).

However, the argument here (reflecting Weiss and Pawson's emphasis on theory-based evaluation, process and mechanisms outlined in Chapter 3) is that M&E has a much wider and fundamental developmental role and is about much more than simple accountability and outcome measurement, however defined (Coalter, 2006). Shah *et al.* (2004) argue that M&E should provide the basis for a dialogue, both between organizations and sponsors and *within* organizations. Further, in societies with weak civic structures it should recognize the importance of organizational development, as much as narrowly defined outcomes. Although it could be argued that such an approach to M&E is generic – it should apply in all contexts – it has a particular relevance to sport-in-development organizations because they are important *as organizations* within varying types of civil society. Such organizations frequently seek to compensate for wider failures of national and local states, weak civic structures and disintegrating families. They seek to develop forms of social capital by providing young men and women rare opportunities to participate in decision-making, confront exploitative gender relations, encourage ambition and recognize the value of education, develop relationships based on trust and reciprocity and provide opportunities for the development of human capital.

Consequently, the importance of such organizations qua organizations (as well as their programmes) means that it is essential that M&E are not summative but *formative*. Summative evaluations tend to be conducted for the benefit of funders and be concerned with determining the (narrowly defined) 'effectiveness' of programmes in terms of desired intermediate impacts, such as the ubiquitous self-esteem and HIV/AIDS knowledge (with the problems associated with simple correlations, intervening variables and attribution frequently ignored). However, formative evaluations are concerned with examining ways of improving and enhancing the implementation and management of interventions. This approach to M&E seems to be accepted by the UK government's Department for International Development (2005: 12), which states that 'the over-arching goal for evaluation in international development is to foster a transparent, inquisitive and self-critical organisational culture ... so we can learn to do better'. Further, SCORE (Sport Coaches Outreach, 2005: 3) argues that:

> The issue of internal capacity at organisational ... level is one of the greatest challenges for the effective implementation and sustainability of projects ... sufficient internal capacity is essential for long term success ... stronger organisations will lead to better implemented projects and better results in the long term.

It is argued that such aims can only be achieved via formative evaluation, which is both participatory and process-led.

Participatory M&E: developing people and programmes

As we have noted, most sport-in-development programmes are based on the development of *youth peer leaders*. In other words, people (or 'responsible citizens') are a major *outcome* of such organizations and they might be regarded as crucial to the promotion of 'development values and outcomes' (SCORE, 2005: 13; Nicholls, 2007). However, this is not normally the subject of evaluation (in traditional sports development programmes leaders and coaches are usually regarded simply as *inputs*). Such an approach necessarily leads to a participatory approach to M&E, which contributes to organizational and personal development in a number of ways – reminiscent of Coleman's concept of social capital and its relationship to the development of human capital (see Chapter 4). When organizations involve their members in M&E this is likely to lead to the following.

- Capacity-building: to achieve sustainability, to achieve their many aims and to improve their programmes, organizations need to develop internal capacity (SCORE, 2005).
- Greater ownership, understanding and integration: a broad agreement about, and understanding of, the relationship between aims and objectives can provide the basis for an integrated and coherent organizational culture and associated programmes (see the MYSA case study above; Weiss, 1997).
- An ability to reflect on and analyse attitudes, beliefs and behaviour (Shah *et al.,* 2004): the involvement of staff in the monitoring and evaluation of all aspects of organization and programme delivery contributes to the development of a self-critical and self-improving organizational culture (DFiD, 2005).

- More fundamentally, some argue for such participatory processes as 'a direct assault on hegemonic knowledge' (Elabor-Idemudia, 2002: 232). This in part reflects the view that 'peer educators are infrequently and inconsistently involved in the production of knowledge; subsequently their needs and contributions are rendered invisible' (Nicholls, 2007: 2). In this regard Nicholls (2007) argues that, if participatory approaches are not adopted, then vitally important issues of national and cultural diversity are ignored, with the attendant danger of homogenizing problems of, and solutions to, such issues as poverty and HIV/AIDS.

Process-led M&E: why do our programmes work?

Finally we return to issues raised in Chapter 3 in relation to theory-based evaluation and argue for its special relevance to sport-in-development work. Although summative, outcome-based evaluations may provide some indication as to the effectiveness of the programme – for example, the extent to which self-efficacy has been improved, HIV/AIDS knowledge has been increased, values and attitudes have been changed – such an approach has two major limitations.

First, it is difficult to overestimate the difficulties in undertaking such work in the often chaotic circumstances in which many sport-in-development programmes work. Limitations on financial resources (barely enough for programme delivery), lack of research expertise, the relatively chaotic lives and irregular attendance of many participants, all combine to raise significant questions about the logistics of meaningful outcome measurement and evaluation (leaving aside the generic methodological issues associated with intervening and confounding variables).

Second, as Pawson (2006) and Weiss (1997) argue, such evaluations can rarely answer the question as to 'why' programmes achieve either desired or unwanted outcomes. The simple measurement of outcomes fails to address Patriksson's (1995) questions about which sports and sports processes produce which outcomes for which sections of the population and in what circumstances – a significant set of issues given the multifaceted nature of many sport-in-development interventions and the wide variety of contexts within which they operate. The answers to such *process* questions are central to increasing the effectiveness of programmes, to the development of organizational understanding, capacity and coherence and, more generally, to the further growth and development of sport-in-development programmes (Kruse, 2006).

As argued throughout this text, 'sport' does not have causal or magical powers; it is the *processes of participation*, how it is provided and experienced and the combination of a variety of factors, which explain outcomes: 'outcome patterns are contingent on context' (Pawson, 2006: 25). Such an analysis leads to a process-led, formative, approach to M&E, as it enables (in fact requires) *theory-driven evaluations*, rather than the more traditional quantitative approach to output and outcome measurement. As detailed in Chapter 3, this requires a clear understanding and evaluation of the conceptualization, design and delivery of a programme. Further, the *participatory* nature of such an exercise is essential to ensure the inclusion of local knowledge which, as Diawara (2000) argues, includes both practical and theoretical knowledge and encompasses the cultural and social interpretations connected to this knowledge, which will underpin how programmes are received and heavily influence their relative effectiveness (also Burnett, 2001).

Although such an approach has a general applicability, it has clear relevance to sport-in-development programmes. It not only has the potential to contribute to organizational and community development, but also provides the basis for a *dialogue* between funders and sport-in-development organizations. This requires both to articulate clearly and precisely the nature of their assumptions about sports programmes (their programme theories) and how participation is presumed to lead to specific *intermediate impacts* and, more ambitiously, *outcomes*. Such an approach could lay the basis for exploring aspects of 'hegemonic knowledge' (Elabor-Idemudia, 2002) and 'colonial discourses' (Nicholls, 2007), question the possibly overly functionalist views of Giulianotti's (2004) 'sports evangelists', acknowledge concerns about diversity of cultures and problem definition and solution (Diawara, 2000) and provide a basis for the necessary real north–south dialogue (Nicholls, 2007) – at least on a programme-by-programme basis. It could also help to begin to address Kruse's (2006) questions about how to understand the relationships between forms of sport, forms of organization and forms of development, *or the extent to which such relationships can exist*. Certainly, in the area of sport-in-development we can clearly see the truth of Pawson's (2006: 5) assertion that 'social interventions are always complex systems thrust amidst complex systems'.

6 Sport and educational performance

Scoring on the pitch and in the classroom?

Introduction

The 'sport leads to positive outcomes' perspective received a substantial boost via a combination of New Labour policies. First, their main election slogan was 'education, education, education'. Second, although education is not a specific criterion in official definitions of social exclusion, it clearly underpins factors such as poor skill levels, unemployment and low income and forms a central component of the new emphasis on responsibilities – helping the poor to help themselves. In this context Policy Action Group 10 (DCMS, 1999: 23) stated that 'sport can contribute to neighbourhood renewal by improving communities' performance on four key indicators – health, crime, employment and education'.

In 1994 the then Conservative government had introduced the concept of specialist schools, which were state schools who applied to government for a subject specialism, raised private sponsorship money and submitted a development plan with agreed targets. If successful, they received additional capital funding and additional money per pupil. The first specialist area was technology, followed by languages and in 1997 sports and arts specialisms were introduced (Levacic and Jenkins, 2004). The extension of the policy was part of the New Labour government's broader plans to raise standards in secondary schools and in 2005 about two-thirds of pupils in the non-selective state sector were in such schools (Jesson and Crossley, 2005). Evidence is quoted that academic performance in sports colleges is improving over time (particularly for boys), especially when compared to non-specialist schools (Rudd et al., 2002) and that technology and sports schools are the only types to add value to subjects other than their own (Levacic and Jenkins, 2004). The evidence indicates that, in general, specialist schools are more effective than non-specialist (especially in schools with high proportions of pupils eligible for school meals), but that their effect is modest in size. Further, analysis indicates that specialist schools were not a random sample of all schools, presenting a clear problem of selection bias when comparing with non-specialist schools. On the basis of this analysis Levacic and Jenkins (2004: 27) conclude that 'the evidence points to specialist schools being more effective as a consequence of being specialist schools, but it is by no means adequate for establishing causality'.

For example, Judkins and Rudd (2005), acknowledging that specialist schools have a modest effect in improving exam grades, suggest a series of *generic* mechanisms such as a new whole-school ethos, teachers 'going the extra mile', innovative use of staffing, a greater focus on the individual student, a broad and flexible curriculum and additional resources and improved status. Such analyses suggest that the particular nature of specialist schools is more important than its particular specialism. These dilemmas partly illustrate some of the issues explored in this chapter: the relationship between sports-specific effects and a range of other factors known to be associated with educational performance.

Failing most of the tests

In this chapter we consider the evidence relating to the presumed relationships between sport and educational attainment. Miller *et al.* (2005) indicate that the debate divides broadly into two approaches. The first is a 'zero sum' approach, which is often a concern of parents, which suggests that time and energy devoted to sports come at the cost of academic performance (Coleman, 1961). The second perspective can be subdivided into two. First, participation in school sports (or PE) tends to be associated with a range of positive outcomes such as reduced absenteeism, a stronger commitment to the school and improved discipline (Keays and Allison, 1995). Second, such positive outcomes lead to higher academic performance among sports participants than non-participants. However, as we will see, there is a third broad perspective which states that, while it is very difficult to prove positive cause and effect relations between sports participation and academic performance, at the least it does not detract from such performance and should be encouraged because of direct physical and health benefits (Sallis *et al.*, 1999; Shephard, 1997; Lindner, 1999).

In this area we are confronted with a familiar range of methodological and conceptual issues. Longitudinal studies generally appear to support the suggestion that academic performance is enhanced, or at least maintained, by increased habitual physical activity (as in many other areas, much research relates to physical activity rather than more narrowly defined 'sport'). However, critics suggest that, for a variety of reasons, many of these studies do not provide definitive evidence of cause and effect (or an understanding of the possible mechanisms involved). Not all studies use randomized allocation of pupils to experimental and control groups to control for pre-existing differences relevant to both sports participation and educational performance. For example, Trembaly *et al.* (2000) explain the apparently positive relationships between sports participation and academic success as reflecting the fact that both may be influenced by genetic endowment and early developmental experiences, encouraged and maintained by supportive parents. Others point to the fact that sports participants are often disproportionately from higher socio-economic groups, those who are also most likely to achieve academically. Many studies also use somewhat subjective teacher-assigned grades to assess academic achievement, rather than standardized and comparable tests. In addition, some programmes (especially PE) often include parallel interventions (e.g. health information, community involvement, extra nutrition), making it difficult to isolate sport-specific effects and many are based on pupil self-reporting of activity levels and/or ignore the potential significance of different types of sports (Eitle, 2005). Others point to the lack of tests of the processes or mechanisms hypothesized to mediate between the effects of sports participation and other variables (Marsh, 1993). Consequently, research has produced mixed, inconsistent and often non-comparable results (Etnier *et al.*, 1997; Sallis *et al.*, 1999; Shephard, 1997; Marsh and Kleitman, 2003). Reviewing a range of relevant literature, Lindner (1999: 130) concluded that:

> interpretation problems plague studies attempting to link perceptual-motor training, extra physical education lessons and fitness or motor parameters with academic achievement. Most studies have been unable to specify the nature of any relationship found, and often the conclusions have been speculative.

Shephard (1997: 115) illustrates the problems in assessing cause and effect as follows:

> Even in studies where physically active students have had an unequivocal academic advantage over their sedentary peers, it is unclear whether intelligence led to success in sport, whether involvement in an activity program enhanced academic performance, or whether both academic success and a predilection for physical activity are related to some third factor, such as a genetic characteristic that favors both academic and physical developments.

How is sport presumed to work?

As in other areas relating to sport and its presumed impacts, key theoretical, conceptual and methodological issues relate to the nature of the relationships being posited between (i) participation in various types of physical activity/physical education/sport; (ii) the impact of this on such intermediate factors as cognitive abilities, self-efficacy, self-esteem, attitudes and values; and (iii) the relationship of these intermediate factors (if any) to the desired outcome of improved educational performance. As was emphasized in Chapter 3, the understanding of such issues is central to a thorough theoretical understanding of the nature of causal relations and to any policy-driven attempts to optimize the circumstances likely to lead to the achievement of desired outcomes.

At the most basic level it is hypothesized that there is a positive relationship between physical activity and *cognition* (the mental abilities and processes through which knowledge is acquired). Work in this area divides broadly into two categories (Sibley and Etnier, 2003): physiological changes brought about by exercise and increased fitness and learning/developmental factors. Shephard (1997) speculates that possible physiological mechanisms might include direct, but short-term and relatively small, effects such as arousal in cerebral blood flow and neurotransmitter efficiency (see also Etnier *et al.*, 1997; Fox, 2000). In addition, the calming effects of increased serotonin levels may produce immediate, but short-term, reductions in disruptive behaviour (in which case few educational benefits would be obtained via after-school sport). Longer term, more indirect effects, might include higher levels of physical activity leading to increased intake of nutrients, or the neural activity associated with sports-related motor learning enhancing the development of inter-neuronal connections (Hillman *et al.*, 2005).

In terms of learning/developmental effects, Etnier *et al.* (1997) present a wide-ranging analysis of the relationship between exercise or fitness levels and cognitive functioning (e.g. perception, reasoning, memory). However, their meta-analysis of 134 behavioural studies illustrates familiar methodological issues and produces mixed and inconclusive results. Although both short- and long-term exercise and training programmes had beneficial impacts on cognitive performance, Etnier *et al.* (1997) found, not surprisingly, that the nature and strength of results were affected by the type of measures used to assess cognitive ability (e.g. perceptual skills, verbal tests, maths tests, memory and intelligent quotient) and by the nature and the duration of the exercise. Further, the extent of the measured impact tended to be largest in the weakest research designs (e.g. cross-sectional or simple correlational studies), raising the possibility of pre-exercise cognition differences not controlled for in the research. Etnier *et al.* (1997) regard this as a possibly significant issue, suggesting that people who exercise tend to have higher levels of education (and developed cognitive abilities). Similarly, Coakley (1997) suggests that it is possible that sport and activity participation may attract people with high self-confidence and above-average cognitive abilities.

Conversely, but not surprisingly, Etnier *et al.* (1997) found that the weakest findings in relation to improved cognitive functioning were in the most robust research designs (e.g. where sedentary participants were randomly allocated to treatment groups). Their general conclusion is that the weakness of the research designs of most studies seriously limits firm conclusions regarding the nature and strength of relationships between exercise and improved cognitive abilities. However, despite these reservations, they confirm that measured effect sizes (i.e. improvements in cognitive abilities), although relatively small, were consistently largest for children and young people (6–16).

To explore the relationship between physical activity and cognition in children Sibley and Etnier (2003) examined the combined results of 44 studies. They grouped studies according to their design/methodological rigour, health status and age of subjects, activity characteristics and the nature of cognitive assessment (e.g. perceptual skills, IQ, verbal tests, maths tests, memory). In terms of concerns about both validity and reliability it is worth noting that they identified 57 different methods of cognitive assessment (many created specifically for the particular study). Overall, like Etnier *et al.* (1997), they found a significant positive association between physical activity and a range of measures of cognition, 'suggesting that physical activity may be especially beneficial for children [and] physical activity has a positive relationship with cognition across all design types, for all participants and for all types of physical activity' (Sibley and Etnier, 2003: 251).

Like Etnier *et al.* (1997), the analysis indicated that physical activity had the greatest impact on the cognition of 6–13 year olds, apparently confirming the more general view that movement is especially important in the cognitive development of young children. Their more general finding, that 'any type of physical activity will ultimately benefit cognitive performance' (Sibley and Etnier, 2003: 252) has important implications for policy and provision. Tomporowski (2003), in a review of studies of the role of acute physical activity on children's and adolescents' cognitive functioning, concludes that scheduled periods of physical activity do not interfere with later (in the day) academic performance and in some situations may lead to short-term positive changes in children's behaviour and cognitive performance (related to aspects of information-selection and decision-making). However, the author concludes with the cautionary comment that such effects are unlikely to be global.

More broadly, Etnier *et al.* (2006) explore the nature of relationships between increased *cardiovascular fitness* and improved cognitive performance. They suggest that, although research indicates a positive relationship, much of it fails to test dose–response relationships, giving little insight into the level and intensity required to achieve positive outcomes. Using meta-regression techniques they tested the relationship between aerobic fitness and cognitive performance in 37 studies and found that, although *physical activity* is associated with reasonably reliable, but small, cognitive effects, overall the data did not support the 'cardiovascular fitness hypothesis'. The difficulties of untangling the issues involved are demonstrated by the fact that, in cross-sectional studies, aerobic fitness was negatively predictive of cognitive performance for children and young adults, but in the more rigorous pre–post tests it was not a significant predictor. While admitting the methodological limitations of the meta-analytic method (e.g. combining summary statistics from a range of different studies reduces the ability to make cause–effect judgements), their conclusion is that 'variables other than aerobic fitness may play a more important role in predicting cognitive performance' (Etnier *et al.*, 2006: 125). Consequently, like others, they emphasize the need to understand better the processes and linking mechanisms involved. Making a distinction between necessary and sufficient conditions, they conclude that:

> aerobic fitness may be the first event in a cascading series of events that ultimately impact cognitive performance. If this is the case, then changes in aerobic fitness might in fact be necessary for changes in cognitive performance to occur, but aerobic fitness itself might not be a sensitive indicant of the cognitive benefits that can be obtained through physical activity participation.
>
> (Etnier *et al.*, 2006: 125)

Like others, they hypothesize that there are poorly understood physiological or, more likely, socio-psychological explanations for the measured positive relationships between physical activity and improved cognition. This reflects Sibley and Etnier's (2003: 252) earlier conclusion that perhaps 'psychological mechanisms are the best for explaining the cognitive gains'. Similarly, Vance *et al.* (2006), in a study of physical activity and cognitive functioning in older people, provide partial support for a 'social stimulation hypothesis' that exercise promotes social contact which stimulates the brain (we will return to the issue of social processes below).

Grissom (2005) moves beyond issues of cognitive performance and reports on a study of the relationship between physical fitness and *educational performance*, using a very large sample (n = 884,718) of 5th, 7th and 9th grade Californian school students. The analysis was undertaken via matched samples from the state-wide Standardised Testing and Reporting Program (reading and maths) and the Physical Fitness Tests (aerobic activity; body composition; upper body and trunk strength; flexibility). The initial analysis appears to confirm the findings of other studies (e.g. Dwyer *et al.*, 2001) that there is a consistent, statistically significant, positive relationship between overall fitness and academic achievement. The relationship was especially strong for females and for students of higher socio-economic status. However, as these relationships imply, it is a strong possibility that the relationship between fitness and academic achievement is mediated by factors known to be directly associated with educational achievement. For example, irrespective of fitness levels, higher social class is widely associated with better general health and levels of academic achievement. Grissom (2005: 24) admits that these correlations cannot prove a causal relationship between fitness and academic achievement, stating that 'improved aerobic capacity by itself is not going to improve reading achievement'. Nevertheless, it is suggested that 'physical and other activities that promote good health seem to promote intellectual capacity'. Dwyer *et al.* (2001: 235), in an Australian study of randomly allocated 7–15 year olds, also found significant associations between school ratings of scholastic ability and measures of fitness (e.g. cardio-respiratory endurance, muscular force and power), but concluded that all correlations were low and 'physical activity and fitness would at best make a modest contribution to academic performance'.

Although not rejecting this conclusion, Coe *et al.* (2006) raise the relatively unexplored possibility of a 'threshold of physical activity' (which might be part of the explanation for inconsistent findings). In their study of 6th grade students they found that, on average, only 19 minutes in a 55-minute physical education class were spent in moderate to vigorous physical activity. Consequently, they suggest that higher levels of vigorous activity might be necessary to contribute to increased educational achievement. In their study only (self-reported) out-of-school vigorous activity appeared to be correlated with higher educational achievement. The fact that this was attained via sports participation leads Coe *et al.* (2006: 1518) to speculate that 'sports participation provides an adequate intensity level to meet the threshold necessary to see desirable effects of physical activity on fitness and academic achievement'. However, despite such interesting speculations, the authors (like many others) concede that the key explanatory variable might be socio-economic status, for which they had no data.

Lindner (1999: 138) reports on a Hong Kong study of the relationship between self-perceived academic performance and frequency and duration of sports participation among 4,690 pupils aged 9–18, and concludes that:

there is a curvilinear relationship between frequency of sport participation and academic performance for at least the older groups, in which regular exercise is associated with relatively good academic performance, while lack of activity or very frequent and intense participation shows lower academic performance.

However, he concludes that students with more confidence in their academic ability were the group with stronger motives for involvement in sports and physical activities. Further, no evidence could be deduced that regular exercise *causes* good academic performance, or that lack of exercise or excessive participation causes poor school results (Lindner, 1999). Further, the recorded correlation is between a particular frequency of activity and *perceived* (i.e. self-reported) academic performance.

More generally, Grissom (2005) admits that the understanding of these issues will probably not be achieved via experimental or correlational designs and suggests that there is an urgent need for 'naturalistic' research to understand mechanisms and contribute to the building of theory (a matter to which we will return).

Maybe it is feeling better about yourself

In addition to explanations based on physiology, biochemical changes, improved cognition and fitness, Shephard (1997) also suggests some socio-psychological, indirect, possibilities (also hinted at by some of the authors reviewed above). It is possible that an increased sense of *self-efficacy* (i.e. a belief in one's ability to execute courses of action to achieve desired goals (Bandura, 1986)) might be developed via increased motor skills and a sense of achievement in physical activity or sport. This, in turn, might lead to increased *self-esteem*, which, more problematically, might in turn lead to improved behaviour and an increased desire to learn (accompanied by an increased belief that learning is possible). For example, in a meta-analysis of 65 studies, Gruber (1986) concluded that the self-esteem of elementary school children was positively influenced by physical education programmes and Harter (1982) found a relationship between a sense of physical competence and self-esteem. On the other hand, in a more recent systematic review of 23 randomized control trials exploring the relationship between exercise and self-esteem in children, Ekeland *et al.* (2005) found that only one of the studies could be viewed as having a low risk of bias, with eight having a moderate risk and 14 exhibiting a high risk – greatly limiting the researchers' ability to make definitive general statements about the precise statistical relationship between exercise and self-esteem.

Similar to the concerns about self-selection in the research on cognition, Lindner (1999) cites longitudinal studies which appear to find that high school athletes were different from non-athletes *before* they entered high school (with those with lower abilities and/or low self-esteem dropping out of sport). This type of dilemma is acknowledged by Biddle and Mutrie (2001: 184) who distinguish between two perspectives on the relationship between self-esteem and physical activity. The 'motivational approach' (or 'self-development hypothesis') postulates that individuals with high self-esteem (or physical self-worth) 'are more likely to exercise, as this is an area where competence and self-worth can be maintained or enhanced'. On the other hand, the 'skill (personal) development hypothesis' is that self-esteem is an outcome of participation in physical activity, and that self-esteem can be changed through experience. However, Biddle and Mutrie (2001: 185) suggest that these two perspectives are not mutually exclusive, 'as initial involvement in physical activity, which may be externally motivated, may lead to enhanced self-perceptions of esteem and worth which in turn, become motivators of subsequent activity'.

Spence *et al.* (2005), in a systematic review of 113 studies of the relationship between exercise and global self-esteem (GSE), found that exercise participation appears to lead to small, if significant, increases in GSE. However, they conclude that, overall, 'the benefits of exercise for GSE are overstated' (Spence *et al.*, 2005: 322), in part because most of the studies reviewed were 'generally undersized and underpowered' (Spence *et al.*, 2005: 323) – i.e. small sample sizes limited the ability to measure effects. In this regard Spence *et al.* (2005) raise an issue not always addressed systematically in the literature (or in policy rhetoric): the nature of the relationship between aspects of physical self-concept (perhaps improved via physical activity) and the broader and more complex concept of GSE (and, of course, the even more difficult issue of its relationship to educational performance).

Here they draw on Sonstroem and Morgan's (1989) hierarchical, competence-based model of self-esteem, in which the lower levels are situation-specific and susceptible to change. Such an approach is based on the acceptance that the concepts of 'self' and 'self-esteem' consist of multiple components (each of which is not of equal importance to all individuals). For example, Harter (1988) suggests that some of the components of self-esteem are perceived intelligence, scholastic competence, social acceptance, athletic competence, physical self-concept and physical appearance. From this perspective, the hypothesis is that the lower level development of *physical self-efficacy* (based on personal judgements about competence to perform particular tasks) may lead to a sense of *physical competence* (a general evaluation of the self as possessing overall physical fitness based on feelings of self-efficacy via specific exercise activities) and *physical (self) acceptance* (a more general satisfaction with various aspects of the body), which in turn is one component of global self-esteem. Sonstroem and Morgan (1989) also speculate that *perceived physical appearance* may be an important aspect of self-acceptance. In this regard Leith (1994) argues that the close link between body image and self-image may help to explain the apparently strong (theoretical) link between exercise and self-esteem, especially for many young women (although this is also increasingly so for some young men) (see also Fox, 1999). Ferron (1997) suggests that this reflects the experience of bodily changes and growing interest in the opposite sex and Harter (1990) argues that for adolescents (especially girls) physical self-esteem is consistently an important predictor of global self-esteem (McDermott, 2000).

The importance of this hierarchical model for Spence *et al.* (2005) is that, in their systematic review, the smallest measured changes (i.e. the weakest 'sports effect') occurred at the level of global self-esteem. They suggest that this may be explained by the fact that 'exercise participation is thought to have its greatest influence on self-esteem at domain-specific levels (e.g. physical self-worth, physical competence)' (Spence *et al.*, 2005: 321) and that this effect is subsumed in more general measurements of self-esteem. Harter (1999) argues that, if we aggregate these quite specific self-evaluations into a single global score, then we are not able to explore participants' subjectively meaningful distinctions across a range of sources of self-esteem. Of course, the relationship between enhanced physical self-worth and global self-esteem is not straightforward and the impact of notions of physical self-image will vary, depending on the relative importance of sport and physical activity to individuals compared to other sources of self-esteem. For example, Zaharopoulos and Hodge (1991) found that, although school athletes had higher levels of physical ability self-acceptance than non-athletes, they did not have higher global self-esteem and Bowker *et al.* (2003) report no significant direct relationship between sports participation and global self-esteem for senior high school students.

In this regard Fox (1992), while agreeing that participation in sport may lead to outcomes such as a sense of competence or physical strength, emphasizes that the effect of these on physical self-worth and *then* self-esteem are filtered by the importance attached to them by each individual. For example, in a large-scale survey of English school pupils, Mason (1995) found that boys placed a much higher emphasis than girls on sport and physical education in terms of their self-definition, preferred areas of achievement, sources of social acceptance and friendship networks.

Miller *et al.* (2005) explored some of these issues by examining the extent to which being a sports participant formed part of a pupil's identity among 600 adolescents in New York. They distinguish between a simple sports participant – the majority of their sample – and self-defined 'jocks' (which might be regarded as a form of over-identification) and explore the extent to which such identification varies by gender and race and its relationship to self-reported academic outcomes and school misconduct. Their findings were rather mixed, with female athletes reporting higher grades than female non-athletes, whereas male athletes reported marginally lower grades than male non-athletes. In contrast, self-identified female jocks reported lower grades than female non-jocks. Female athletes were more likely to miss class than female non-athletes, although there were no differences between both types of males. The perhaps not surprising conclusion was that the strength and direction of the relationship between identification with school sport and positive academic outcomes 'appear to be contingent on the gender and race of the adolescent; the dimension of athletic involvement … and the time span over which predictor and outcome are measured' (Miller *et al.*, 2005: 187). However, the authors suggest that their findings constitute a warning about the dangers of 'over-identification' and that school-sponsored athletic programmes 'are no panacea, particularly when they promote a "jock" ethos … they must be tailored in such a way as to discourage engendering a jock identity' (Miller *et al.*, 2005: 191).

To address some of these issues Fox and Corbin (1989) developed a multidimensional approach to examining the relationship between physical activity and self-esteem via the *Physical Self-Perception Profile* (PSPP) (Fox, 1990). This provides a measure of various aspects of physical self-worth, via the four subdomains of self-assessed perceived sport competence, body attractiveness, perceived strength and physical condition. Also, reflecting the issue of the relative importance of physical self-perceptions, the PSPP has sometimes been combined with a Perceived Importance Profile, although Biddle and Mutrie (2001) note that few studies have exploited the full potential of these interrelated measurement tools.

Fox (2000) offers broadly positive, but cautious, conclusions about the benefits of exercise to self-esteem. His review of existing research seems to indicate that, from late adolescence onwards, taking part in regular sport or exercise is moderately associated with more positive physical self-perceptions, including body image. Further, being fit and slim are weakly associated with positive physical self-perceptions, body image and, in some populations, body satisfaction. However, sport and exercise are weakly and inconsistently associated with global self-esteem, as this relationship seems to be wholly dependent on context: the nature of population involved, the nature of the environment and even individual characteristics. Fox (2000) summarizes the general practical implications of existing knowledge as follows (see also Biddle and Mutrie, 2001):

(i)   The greatest improvements in self-perception/self-esteem are likely to occur in those groups who have the most to gain physically from exercise participation, such as the middle-aged, the elderly and the overweight and obese. In this regard Spence *et al.* (2005) suggest that the biggest effects on self-esteem will be among those with the lowest initial levels of physical fitness.

(ii) The greatest improvements are likely to occur in those who are initially low in self-esteem, physical self-worth and body image (see also Spence *et al.*, 2005).

(iii) The 'attractiveness' factors which make people stay with such programmes cannot be separated from those that promote self-esteem: for example, the qualities of the leader, the exercise setting and relationships with other participants.

This last point raises fundamental issues about context and process. For example, Biddle *et al.* (2004) suggest that, while physical activity may enhance psychological well-being, it is likely that the prevailing psychological climate and social interactions will be more crucial than actual physical activity. Sonstroem and Morgan (1989) also accept that the social and psychological processes involved in participation may be as important as any objective, or even subjective, improvements in fitness or physical competence. In this regard, Fox (2000) hypothesizes that the relationship between exercise and any measured increases in self-esteem may be explained by perceived autonomy and personal control and/or a sense of social belonging and significance within the group.

With regard to autonomy and control, Biddle (2006) argues that the enhancement of physical self-efficacy and (possibly) self-esteem is most likely to be achieved in a 'social climate' which seeks to develop intrinsic motivational approaches based on a task-oriented, mastery orientation, in which participants' skills are matched with the challenges they face, which facilitate clear experiences of personal success and provide positive encouragement. In other words, for many of the groups likely to benefit most from improved physical self-worth, body image and self-esteem, the traditional competitive, ego-centred, sports might not be effective. As we will see in Chapter 7, research on the impact of sport on recidivism indicates that the nature of the process – rules, regulations, degree of informality, task-orientation, protective factors and leadership – is central to understanding the nature of change and outcomes (Sugden and Yiannakis, 1982; Serok, 1975; Rijpma and Meiburg, 1989; Witt and Crompton, 1997; Taylor et al., 1999). Similarly, we have already noted Etnier et al.'s (1997) suggestion that any positive cognitive impacts associated with physical activity may be related to (not fully understood) socio-psychological mechanisms independent of aerobic fitness and exercise.

Biddle's (2006) emphasis on task and mastery orientation and less competitive environments relates to literature on female sports participation and evidence that many young women are more likely to prefer such approaches (see review in Biddle et al., 2005; Wang et al., 2002). In this regard, Bowker et al. (2003) seek to explore the important distinction between sex and gender-role orientation and the effect that this has on attitudes to, and outcomes associated with, sport. In their study of 100 white middle-class Canadian teenagers (60 girls, 40 boys) they explored gender differences in domain-specific and global self-esteem and the role of sports participation and gender-role orientation in predicting any differences. They provide three main findings. First, although boys were more satisfied with their weight, appearance and perceived physical attraction, there were no significant gender differences in global self-esteem. The conclusion that they draw from this, and in agreement with Mason's (1995) findings, is that for girls competence in other domains may be 'compensating' for the lower scores on satisfaction with physical appearance. Second, gender role orientation, rather than sex, predicted feelings about appearance and athletic competence – those with the most 'feminine orientation' felt least positive about their appearance. Third, the nature of one's gender orientation affects the extent to which a more or less competitive environment benefits the sense of self (Biddle et al., 2005). However, it also worth noting Videon's (2002: 421) comment that girls might benefit from sport more than boys because 'sport socialization deviates from girls' gender socialization ... athletic participation emphasizes competition, independence, and achievement orientation, which are not traits that are encouraged in girls' socialization experiences'. Consequently, it is possible that participation in sport might have greater impact on academic outcomes than for males (Miracle and Rees, 1994) – although only one, rather limited, study has found this to be so

(Hanson and Kraus, 1998). Nevertheless, it is possible that providing activities which simply confirm gendered attitudes and modes of behaviour might, in certain circumstances, disadvantage young women (Scraton, 1989).

Ekeland *et al.* (2005), in a systematic review of 23 randomized control studies of the relationship between exercise and self-esteem in children and young people, emphasize the limitations of current research (and perhaps the methodology of systematic reviews: see Chapter 3). They conclude that the studies they reviewed 'cannot tell us anything about what kind of exercise might give positive effects and in which setting' (Ekeland *et al.*, 2005: 797). Further, the limitations of cross-sectional and experimental approaches have led many researchers to emphasize the need to explore issues of process and the mechanisms involved in the relationships between sports participation, physical self-esteem and global self-esteem and the possible relationship between these intermediate impacts and educational performance (Sibley and Etnier, 2003; Etnier *et al.*, 1997; Grissom, 2005; Bailey, 2005; Bailey *et al.*, in press). For example, in relation to the relationships between physical activity and well-being/self-esteem, Fox (1999) concludes that current evidence suggests that the social nature of the processes of participation may be more significant than physiological adaptations, or 'the quality of these encounters will ultimately determine whether self-perception outcomes are positive or negative' (Fox, 1992: 50).

The relatively weak and inconsistent relationship between sport and exercise and global esteem (dependent on the nature of the populations, individuals, activity contexts and processes) leads Fox (1992: 50) to argue that, because the physical self is only one component of the multidimensional self-esteem construct, 'it would be a political mistake for physical education to build its case on self-esteem promotion, because this fails to identify its unique contribution ... the physical self and physical competence, fitness and physical appearance'.

This argument also has some force when we look at the more important issues about the relationship between various aspects of physical self-worth, self-esteem and academic performance. For example, Taras (2005) points out that, although some studies found that physical activity can lead to improved physical fitness and self-concept, this often had little or no effect on long-term academic performance (MacMahon and Gross, 1988). Marsh (1993) refers to research which seems to indicate that academic achievement was strongly correlated with *academic self-concept*, but showed little relationship with more general domain-specific, self-concept measures. Trembaly *et al.* (2000) report on a Canadian cross-sectional study of about 5,000 Grade 6 pupils which compared self-report estimates of participation in physical activities (in and out of school), body-mass index, family background (students' possessions and family cultural activities) and self-esteem with the students' academic test scores (reading, mathematics, science and writing). Self-reported physical activity levels were significantly related to self-esteem, with increases in vigorous physical activity levels associated with progressive improvements in self-esteem for both males and females. However, increased levels of physical activity had a very weak relationship with academic achievement.

Emler (2001a: 27), in a major review of all aspects of self-esteem, summarizes the more general research evidence about the relationship between self-esteem and educational attainment as follows:

> Over many years of research, a consistent pattern is apparent. Self-esteem and educational attainment are related. But they are not strongly related. The strength of the association varies with age; with the educational outcome considered; with the sex, ethnic origin and socio-economic background of the individuals concerned; and with the measures of self-esteem used.

In fact, Emler (2001b) contends that longitudinal studies of the relationship between self-esteem and educational attainment indicate that the latter causes the former and not vice versa (although one assumes that this may be because academic self-concept is a major factor in general self-concept: Sonstroem and Morgan, 1989).

Depends on your sport?

Eitle and Eitle (2002) note that much research on sport, self-esteem and academic achievement treats sport as monolithic, with little exploration of the differential impacts of different sports and how this is mediated by such factors as gender, race and class (see also Eitle, 2005). They hypothesize that previous inconsistent findings about the relationship between sports participation and academic achievement may be explained partly by a failure to analyse sports-specific effects (i.e. that broad generalizations may mask differential impacts of particular sports on different types of participants). However, in seeking to explore this issue, they illustrate the complexity of the processes mediating the relationships between the choice of sport, participation in that sport and academic achievement. They suggest that insufficient attention is paid to the strong possibility that the association between sports and academic achievement may differ between social groups. For example, they point to research in the USA indicating that while sports participation was positively associated with educational outcomes for white students, no such effect was present for black students (e.g. Sabo *et al.*, 1993). Consequently, they argue that such relationships are mediated by factors associated with race, class, cultural capital (an important concept which is often weakly defined via surrogate measures, such as trips to museums), educational resources (e.g. books in home; computer; study space) and the choice of sports.

Via a secondary analysis of a sample of 5,000 black and white male high school students drawn randomly from the National Education Longitudinal Study in the USA, they explored potential differences in the effects of family factors on participation in types of sports. They concentrated on participation in American football and basketball (which offer a possible professional career) and the impact on academic outcomes (standardized composite 10th grade tests and self-reported grades). Their data seem to indicate that, between 8th and 10th grades, participation in basketball and American football was associated with a decline in academic achievement, especially when compared to participants in other sports. However, although they state that 'participation in different sports has differential consequences for academic achievement' (Eitle and Eitle, 2002: 141), their data suggest a more subtle explanation than this simple correlation. For example, their data indicate that those most likely to choose to take part in basketball and American football, both black and white, tend to have lower 'cultural capital' and academic resources (see also Eitle, 2005). In other words, rather than sports simply serving as a drain on energies that could be spent on maximizing academic achievement, certain economically and culturally disadvantaged males may pursue some sports because they lack the resources necessary to perform well academically, which only serves to further disadvantage them – as argued some time ago by Edwards (1986). In a follow-up study Eitle (2005) illustrated that although, understandably, participation in basketball reduced rates of early drop-out from school, this did not guarantee improved educational performance. As Eitle and Eitle (2002: 141–2) state:

> The temporal ordering of the relationship between involvement in sports and academic achievement may be more complicated than some have previously assumed … cultural disadvantage may contribute to an increased interest in and dependence on particular sports and that this dependence on sports may have additional adverse consequences for its participants in terms of academic achievement.

A related speculation by Eitle and Eitle (2002) is that participation in sport might increase various forms of human, social and cultural capital via mixing with a variety of different types of people – akin to Putnam's (2000) bridging capital or Coleman's (1988–9) version of social capital and the development of human capital. However, if certain sports differentially attract participants from disadvantaged backgrounds, then the possibility of developing educationally relevant social capital may be more limited, rather like Putman's (2000) more limiting, bonding social capital (McNeal, 1999). Likewise, they speculate that sports may differentially assist those who are already advantaged and/or the advantages of sports participation are likely to be used more effectively by the already advantaged (Sabo *et al.*, 1993) – in other words, in certain circumstances sports participation may result in the reinforcement of social and educational disadvantage. In this regard Taras (2005) speculates that the beneficial effects of physical activity and sport on academic performance may only exist in certain subpopulations. These speculations about types of sport and related social capitals bring us to research which suggests that the key to understanding any relationships between sports participation and academic performance might lie in the social relationships associated with participation and the meaning that they have for participants.

It's not what you do, but who you do it with

Snyder and Spreitzer (1990) outline six, interrelated, largely sociological hypotheses as to why school sports participation might lead to an improvement in educational performance.

(i)   A participation-identification model (Finn, 1989) which leads to increased interest in the school and its core academic values and pursuits. For example, Taras (2005) suggests that children who learn to cooperate, share and abide by rules of group physical activities are likely to feel more committed to their school and community and want to challenge themselves. Eitle (2005) views this as a 'functionalist' argument, based on notions of pattern maintenance (participants are socialized into mainstream expectations), integration (players are connected with academically oriented students and role models, increasing their attachment to the school) and goal orientation (achieving within boundaries of rules).

(ii) Increased self-concept generalizes to academic achievement. For example, Spady (1970) suggests that participation in sport could lead to an increase in perceived social status and Grabe (1981) suggests that this was most likely in small schools. Videon (2002) argues that feelings of popularity have been shown to mediate the relationship between sports participation and expectations to attend university in the USA. As peer acceptance is central to development, such acceptance is most likely if a child is good at something valued by peers. Being a competent athlete is likely to be regarded as a strong social asset and physical education may provide a means of enhancing the peer status and social integration of unpopular children (Evans and Roberts, 1987). Marsh (1993: 25) suggests that 'the most consistent effect of participation in sport appears to be an increase in perceived social status (or perceived popularity [and it] does appear to have positive effects on educational aspirations' (if not educational performance). More generally, Lipsky (1981) suggests that merely being interested in, and knowledgeable about, sports can facilitate social acceptance.

(iii) Increased attention from coaches, teachers and parents as a result of sports participation encourages academic achievement. Videon (2002) also suggests that greater attention, encouragement and advice lead to an increased attachment to school among athletes.

(iv) Sport leads to membership of elite groups with an orientation to academic success (a form of social capital). However, as we have noted, Eitle and Eitle (2002) illustrate that, if certain sports differentially attract participants from disadvantaged backgrounds, then the possibility of developing such educationally relevant social capital may be more limited.

(v)   Eligibility to take part in sport (especially representative teams) may depend on, and therefore encourage, educational performance (see also Eitle and Eitle, 2002).

(vi) The expectation of participation in university sports (which in the USA provide an entry to certain professional sports) serves as an incentive to obtain appropriate qualifications.

Marsh (1993) sought to explore some of these issues via a major longitudinal study in the USA looking at the effects of sports participation during the last two years of high school, with a sample of over 10,000 drawn from the national High School and Beyond survey. Data from sophomore (second year) and senior years were used to compare sports participation, standardized achievement tests, post-secondary outcomes and background/demographic variables (e.g. race, gender, socio-economic status, school size). Marsh's (1993) overall conclusion is that participation in sport has many (robust) positive effects, with no apparent negative ones. However, although the biggest effect was related to 'self-concept', as in other research, this had little impact on educational achievement. Marsh (1993) suggests that the relationship between sports participation and academic achievement is mediated by smaller effects on academic self-concept and educational aspirations (which were equally strong for males and females) and contends that this supports the participation–identification model (Finn, 1989) and notions of investment in school.

This 'participation–identification' hypothesis is given further support in later work by Marsh and Kleitman (2003). Using a sample of 4,250 pupils from the USA National Education Longitudinal Study data they report on a six-year longitudinal study of the effects of athletic participation (in intra- and inter-mural and individual and team games) on growth and change during high school. The authors explore three hypotheses. First, the zero-sum model, which suggests that varying amounts of time devoted to academic, social and athletic activities are in competition with each other. Second, a 'threshold model' in which small to moderate amounts of athletic participation have benefits, but with diminishing returns after a certain level of participation. Third, the 'identification/commitment model' which suggests that athletic participation enhances identification with school, involvement and commitment in a way that enhances academic outcomes. In all cases they controlled for pre-existing differences and background variables. Regression analysis indicated that participation in high school sports had positive effects on many Grade 12 and post-secondary outcomes: school grades, coursework selection, homework, educational and occupational aspirations, self-esteem, university applications, subsequent college enrolment and eventual educational attainment. In contrast to the zero-sum and threshold models, these positive effects generalized across academic and non-academic outcomes, across the range of athletic participation levels and across different subgroups, with the positive effects of athletic participation almost completely linear. Once again, sports participation is hypothesized to increase identification/commitment to school and school values which mediate the participation effects, particularly for narrowly defined academic outcomes not directly related to sports participation. Consistent with this identification/commitment model, extra-mural sport (and to a lesser degree team sports) had more positive effects than intra-mural and individual sports.

This identification/commitment model is also given some support by a suggestive, but limited, three-year study of social capital, group cohesion and pro- and anti-social behaviour in 21 US high schools. Langbein and Bess (2002) used school records of serious incidents and suspensions to examine the impact of participation in interscholastic sport programmes on delinquency in schools, controlling for school size. The authors conclude that, although larger schools have more disturbances, bigger interscholastic sports programmes mitigate these effects. The impact of sports participation increases disturbances in small schools but, at some point of inflection, as schools grow larger, sports participation decreases disturbances. However, when the sports participation rate is below a certain threshold, the effect of greater school size is to increase the disturbance rate. For most schools varsity and junior varsity athletic programmes reduced the rate (and number) of disturbances. As schools get larger, participation in the elite and glamorous inter-scholastic sports mitigated disturbances. The authors suggest that, in respect of fostering pro-social behaviour, either the schools should be smaller, or opportunities for numerous and diverse interactive smaller groups within the larger schools should be expanded. However, the authors point to a number of limitations with the study – in particular, it is not clear if sports participants or non-participants are most involved in disturbances!

But at least it does no academic harm

We have already noted Fox's (1992) warning about the political dangers in claiming too much for physical education and thereby ignoring its unique (and measurable) contribution. In the context of mixed, inconsistent and largely non-cumulative evidence about the positive educational impacts of physical education and sport, those committed to increasing (or retaining) them in the school curriculum have recourse to a similar position. Shephard (1997) reviews more general evidence about the relationship between daily physical education and the academic performance of primary school pupils, using one cross-sectional and three longitudinal studies which used experimental and control groups in France, Australia and Canada. One of these is the seminal and much quoted Canadian Trois Rivières quasi-experimental study. This was a six-year study of 546 primary school students from one urban and one rural school. The experimental group was given one extra hour of physical education per day by a specialist physical educator, with the others receiving only the standard physical education programme delivered by their class teacher (meaning that the experimental group had about 14 percent less academic instruction time). Overall, in grades 2 to 6 the experimental students academically outperformed the control group in maths and English (in a French-speaking school), with the effect strongest among girls. However, the effects were not consistent and varied substantially between subject areas. Shepherd and Trudeau (2005), in a retrospective evaluation, suggest a rather complex interaction of factors to explain the higher marks of the experimental group. In addition to the direct impact of physical activity (better behaviour – also reported by a wide range of studies – and an arousal-induced increase of attention) they also speculate that there might have been 'more effective academic teaching because the staff gains a break from instruction over the course of the day' (Shepherd and Trudeau, 2005: 118). The Australian study (Dwyer *et al.*, 1983) involved random allocation of primary school pupils to different levels of daily physical activity. No differences in academic performance were recorded – i.e. the group allocated the extra hours of physical education illustrated no significant differences in educational performance compared to the other group.

Shephard (1997) highlights methodological limitations in each of the studies, such as small experimental groups, lack of detail about the criteria for matching experimental and control groups on factors which might affect educational performance (e.g. socio-economic status) and short experimental time periods. Although there are some indications of a correlation between increased curriculum physical activity and *some* improvement in educational performance, Shephard's (1997: 127) overall conclusion is that 'daily programs of physical education should not be introduced with the expectation that they will lead to major gains in academic performance'.

Sallis *et al.* (1999) report on a study in seven Californian schools of the effects of a two-year health-related physical education programme on standardized academic achievement scores for 754 children in 4th, 5th and 6th grades. The schools were randomly assigned to three groups:

Group 1. Certified PE specialists taught the Sports, Play and Active Recreation for Kids (SPARK) curriculum. This is a three days per week programme which includes physical activity, self-management skills and parental involvement. Its aim was to promote high levels of physical activity, movement skills, encourage positive socialization and, via self-management, promote physical activity outside school.
Group 2. Classroom teachers were trained to implement the curriculum and develop classroom management and instructional skills.
Group 3. A control group continued with their usual programme.

All children were pre- and post-tested on nationally accepted achievement tests (reading, mathematics, language and a composite score). The study produced no robust evidence that the *specialist provision* had favourable effects on academic performance, although both the specialist and classroom teacher groups performed better than the control group (with the maximum academic contact time). In fact, over the two-year period *all* post-test scores decreased. However, the study produced an interesting insight with important implications for consideration of the social processes involved. The students in the trained classroom teacher group performed better than students in the control group, leading Sallis *et al.* (1999) to conclude that the training received by classroom teachers may have improved their ability to manage children and/or increased their confidence in the teaching of academic subjects and/or improved their relationships with pupils via the less formal situations in PE (this is also implied by Lindner's (1999) findings).

Overall, Sallis *et al.* (1999) suggest that their findings confirm the conclusion of other studies, that spending more time in physical education did not have harmful effects on academic achievement. Consequently, devoting substantially increased school time to health-related physical education does not have a detrimental effect on students' academic performance, while conferring physical and mental health benefits (for the same firm conclusion see Marsh, 1993; Shephard, 1997; Lindner, 1999; Sibley and Etnier, 2003).

Maybe it's sport plus

Projects using sport to address issues of anti-social behaviour and recidivism are increasingly using a *sports plus* approach (Chapter 7), based on an increasing recognition that desired outcomes cannot be taken for granted, are rarely guaranteed simply by sports participation and that there is a need to 'manage for outcomes'. For example, Danish and Nellen (1997) argue that, if sport is to provide young people with some of the desired life-skills, a more focused and analytical approach is required. They draw on their experience in the USA of the *Going for the Goal* programme (a 10 hour, 10 session programme) and the *Sports United to Promote Education and Recreation* (SUPER) programme, in which instructors are told to focus on *how* participants are participating, rather than on how well they are *performing*. They suggest that specially designed sports-based programmes can be delivered to develop a range of transferable skills (e.g. goal-setting; communication; handling success and failure) and enhance self-perception and social competence. However, in order to achieve these outcomes, there is a need for specially trained personnel who concentrate on process and task, rather than the more traditional approach of performance and outcome behaviours (see also Biddle, 2006).

Petitpas *et al.* (2004) illustrate some of these general issues via an analysis of the *Play it Smart* programme in the USA. This broad-based community programme, funded by the National Football Foundation, uses specially trained academic coaches to establish academic, counselling and coaching relationships with American football players in inner-city areas. Its three broad aims are (i) to improve grade point averages and graduation rates; (ii) to increase involvement in community service activities; (iii) to improve knowledge and use of health-enhancing behaviours. In addition to coaching football, these coaches provide many of the services typically seen in guidance or academic counselling programmes and seek to establish a positive gang experience and foster close relationships with community organizations and parents. The results of the two-year pilot programme indicated that grade point averages increased and were above the general school average, standard academic scores were above the general school population and the matriculation rate into higher education was double that of the general school population. Petitpas *et al.* (2004) acknowledge that the lack of a control group limits their ability to attribute the results solely to the programme (although it has now been extended to 88 high schools).

The salience of sport for many young people has been used in partnerships with educators and youth workers to attract young people deemed to be at risk to educational environments that they might otherwise not attend. For example, the *Midnight Basketball* initiatives use access to high-quality basketball facilities and leagues to attract young people to classes in drug counselling, personal development and so on (see Chapter 7). In Chapter 5 we noted the success of sport-in-development organizations in attracting large number of young people, enabling them to address issues of HIV/AIDS education (although their ultimate effectiveness has still to be proven).

One specifically educational example of such a partnership is the UK-based *Playing for Success* programme, in which sport is used to help to motivate young under-achieving pupils to attend out-of-school-hours study-support centres at professional football clubs (Sharp et al., 2003). This programme was established in 1997 as a partnership between the Department for Education and Skills (DfES), the Football Association, Premier League, Nationwide League, their clubs and local authorities. In 2006, 154 clubs were involved (not just football), with a target of 55,000 pupils per year attending the centres. Centres are equipped with the latest ICT facilities and are open after school hours, at the weekend and during school holidays. Typically, each pupil attends a weekly two-hour session for 10 weeks. A centre manager (a qualified and experienced teacher) is supported by higher education and further education students and members of the local community working as mentors. Pupils are nominated by their schools, although attendance is voluntary. The variety of selection criteria includes: pupils who would benefit; children who have low self-esteem/lack confidence; pupils who are under-achieving in terms of their ability; pupils who showed an interest; pupils lacking motivation toward school work (Sharp et al., 2003). This led to pupils with initial numeracy and reading comprehension scores well below the level expected for their age, with just over half (54 percent) being boys and a quarter from ethnic minority backgrounds (Sharp et al., 2003). Part of the attraction is clearly the opportunity to attend the ground of a major local professional football team and the possibility to meet players and be presented with certificates and prizes by members of the management and players. Importantly, attending classes in such high-status environments may also serve to reduce any sense of stigma associated with study support, with Sharp et al. (2003: 8) concluding that the pupils 'felt privileged to be selected, rather than singled out as in need of extra help'.

The evaluation of the fourth year of operation of the scheme (Sharp et al., 2003) is based on a mixture of data on pupil outcomes on nationally standardized tests, self-completion questionnaires and control groups of similar students who did not attend. The findings indicate the following:

- Despite sessions being held after school, most attended for 80 percent or more of the course.

- On average, primary pupils improved their numeracy scores by the equivalent of 17 months and secondary pupils by about 24 months.
- Performance in reading comprehension improved, although the progress of primary pupils did not reach statistical significance. Secondary pupils' reading comprehension scores improved significantly, by the equivalent of eight months.
- Compared with the control group, the changes of greatest educational significance were evident in pupils' independent study skills and self-image.

Clearly this is an educational initiative within a sports context, with the football clubs proving to be attractive and a strong element in motivating pupils to attend the classes. For example, only 5 percent of girls and 1 percent of boys stated that they were not interested in sport (although there were significant gender and ethnic differences in the type of favourite sport). However, it is clear that the nature and quality of the educational environment is the key to success. High-quality facilities, lower pupil/teacher ratios (providing pupils with immediate help), the use of student-centred target-setting and independent, supported, learning are all identified as keys to success. More generally, Sharp *et al.* (1999: 8) suggest that 'attending an educational setting other than school gave underachieving youngsters the opportunity to make a "fresh start"'. Nevertheless, although the outcomes are clearly related to a distinctive learning environment, the *Playing for Success* initiative illustrates the potential contribution which sport (in this case professional football clubs) can make to multi-agency programmes aimed at wider aspects of personal, educational and social development.

The exam results

Despite a range of studies which appear to indicate varying degrees of correlations between (often self-reported) participation in physical activity and sport and enhanced academic performance (variously defined and measured), it is not possible to draw definitive conclusions and policy recommendations. In part this is because of the widespread difficulties in controlling for the variety of factors which influence educational achievement and the problems of assessing the direction of cause and effect. For example, Shephard (1997) suggests that it is unclear whether intelligence leads to success in sport, whether participation in sport enhances academic performance, or whether both academic success and a predilection for physical activity are related to some third set of physiological, psychological or sociological factors. Several researchers point to a 'selection effect' and suggest that when background characteristics (e.g. social class, sex, ethnicity, cultural capital) are taken into account, the correlations between sports participation and academic performance are much weaker (Miller *et al.*, 2005; Holland and Andre, 1987).

In terms of the overall concerns of this book, a key issue is the increasingly widespread recognition that, even where strong correlations are measured, there is an inability to specify the nature of any relationships, process or mechanisms, with many researchers resorting to speculation (Etnier *et al.*, 1997; Sallis *et al.*, 1999; Marsh and Kleitman, 2003; Eitle and Eitle, 2002). If participation in sport is related to improved academic performance, it can only be via its ability to develop and/or strengthen a series of *intermediate factors* (speculatively ranging from cerebral changes via social acceptance to forms of social capital), which are presumed to be related in some ways to performance in the education system. This raises important questions as to the extent to which 'sport' can develop these intermediate factors and the contention that much research is limited by a tendency to treat sport (and the associated processes) as somewhat monolithic (Eitle and Eitle, 2002; Eitle, 2005), with a lack of systematic research on the possible different effects of different types of sport on different subpopulations. These are clearly not solely 'academic' questions, as they have major implications for policy, investment, provision and management. It is for this reason that many researchers and practitioners are arguing that there is a need to understand processes – the mechanisms by which such outcomes are achieved for which groups in which circumstances. For example, in a major review of the educational benefits claimed for physical education and school sport (PESS), Bailey *et al.* (in press: 27) conclude:

> One concerning omission from the existing literature is that which offers a coherent analytical framework for explaining possible effects associated with PESS/ physical activity ... few studies seek to explore the precise mechanisms that might cause cognitive benefits, or the ways in which different types of activity and different ways they are presented might initiate those mechanisms. Some of the studies also fail to distinguish sufficiently between correlation and causation. In light of the evidence of the influence of socio-economic factors, parental investment, the social context of playing and other variables on participation in many activities ... it is not warranted to move from a finding that two types of measures are *related* – such as physical activity and school performance – to the claim that one *caused* the other.

For the authors the way forward, in line with the position adopted in this book, 'would be to adopt a theory of change approach to PESS' (Bailey *et al.*, in press: 31) in order to question assumptions and implied causal links and 'in an accountability framework, it is self-evident that any changes made should be based on robust research evidence' (Bailey *et al.*, in press: 32). In the context of the information presented in this chapter and Bailey *et al.*'s (in press) conclusions about the existing evidence, it is worth noting that Weiss (1997: 520) argues that 'probably the clearest call for TBE [theory based evaluation] comes when prior evaluations show inconsistent results'.

Finally, a more important set of questions relate to the extent to which any 'sport effects' are in fact related to improved educational performance. For example, we have noted the need to distinguish between the development of physical self-efficacy/worth/esteem, its complex relationship with global self-esteem and Emler's (2001b) contention that evidence tends to suggest that educational success leads to self-esteem and not vice versa. Perhaps the difficulty, or impossibility, of addressing these issues explains the appeal of the 'it does not do any harm position'. In other words, although it is extremely difficult to prove that participation in sport leads to improved academic performance, devoting substantially increased school time to it does not appear to have a detrimental effect on students' academic performance, while conferring physical and mental health benefits (Sallis *et al.*, 1999; Shephard, 1997; Lindner, 1999; Sibley and Etnier, 2003).

More generally Taras (2005) argues that it is probable that any benefits of physical activity on academic performance are subtle (and subgroup related) and can only be detected when extremely large populations of students are studied. This position is given support, and a new light shone on the various methodological difficulties, by Grissom's (2005: 13) argument that the widespread failure of experimental designs to find statistically significant differences between experimental and control subjects

> is due in part to the difficulty in raising academic achievement. It is very difficult to raise student achievement, beyond what might be expected, even when that is the specific focus. A study intended to affect achievement indirectly [i.e. via participation in PE and sport] would encounter even more difficulty.

In a sense the issues dealt with in this chapter could be regarded as generic. Many of the claims related to sport's wider social role relate, implicitly or explicitly, to its presumed ability to develop cognitive skills, self-efficacy, self-confidence, self-esteem, forms of social capital and so on (although as we have seen, the question remains as the extent to which this occurs and the relationship of such intermediate impacts with the desired outcomes). We now turn to a policy area which shares many similar assumptions and desired outcomes: sport and crime prevention.

Sport and crime prevention

Playing by the rules?

Fair cop or fair play?

Vague and unexamined claims about sport's ability to address issues of anti-social behaviour and crime have always underpinned public investment in sport. From nineteenth-century concerns with social order and the moral condition of the new urban working classes (Bailey, 1979); via the 1975 White Paper's (Department of the Environment, 1975: 2) concern to reduce 'boredom and urban frustration' and contribute to 'the reduction of hooliganism and delinquency among young people'; to the establishment of Action Sport in 1981 in response to urban riots and 'the urgency, in view of the social problems, of putting leaders on the street' (Sports Council Annual Report, 1981/2, quoted in Rigg, 1986: 12), the supposed role of sport in combating anti-social behaviour and delinquency has been a key part of the rationale for public sector investment in sport.

The relationship between sport and crime prevention reflects the mythopoeic nature of sport (Chapter 2) and forms a central part of policy-makers' 'established repertoires' (Chapter 3). Sport (usually assumed to be competitive team games) has traditionally been regarded as having a 'moral' component, teaching 'lesson for life', contributing to 'character building' (e.g. honesty, integrity, trustworthiness), the development of self-discipline and deferred gratification and positive moral reasoning, such as a commitment to 'fair play' (although the evidence for the latter is not strong) (President's Council on Physical Fitness and Sports, 2006). These are often reinforced with ad hominem stories about how sport 'saved me from a life of crime'.

The debate about the relationship between sports participation and crime divides broadly into theories about the rehabilitation of offenders and theories about crime prevention (or 'diversion'). The former approach tends to involve small schemes, focused on a limited number of offenders (often based on outdoor adventure activities). They tend to be much less 'product-led' and to be based on an intensive counselling approach, in which the needs of offenders are identified and programmes adapted to suit their needs, aimed at developing personal and social skills and improving self-efficacy, self-confidence, self-esteem and locus of control – which it is hoped will transfer to the wider social context and reduce offending behaviour (Coalter, 1988; Taylor *et al.*, 1999; West and Crompton, 2001; Nichols and Crow, 2004).

Diversionary programmes, which are the predominant concern of social policy, tend to be relatively large-scale, open-access sports programmes targeted at 'youth-at-risk' in specific areas and/or during specific time periods (e.g. summer sports programmes; midnight basketball). Even before New Labour's concern with social exclusion, this approach was part of broader social and urban regeneration programmes. For example, Simmonds (1994) estimated that, in the first round of Single Regeneration Bids, 20 urban regeneration partnerships secured £67 million worth of sports-related initiatives which identified the reduction of youth crime as an objective and were included as part of broader community safety programmes. In 1997 the National Recreation and Parks Association identified over 600 pilot programmes in the USA focused on at-risk youth (Witt and Crompton, 1997).

This approach was reinforced by New Labour's social inclusion agenda. A combination of factors served to place sport more centrally and formally on the 'community safety' agenda: the emphasis on the contribution of all public organizations to cross-cutting agendas; the inclusion of 'living in a high crime environment' as a major component of the definition of social exclusion (both a cause and consequence of socially excluded environments); a diffuse concern with 'active citizenship' and latterly a high-profile political emphasis on a 'respect agenda' which is 'about nurturing and, where needed, enforcing a modern culture of respect' (www. respect.gov.uk). These factors ensured that sport featured strongly in statements about the new cross-cutting approach to social policy. For example, Policy Action Group 10 (DCMS, 1999: 23) stated that 'sport can contribute to neighbourhood renewal by improving communities' performance on four key indicators – health, crime, employment and education'. Even more explicitly, the Scottish Office (1999: 22) claimed that 'arts, sport and leisure activities ... can give young people a purposeful activity, reducing the temptation to anti-social behaviour'.

In this policy environment a range of local initiatives were launched. Many were rather opportunistic traditional sports development schemes, using the reinforced emphasis on crime prevention to obtain funding, but frequently failing to articulate systematically how they would lead to a reduction in crime. The significance of sport in the new cross-cutting social agenda is indicated by the establishment of a national sports-based programme called Positive Futures (www. positivefuturesresearch.org.uk). This was established in 2002, and by 2003/4 it had approximately £6 million funding, as a partnership between the Home Office Drugs Strategy Directorate, Sport England, the Youth Justice Board and the Football Foundation. The initial 24 Positive Future projects were targeted at 10–16 year olds in wards identified as the 20 percent most deprived (the most socially excluded). The intended outcomes were:

- an increase in regular participation in sport and physical activity by 10–16 year olds;
- a reduction of youth offending in the locality of a project; and
- a reduction in drug use among 10–16 year olds participating on the schemes.

Other initiatives were loosely based on 'midnight soccer/basketball' models from the USA (where they seemed to have been associated with reductions in recorded crime: Morgan, 1998; Wilkins, 1997; Hartmann and Depro, 2006). These (and some of the Positive Futures projects) tended to be based on a 'sport-plus' approach, in which sport enters into partnerships with other agencies to combine sport with other developmental activities. The latter approaches in part signify a growing sophistication and understanding of the developmental limitations of simple sports participation. Many of the early projects reflected various combinations of the historical view of sport as a cost-effective 'solution' to complex social problems; traditional professional repertories and self-interest; opportunism and the underfunded nature of most community sports-development programmes and the need for national agencies to be seen to be 'doing something' in the new policy environment (Weiss, 1993). However, as the area has matured (although many of these pressures remain), there is a growing realization that some version of a 'sports plus' approach is needed – a growing realization that such interventions are 'complex systems thrust amidst complex systems' (Pawson, 2006: 5). We now turn to the exploration of some of these complexities.

What is anti-social behaviour?

A major narrative review of the social impacts of sport concluded that, although there appeared to be strong theoretical arguments for the potentially positive contribution which sport can make to the reduction of the propensity to commit crime, 'there is an absence of robust intermediate or final outcome data' (Coalter *et al.*, 2000: 47). A similar review of 11 UK schemes designed to use sport to divert young people from criminal behaviour found that 'information about outcomes was hard to come by' (Robins, 1999: 92); a review of 120 programmes for at-risk youth in the USA found that 30 percent undertook no evaluation and only 4 percent undertook pre/post evaluation of participation-related changes (Witt and Crompton, 1996a).

The absence of systematic evidence of the effectiveness of such programmes can be explained by a number of factors. At the level of practice there has been an absence of a culture of monitoring and evaluation, bolstered by a range of factors: a simple belief in the efficacy of such interventions; limited project funding is concentrated on provision rather than evaluation and a general lack of research expertise. However, most fundamentally there has been a widespread lack of clarity about the nature of outcomes and their measurement; substantial methodological difficulties in controlling for intervening variables and assessing cause and effect relationships (Taylor, 1999; Nichols and Crow, 2004; Coalter *et al.*, 2000; Witt and Crompton, 1996a; Morris *et al.*, 2003). Witt and Crompton (1996a: 12) state that 'the lack of specific objectives written in an operational format leads to the inference that many agencies have not identified specific standards by which to evaluate the success of their programmes' (Witt and Crompton, 1996a: 12).

Such problems are also evident in the more focused, small-scale, rehabilitation programmes. For example, West and Crompton (2001), in a review of North American outdoor recreation programmes, reported that of 14 programmes reporting recidivism rates, eight reported reduced rates and of the 16 reporting changes in self-concept, 14 showed significant positive changes. However, the authors gave only tentative support for such approaches because of a lack of internal validity, lack of consistency in defining recidivism and self-concept and a lack of control groups. More fundamentally, Taylor (1999) argues that the major problem in identifying and measuring the effects of sport on criminal behaviour (if any) is that the influence on behaviour is indirect, working through a number of intermediate outcomes or processes, such as improved fitness, self-efficacy, self-esteem or locus of control and the development of certain social and personal skills. It is clearly not sufficient to measure changed behaviours and simply to assume that these are 'sports-effects'.

A major study of British rehabilitation programmes concluded that evaluation was variable and that performance indicators ranged from the simple monitoring of attendance, via the use of anecdotal evidence, to a few who estimated reconviction rates. The conclusion illustrates many of our more general concerns with policy dilemmas, programme processes and mechanisms and methodological limitations:

> Programme managers ... feel that quantitative indicators are insufficient to capture the essence of the outputs [and] that this reflects the difficulty of not only determining the significant variables but also measuring the precise effect they have ... there is a problem finding qualitative evaluation techniques which are feasible with limited resources, but which adequately monitor the complex outcomes which most of the programmes aspire to. All programmes agree that physical activities do not by themselves reduce offending. All agree that there are personal and social development objectives that form part of a matrix of outcomes. These developments may, sooner or later, improve offending behaviour, but their impact is unpredictable in scale and timing.
>
> (Taylor *et al.*, 1999: 50)

Such tentative conclusions relating to highly focused and small-scale projects clearly raise major issues when we consider large-scale, open access, diversionary programmes. It has consistently been noted that many of these have a number of common weaknesses, such as vague rationales, overly ambitious objectives and a relatively unsophisticated understanding of the variety and complexity of the causes of criminality (Coalter *et al.*, 2000; Robins, 1990; Utting, 1996). For example, in considering the causes of crime, Asquith *et al.* (1998) identify a complex and interdependent range of socio-psychological 'high-risk factors' which include: hyperactivity, high impulsivity, low intelligence, poor parental management, parental neglect, offending parents and siblings, early child bearing, deprived background, absent father and maternal substance abuse in pregnancy. In most cases there is little recognition of such complexity and little attempt to outline the variety of causes of the variety of behaviours which sport is meant to change. Allied to this are frequently vague definitions of the various forms of 'anti-social behaviours' with which projects seek to deal and which raise significant issues of validity and comparability when seeking to identify the 'stubborn empirical generalisation', the 'best buy' in policy terms (Pawson, 2001a: 6). These issues are illustrated by a study by Begg *et al.* (1996) which includes such wide-ranging behaviours as shoplifting, car theft, burglary, hitting parent/partner, fighting in the street or using a weapon in a fight. It is clearly a possibility that each of these behaviours reflects different values, attitudes and circumstances and that the nature of the 'sporting cure' (if there is one) might differ.

Related to the definition of 'anti-social behaviour' is the interesting question about the extent to which many young people may not accept that their behaviour needs to change (a major factor influencing the potential for the success of interventions). For example, Fitzpatrick *et al.* (1998) found that young people defined the issues in terms of *police harassment*, with the associated desire to gain adult respect and tolerance and to change other people's attitudes towards them and their neighbourhood. This finding was confirmed in a survey of 892 young people in Edinburgh in which only half (49 percent) thought that the police had a good understanding of the problems faced by young people, and only slightly more (54 percent) felt that the police treated young people fairly (Asquith *et al.*, 1998). It is clear that, among such young people, the philosophy and approach adopted may have a significant bearing on its attractiveness and effectiveness. As Pawson (2006: 27) argues, all social interventions are 'active interventions to *active* subjects', who may choose to accept the intervention's definitions and adopt them, thus changing behaviour in a favoured policy direction – or not.

These issues are related to a more general problem that the design of many programmes is not informed by any clear 'theory of change' (Granger, 1998). For example, an Australian study of 175 programmes (and 22 case studies) for at-risk youth concluded that (Morris *et al.*, 2003: 72) 'there is no significant relationship between program conception, delivery and intended outcomes in the type of activity provided' (see also Witt and Crompton, 1996a). Further, Purdy and Richards (1983) suggest that that both diversionary and rehabilitation programmes frequently ignore vital issues relating to the length, intensity and priority (the age of starting) of participation required to change values, attitudes and behaviour. In this regard McKenzie (1997) argues that interventions must directly address characteristics that can be changed and that are associated with an individual's criminal behaviour. The broad implication is that many programmes fail to address systematically the *causes* of the behaviour that they wish to change and the relationship of these causes to programme content and process. As Pawson (2006: 9) comments, programme design is frequently 'a research free zone'. For this reason we now turn to a consideration of some of the theories about the presumed nature of relationships between participation in sport and the propensity to participate in anti-social or criminal behaviour.

Theories of crime and theories of sport's processes

One way of illustrating the issues at stake is via a typology developed by Schafer (1969), which seeks to combine the interrelated issues of theories of the causes of delinquency and theories about the nature of sport's contributions to the reduction, or change, of such causes. He outlines five elements underpinning the 'therapeutic' potential of sport which are based on rather broad theories about causes of delinquency (boredom, peer group affiliations and differential association, educational failure and blocked aspirations and low self-esteem, lack of self-discipline and adolescent development needs). The theories of the causes of anti-social behaviour are rather crude and underdeveloped (they certainly do not address the complexities of Asquith *et al.*'s (1998) complex and interdependent socio-psychological and environmental factors). However, the approach serves to illustrate the need to understand the causes of behaviours that sport is trying to change, the nature of sports processes/mechanisms and how they are assumed to have the potential to achieve positive outcomes in relation to particular factors.

This general approach provides the basis for the development of 'theory-driven evaluation' (Pawson, 2006; Weiss, 1997) in which programmes are regarded as theories based on broad hypotheses about causes and cures. Clearly this requires some statement of the presumed causes of the type of behaviour that programmes wish to change and how they will seek to achieve this. Such understandings should enable programmes proactively to 'manage for outcomes'. The systematic articulation of the theory informing the programme also provides the basis for evaluation, especially where the precise measurement of outcomes is difficult (as is the case in most diversionary and many rehabilitation schemes). Evaluation can then be based partly on the articulation of the core theory of how the programme is supposed to work and an evaluation made as to whether the programme is sound, plausible and valid and delivered as intended (see Chapter 3).

We return to Schafer's (1969) typology.

Antidote to boredom

The most widespread, common-sense, assumption underpinning policies to combat anti-social behaviour is that 'the devil makes work for idle hands'. From this perspective much adolescent crime is opportunity-led and giving young people something (hopefully constructive) to do 'keeps them out of harm's way'. For example, the Scottish Office (1999: 4.34) promoted sport as part of its social inclusion strategy because it could provide young people with 'a purposeful activity, reducing the temptation to anti-social behaviour'. More general analyses suggest that perceived boredom may be related to alcohol use and in turn to crime (Orcutt, 1984), that it is related to depression, hopelessness and loneliness (McGiboney and Carter, 1988) and that it may be related to deviant behaviour at school (Wasson, 1988).

Such analyses inform investment in the widespread use of diversionary sports programmes which aim 'at the casual integration of youth at risk, in order to reduce delinquency rates by encouraging the positive use of their leisure time' (Robins, 1990: 19). One such programme was the much-publicized open-access summer Splash programme (Schools and Police Liaison Activities for the Summer Holidays), founded by £2 million government investment and administered by the

Youth Justice Board. It concentrated on a core of at-risk 13–17 year olds in high-crime housing estates in England and Wales. Evaluations of the Splash programmes claim that they led to an aggregate reduction in 'youth crime' (Loxley *et al.*, 2002; Cap Gemini Ernst and Young, 2003). For example, in 2003 it was reported that in ten areas total recorded crime reduced by 7.4 percent and 'juvenile nuisance' increased by only 0.1 percent (compared to 13.2 percent in an equivalent period prior to the scheme). However, it was admitted that such conclusions were based on small samples and that a robust analysis of local crime figures was difficult because of changes in approaches to recording and the different sizes of areas covered.

Nichols and Crow (2004) argue that such 'primary programmes', and more targeted 'secondary programmes' aimed at deterring criminal behaviour among identified at-risk youth, face substantial methodological problems in attempting to evaluate their effectiveness. First, they are rarely able to collect details of participants, certainly not definitive evidence about their 'at-risk' status (unless it is assumed that all young people in deprived areas are at risk). Another issue relates to the widely acknowledged limitations of *recorded* crime statistics – what is detected, reported and recorded often bears little relationship to actual levels of crime or anti-social behaviour and the areas to which they refer are often not co-terminal with the programme areas (see Loxley *et al.*, 2001; Cap Gemini Ernst and Young, 2003).

The most significant, generic, methodological issue relates to attempts to impute causal relations between such inclusive programmes and crime statistics. It is noticeable that, while apparent reductions in recorded crime statistics are frequently used as an indicator of the effectiveness of such programmes, they are usually accompanied by an admission of the limitations of such an approach (Cap Gemini Ernst and Young, 2003). A Home Office evaluation (Heal and Laycock, 1987) of summer programmes found it extremely difficult to prove that statistically insignificant reductions in crime were *caused* by the programme. Coalter (1998) quotes an internal police review of a summer programme which acknowledges that the evidence of the impact of the programme on recorded crime was inconclusive, but argues that it still had a value because it increased the choice of the type and number of *non-criminal opportunities* available to young people during school holidays. However, Heal and Laycock (1987) concluded that such schemes will become less effective as the initial novelty declines and, despite a possible short-term diversionary effect, there was no evidence about the longer term impact on the attitudes and behaviour of participants. A Home Office review of such programmes (Utting, 1996) concluded that 'it is difficult to argue that such activities have in themselves a generalisable influence on criminality. The lack of empirical research means important practice issues remain unresolved.'

It is interesting to note that as such diversionary schemes have developed, some have moved to a 'sports plus' model by including more focused and structured developmental activities, such as advice on anger management, alcohol and drug abuse, personal health and hygiene, and vocational training. We will return to this below.

Differential association

From this perspective anti-social behaviour is learned behaviour, which is developed in and supported and rewarded by delinquent peer groups. Consequently, it is suggested that sport provides an alternative social milieu via which such behaviour can be 'unlearned'. This seems to be based vaguely on social learning theory (Bandura, 1962; Bandura and Ribes-Inesta, 1976; Payne *et al.*, 2003), in which people learn by imitating their observations of others' behaviours in an environment which rewards and reinforces such behaviours. Consequently, via the social processes and relationships involved in participation in sport, participants are influenced by 'significant others' (coaches, teachers, other participants) who provide appropriate, alternative, role models and espouse more conventional values. Further, participation can reduce or eliminate association with delinquent peers – either by reducing available time, or changing participants' interests and attitudes. This is also related to Schafer's (1969) theory that the sports environment emphasizes traits such as deferred gratification and hard work, which lead to increased self-discipline and self-control (which it is presumed then lead to a reduction in the propensity for anti-social behaviour). Such a perspective is clearly based on a narrow and traditional definition of 'sport' associated with a desire to improve performance, rather than simply to participate for recreational or social purposes.

Clearly, the outcome of such processes will be contingent on a range of factors. For example, Segrave and Hastad (1984) found that formal participation in sport was not enough to generate commitment to institutions and non-delinquent values – sports were only one of a number of priorities and social experiences which influenced attitudes and behaviour. This, of course, is compounded by Fitzpatrick *et al.*'s (1998) analysis that young people often reject definitions of their behaviour as needing to be changed.

A more fundamental concern is that there is a clear assumption that sporting subcultures and relationships necessarily generate positive and 'pro-social' behaviour (a core belief underpinning sports policy rhetoric). However, in simple common-sense terms Patriksson's (1995) argument that sport, like all activities, is not a priori good or bad, but has the potential to produce both positive and negative outcomes seems obvious – especially when we consider the diversity of sport and sporting contexts. In a review of research on sport and moral reasoning, the President's Council on Physical Fitness and Sports (2006) reported on a series of studies which found that the maturity of moral reasoning and judgements among athletes was often less than that of non-athletes (although this varied slightly between types of sports). The broad conclusion is that there is a need for a 'sports plus' approach, with more systematic discussions between coaches and players of moral and ethical issues relevant to sports, teams and broader social issues.

Endersen and Olwens (2005) report on a two-year longitudinal cohort study of 500 11–13 year old males in 37 schools in Bergen. Using a social learning theory perspective they examined relationships between participation in power sports (boxing, weightlifting, wrestling and oriental martial arts) and self-reported violent and anti-social behaviour. The data indicated that participants in power sports had higher levels of self-reported, anti-social involvement than non-participants. Further, 'enhancement effects' were found, with the results indicating that stopping participation in power sports may lead to a relative reduction in anti-social behaviour. No self-selection effects were found, with the same type of behaviour found in novices and for boys with one-year prior experience. The strongest relationships were found for boxing and weightlifting, with the correlation between boxing and self-reported violence particularly marked. The weaker correlations for martial arts were explained as resulting from their philosophy of non-violence. While admitting the limitations of self-reporting, the authors explain these outcomes as a result of the combined effects of enactive learning, violent role models and acceptance/reinforcement of violent and aggressive behaviour from coaches and peers. However, indicating the nature of the general methodological problems, the authors admit that issues relating to confounding variables are not adequately addressed, although the results could not be explained as a consequence of alcohol or drug use, gang membership or stage of pubertal development. The authors also admit that the study has restricted external validity and their ability to generalize from these results is limited.

Another longitudinal, self-report, study by Begg *et al.* (1996) examined the relationship between general participation in sport and 'serious delinquency' (shop-lifting, car theft, burglary, assault). After controlling for delinquent behaviour and psycho-social factors, the authors concluded that, at age 15, females with moderate or high levels of sporting activity were significantly more likely to be delinquent at age 18 years than those with low levels of sporting activity. Males with high levels of sporting activity were significantly more likely to be delinquent at age 18 than those with low levels of sporting activity. The authors conclude that the best predictor of delinquent behaviour at age 18 was delinquent behaviour at age 15, irrespective of involvement in sporting activity.

Clearly, simple participation in sport does not guarantee non-involvement in anti-social behaviour. In this regard, Begg *et al.* (1996) argue that deterrence requires a range of strategies which take into account the special needs and norms of delinquents – a position which is much more likely to be able to be addressed in small-scale focused programmes than broad open-access diversionary schemes. In this regard it is worth noting that Utting (1996), in a review of UK initiatives, stressed the important role of youth workers in the delivery of sporting programmes. More generally, there is clear evidence that the nature of the relationships formed between participants and providers in such programmes plays a significant role in maximizing the potential for the achievement of positive outcomes. For example, Nichols and Taylor (1996) report on a sports counselling programme for young probationers and suggest that the skills of the sports leaders and positive relationships between them and participants were part of the explanation for its relative success. Witt and Crompton (1996a: 16), in a review of programmes in the USA, conclude that 'leadership is perhaps the most important element in determining the positive impact of a program, since it shapes what participants derive from their experience'. More generally Svoboda (1994) asserts that positive effects are most likely to occur in the presence of 'appropriate' supervision, leadership or management.

Such comments indicate that, while sport might provide the context for the development of positive experiences, the social *process* of participation is the key to understanding what is happening. It is worth noting that these analyses have strong similarities with material presented in Chapter 6, which hypothesized that the development of cognitive abilities and feelings of efficacy and self-worth may be explained as outcomes of social processes and not simply (or even) the activity (Fox, 2000; Biddle, 2006). Further, Nichols and Taylor (1996) also identify a wide range of other factors which contribute to the relative success of the sports counselling programme (a reduction, but not abolition, of recidivism). These included the voluntary nature of participation, measured improvements to self-esteem and perceptions of fitness, the length of the course (the longer the better), involvement with a new peer group and access to employment-orientated training courses. In a broadly similar vein, West and Crompton (2001), in a North American review of the role and effectiveness of outdoor recreation programmes, emphasize the importance of what they refer to as 'protective factors'. These refer to the environment in which such activities take place and include participants knowing that adults support their positive development; the provision of places to spend free time in a positive, productive environment in their home area; opportunities to work in a group and to learn how to resolve conflicts constructively; the opportunity to be around peers consistently who are demonstrating positive conventional behaviour and placing a value on achievement (Witt and Crompton, 1997). Sandford *et al.* (2006: 262), in a review of research on the role of physical education programmes in re-engaging 'disaffected youth', state that 'it has been argued that the social relationships experienced during involvement in physical activity programmes are the most significant factor in effecting behavioural change'.

The findings of Nichols and Taylor (1996) and Witt and Crompton (1997) about relationships and process in small-scale rehabilitation projects are confirmed by Payne *et al.* (2003), who deal with the broader issue of the extent to which sports people act as role models and have a positive impact on individuals and the broader community. Importantly their review of research indicates that, in line with self-efficacy theory, sporting (or any) role models are more likely to influence learners if there is a perceived similarity with the learner – and this will vary by such factors as age, sex, gender, class and culture. Payne *et al.* (2003) suggest that learning will be most likely to occur when the learners perceive that they are capable of carrying out the behaviour (self-efficacy expectancy), think that there is a high probability that the behaviour will result in a particular outcome (outcome expectancy) and if the outcome is desirable (outcome value). Their conclusions of relevance to our concerns are that, while there is ample evidence to support the idea of (positive) role model programmes, the most effective are those that focus on developing a long-term mentor relationship, particularly for individuals from socially disadvantaged groups and at-risk groups. This approach focuses on the needs of the people involved, with attention paid to the selection and training of mentors and ongoing support. With regard to the latter point, Morris *et al.* (2003: 4) remind us that, after participation in programmes, most participants will return to their previous environment and that 'a program on its own cannot effectively produce lasting changes in antisocial behaviour by young people – there is a need for continual care in the community that encourages maintenance of positive behavioural change'.

The emphasis placed by various researchers on the importance of reinforcement, leadership styles and establishing a sense of self-efficacy (Witt and Crompton, 1997; Svoboda, 1994; Maugham and Ellis, 1991) brings us to another of Schafer's (1969) perspectives: that sport can compensate for blocked aspirations, low educational achievement and low self-esteem – all presumed to explain anti-social behaviour.

Blocked aspirations, achievement and self-esteem

From this perspective anti-social behaviour is a form of adaptation, adjustment to and compensation for *blocked identity formation and status achievement*, usually resulting from educational failure and unemployment. A number of writers have pointed to the apparent association between low educational attainment and increased risks of delinquency (Rutter and Giller, 1983; Elliot and Voss, 1974; Utting, 1996). Emler (2001b) suggests that such arguments are variously based on a notion that people with low self-esteem have little to lose from any opprobrium they might attract by breaking the law; young people with low self-esteem are susceptible to influence from less law-abiding others (differential association); delinquency is a method for raising low self-esteem, especially in particular subcultures which value and reward various behaviours. From this perspective, achievement through sport is viewed as a sort of 'functional alternative', an alternative way of feeling a sense of achievement and developing self-esteem (a widespread theme in sport-related social policy).

More generally, Reid *et al.* (1994) quote evidence that regular physical activity can promote self-esteem (Calfas and Taylor, 1994) and that inactive subjects had three times the risk of depression compared to the active. This finding underpins their assertion that physical activity/recreation programmes can assist in the reduction of behavioural risk factors for young people. Carlson and Petti (1989) and MacMahon (1990) suggest that depression may be reduced and self-esteem increased via intensive aerobic exercise (see also Raglin, 1990; Steptoe, 1992). Fox (2000: 99) in a review of 36 studies concludes that there 'is a robust and significant finding [of] clear evidence that exercise helps people see themselves more positively'.

As we saw in Chapter 6, there is a large volume of research on issues relating to physical activity, sport and self-esteem and its apparently weak relationship with educational performance. The literature illustrates the complex and multifaceted nature of general, or global, self-esteem, pointing to the relative importance of performance in a variety of roles in several life domains which may contribute to self-concept and self-esteem (e.g. work, school, family, peer acceptance). Physical self-efficacy and physical self-worth, feelings of self-determination and personal control can be developed via improved sporting competence. They are only components in this system and their relative importance seems to vary between individuals and by age and gender, although Fox (2000) argues that because the physical domain features strongly in the value system of western culture, it is consistently included in models of self-esteem, with physical skills, fitness and sport competencies important to many young people. However, he argues that self-acceptance – the degree to which we accept our strengths and weaknesses – may also influence self-esteem. The issue of self-acceptance is an important factor in the design of interventions to promote self-esteem because, 'it is possible … that self-esteem can be lowered through experiences in the physical domain if the conditions raise awareness and self-criticism without increasing perceived competence' (Fox, 2000: 94) – a risk for those already 'at risk'.

Further, reflecting some of the processes discussed in relation to differential association, Fox (2000) states that research indicates that there are several *mediating* variables to consider, including the degree of autonomy experienced by the exerciser, the centrality or importance of exercise or sport to the individual, the nature of the exercise leadership and the 'motivational climate' (akin to Witt and Crompton's (1997) 'protective factors'). In this regard Biddle (2006) suggests that the social climate of sports programmes is central to an understanding of the potential for the development of physical self-efficacy and self-esteem. He suggests that more traditional approaches to sport (competitive and ego-oriented) might not be the most appropriate approach to achieve such outcomes (here it is worth remembering McDonald and Tungatt's (1992) more general argument that social inclusion objectives might not be met via initiatives which incorporate the values of traditional sports provision: see Chapter 4). Biddle (2006) suggests that the enhancement of self-efficacy and self-esteem is most likely to be achieved in a social climate based on a task-oriented, mastery orientation in which participants' skills are matched with the challenge they face, which enable clear experiences of personal success and positive encouragement and seek to develop intrinsic motivational styles. For example, Maugham and Ellis (1991) found that positive verbal reinforcement and rapport with the recreation leader was an important factor underpinning measured improvements in young people's sense of efficacy and competence. Sugden and Yiannakis (1982) suggest that certain adolescents reject organized, competitive mainstream sport because it contains components similar to those which they have already failed to resolve: adherence to formal rules and regulations, achievement of externally defined goals and competitive and testing situations. Serok (1975) suggests that delinquents prefer games with fewer and less specified rules and with fewer requirements for conformity. Reflecting this, Rigg's (1986) analysis of the early Action Sport programmes for the unemployed emphasized the importance of an informal 'drop in' approach to encouraging participation and Robins (1990) refers to a number of diversionary sport projects whose main features were open access and a lack of rigid organization. Rijpma and Meiburg (1989) describe a successful initiative in Rotterdam aimed at marginal youth, based on 'open youth centres' (neighbourhood centres without membership) that provided small-scale facilities for weight-training in an atmosphere which did not place an emphasis on skill.

Andrews and Andrews (2003) report on an eight-month participant observation study of 20 residents (aged 12–17, including 5 girls) in a secure unit in the UK. The authors illustrate the potentially threatening nature of traditional sports for such volatile young people. The ethos of sport and exercise provision involved small group and individual lessons. Where games were played, they had minimal rules and a strong emphasis on fun as an escape from the strict regulations governing the unit. Autonomy and ownership were encouraged by letting the young people construct their own gym programme, based on individual aims and goals and their appraisal of their abilities. To foster self-esteem, peer comparison of physical abilities was not encouraged, emphasis was placed on task mastery, support was not contingent on performance and feedback was fair and appropriate. Further, the authors argue that care needs to be taken in providing aggressive sports which reaffirm adolescent masculine aggression (see Endersen and Olwens, 2005). The authors suggest that traditional sport may not be as effective in cultivating principled moral judgement as theories suggest (Crabbe, 2000; President's Council on Physical Fitness and Sports, 2006). Like others, their general conclusion is that sporting activities should de-emphasize regulations and winning, place an emphasis on choice, with programmes tailored to suit individual needs and the regular use of positive feedback.

Although it is clear that, for some people, appropriate provision and processes of participation in sport can serve to enhance a sense of self-efficacy and physical self-esteem, Fox's (2000: 97) review of research concluded that in general 'participation in sport and exercise was weakly associated with global self-esteem', with the relationship being dependent on the nature of the population, environment and individual characteristics. In a broadly similar vein, West and Crompton (2001) criticized outdoor recreation programmes for having too narrow a focus on the measurement of self-concept, rather than the impact of multiple 'protective factors'.

However, although appropriate processes can be used to enhance the possibility of increasing individuals' self-esteem, there are two major policy-related issues to consider. First, MacMahon and Gross (1988) warn that, as with all short-term programmes, it is not clear whether improved self-esteem transfers to the necessary social skills required to improve behaviour and they argue that much more work is required to specify which groups benefit most from such programmes (see also Taylor, 1999; Nichols and Taylor, 1996).

Second, and much more significantly, Emler questions the policy relevance of such an approach, arguing that existing evidence shows that relatively low self-esteem is not a risk factor for delinquency, violence towards others, drug use, alcohol abuse, educational underachievement or racism. Commenting on his review of research, Emler (2001a) states that,

> Many of the claims made about self-esteem are not securely rooted in hard evidence. Indeed where many of the biggest and most expensive social

problems are concerned – crime, violence, alcohol abuse and racism – there is no warrant for the view that low self-esteem plays a significant role.

His conclusion is clear: 'no study to date has shown that low self-esteem leads to delinquency' (Elmer, 2001b: 19). In fact, 'young people with very high self-esteem are more likely than others ... to reject social pressures from adults and peers and engage in physically risky pursuits'.

However, the difficulties facing evidence-based policy-making in challenging policy-makers' 'established repertoires' (see Chapter 3) are illustrated by an example provided by Emler (2001b: 18):

> The final report of the California Task Force (California Task Force to Promote Self-esteem and Personal and Social Responsibility, 1990) is unequivocal. 'People who esteem themselves are less likely to engage in ... crime' (p. 5). However, their own academic consultants, Scheff *et al.* (1989), find the opposite message in the same evidence: 'the conclusion we draw from the reviews, [that] the relationships reported between self-esteem and deviance have been weak or null' (p. 177).

Despite the wishful thinking of policy-makers and interest groups within sport, it is clear that sport's ability to increase self-esteem is contingent on a range of factors, including the relevance of the experience to particular populations and its relative importance to an individual's sense of self. Further, there is a substantial body of research which indicates that the relationship between increased physical self-worth, global self-esteem and particular forms of pro-social behaviour are at least problematic. Perhaps it is for this reason that McKenzie (1997) argues that raising self-esteem is less important than the need to address the characteristics that can be changed and that, most importantly, are associated with an individual's criminal behaviour (e.g. attitudes, cognitions, peers, substance abuse) (see also Witt and Crompton, 1997).

More generally many writers in this area would agree with Spady's (1970) warning of the dangers involved if sporting activities stimulate participants' status perceptions and future goals without providing the skills and orientations required for occupational success – sport needs to be a *complement* to education and development, not a substitute (we will return to this issue again).

Adolescent development needs

Schafer's (1969) fourth perspective suggests that much adolescent anti-social behaviour is little more than an expression of developmental processes of adventure seeking, of a search for freedom, control and personal identity outwith those ascribed by school and family. In this perspective sport can perform a cathartic function by providing an opportunity for an institutionalized display of force, strength and competitiveness and the opportunity for the display of adolescent masculinity (Maughan and Ellis, 1991; Hendry *et al.*, 1993). However,

Hendry *et al.* (1993) suggest that during adolescence there is a shift in interests away from sport and organized clubs to more casual pursuits. Consequently, there is some evidence to suggest that the period of the highest potential for delinquent behaviour coincides with a decline in the attractiveness of traditional forms of organized sports, especially among those most likely to be non-conformist. More fundamentally, Crabbe (2000: 390) raises important questions about the ability of certain approaches to sport to provide 'functional alternatives' for anti-social behaviour, in particular drug use:

> The fact that the same emotions of excitement, euphoria, celebration, tension and fear are being used does not suddenly result in drugs no longer being seen as 'fun' or worthwhile. Indeed where the competitive nature of sport results in people not 'making the grade' … they may subsequently become disillusioned and alienated by sport to the degree that they may seek solace in the more 'reliable' effects of drug use.

Because of the understandable concentration of diversionary sports provision on young males there is often a failure to consider the interests of young women. Traditionally they have posed less of a problem in terms of criminal behaviour (although this is changing), but if such provision is also concerned to extend opportunities some consideration needs to be taken of their needs. Research evidence suggests that young women are much less likely than young men to base their friendship networks on sport (Mason, 1995), are less likely to be attracted by competitive approaches (Mason, 1995; Roberts and Brodie, 1992), are more likely to have individual, task-orientated competence motivation (Biddle *et al.*, 2005), are more attracted to motor-dominated rather than perceptually dominated sports (Mason, 1995) and are more likely to be attracted by the social aspects of participation. In other words research indicates that many of the presumed 'cathartic' elements of sport are those which many young women find most unattractive. On the other hand, Videon (2002) suggests that young women might benefit from competitive sport as it deviates from gendered socialization processes (see Chapter 5).

If this perspective has some relevance to understanding the nature of some anti-social behaviour, then research points to the need for 'bottom–up' approaches, with locally recruited and credible leaders (Deane, 1998; Witt and Crompton, 1996a). Also, evidence suggests that the potential for success is increased if young people are involved both in influencing the nature of the provision and in its management (Coalter and Allison, 1996; Morgan, 1998; Fitzpatrick *et al.*, 1998; West and Crompton, 2001). For example, Loxley *et al.* (2002) viewed one of the initial weaknesses of the Splash programmes as a lack of consultation with young people, and in an analysis of diversionary sports programmes in the United States, Witt and Crompton (1996a: 22) stated that 'empowerment is an important theme that runs through these case studies. Empowerment enables youth to take ownership and responsibility for their recreational and social activities.'

These comments reflect a widespread acknowledgement that 'it is unlikely that sport and physical activity programs have a major and *direct* impact on reducing antisocial behaviour, [although] they form an important mechanism through which personal and social development may positively affect behavior' (Morris *et al.*, 2003: 56). There is a recognition that much greater care needs to be taken to understand the processes of sports participation; that desired impacts are not an inevitable outcome of participating in 'sport' (Coakley, 2003; Presidents' Council on Physical Fitness and Sports, 2006); that there is need to identify and address the characteristics associated with an individual's criminal behaviour (McKenzie, 1997); that there is a need to provide a range of 'protective factors' (Witt and Crompton, 1997); that, to paraphrase Pawson (2000), complex problems might need complex interventions. As *Game Plan* concluded (DCMS and Strategy Unit, 2002: 60), 'playing sport will not lead to a permanent reduction in crime by itself. Successful programmes require a variety of other support mechanisms to be in place.' Such perspectives can be seen to be reflected in the increasing adoption of 'sport plus' approaches.

Sport plus ... again

Evaluations of both diversionary and rehabilitative approaches suggest that the salience of sport can be effective in attracting at-risk youth to programmes (see Chapter 6 for very similar programmes aimed at improving educational performance). However, there is a need to understand better the causes of particular types of anti-social and/or criminal behaviour and for programmes to be designed more systematically to address these. For example, there may be a need to improve cognitive and social skills, reduce impulsive and risk-taking behaviour, change particular attitudes, increase self-efficacy and self-confidence, deal with substance abuse and improve education and employment prospects (Utting, 1996; Asquith *et al.*, 1998; McKenzie, 1997). An interesting illustration of this approach in relation to the contribution of physical activity to the treatment of drug addiction is provided by Williams and Strean (2006). They argue that physical activity should be selected to be consistent with the function of the overall treatment programme and complement and relate directly to treatment goals (e.g. managing anxiety and stress, mastering psychomotor skills, building confidence). Second, they emphasize the need to understand the context of drug use and its possible relationship with any previous sport or physical activity (e.g. drinking and team games) in order to avoid classical-conditioned response.

As the Positive Futures programme has developed, there has been a realization that the achievement of its crime reduction goals is related to the ongoing personal and social development of participants. As such the programme's objective is to 'widen horizons providing access to lifestyle, educational and employment opportunities within a supportive and culturally familiar environment' (Home Office, 2005: 4). This recognition has 'enabled projects and their many partners to see beyond sport and physical activities, rather than viewing them as an end in themselves. Increasingly, there is an understanding of the potential to introduce a wider programme of interventions' (Home Office, 2005: 5). The wider programme of interventions included training and mentoring, linked educational programmes, healthy lifestyle programmes, drug prevention programmes and leadership training (Leisure Futures, 2002). The much publicized claimed successes of the various *midnight basketball* programmes in reducing recorded crime (Wilkins, 1997: Hartmann and Depro, 2006) are not simply a function of participation in sport, but of a much more complex programme. Although the strong salience of basketball for urban youth is the key to making contact with those at risk, 'the most urgent objective' is education and life learning (Wilkins, 1997: 60). The highly structured programme includes non-traditional education components which seek to develop employment skills, personal development, self-esteem, conflict resolution, health awareness and substance abuse prevention (see also Farrell *et al.*, 1995). Consequently, while sport plays a central role in this programme, the clear conclusion is that diversion must be complemented by *development* and that sport cannot achieve the desired outcomes on its own, especially among those most at risk (for a British example see Deane, 1998).

An interesting and more radical explanation for the apparent effectiveness of the midnight basketball programmes, is provided by Hartmann and Depro (2006), who reject the centrality of individual-level mechanisms. They undertook a statistical analysis of the incidence of property crime and violent crime in cities with and without such programmes and found some tentative support for an association between midnight basketball and a reduction in property crime (but not violent crime). They offer two possible explanations for this which go beyond the direct impact of the programmes on individuals' behaviour. First, such reductions may simply be part of a bundle of crime prevention initiatives (e.g. 'zero tolerance' policies). Their second explanation is their preferred one, and one which has many similarities with Putnam's (2000) perspective on social capital, that:

> midnight basketball may serve to help generate a wider and diffuse sense of community solidarity and trust that serves as a buffer against the anti-social sentiments and behaviours that otherwise contribute to crimes against property and the community at large.
>
> (Hartmann and Depro, 2006: 192)

Interestingly, this possibility does not appear to have been investigated as a possible explanation for some of the (relatively weak) outcomes recorded by similar programmes such as Positive Futures.

Final sentencing

It is clear that, from many different disciplinary perspectives, there is a broad consensus that although 'sport' may prove to be highly attractive for certain at-risk and vulnerable young people, the manner in which it is delivered, the processes and experiences of participation and the social relationships established are the key to achieving certain positive or negative intermediate impacts, even if they are not associated with subsequent behavioural changes. This returns us to Patriksson's (1998) plea for research into the conditions necessary for sport to have beneficial outcomes. However, available research illustrates Pawson's (2001a) point about the limitations of narrative reviews to pursue a 'configurational approach to causality' and identify 'exemplary programmes' in order to inform policy and practice.

For example, West and Crompton (2001) comment that, in many of the studies they reviewed, authors failed to offer details of the variables or procedures involved. They suggest that there is a need to evaluate the differential effects of various aspects of process – the location and duration of activities, the optimal size of groups, participant/staff ratios, the skills of leaders, the importance of voluntary participation, the role of peer acceptance and the importance of various 'protective factors'. In the UK, Utting (1996) commented on the 'shortage of reliable information regarding which aspects of sport, adventure and leisure pursuit programmes are most effective and for how long. It is not clear which interventions are most appropriate for different groups of young people.'

Of course Pawson (2006) suggests that, as social interventions and processes are descriptively inexhaustible, few research reports can contain all relevant information (indeed one might question the extent to which practitioners or researchers will always identify all relevant information!). Nevertheless, most available research supports Segrave and Hastad's (1984) contention that formal participation in sport is not enough to generate commitment to institutions and non-delinquent values – sports are only one of a number of priorities and social experiences which influence attitudes and behaviour. Few would disagree with Shields and Bredemeier (1995: 184) who propose that, 'whatever advantages or liabilities are associated with sport involvement, they do not come from sport per se but from the particular blend of social interactions and physical activities that comprise the totality of the sport experience'. Much of this also seems to support Spady's (1970) contention that sport needs to be a complement to education and development, not a substitute.

The various analyses presented in this chapter clearly point to a need to understand the elements of process and different types of programmes required to maximize desired intermediate impacts for a range of groups (e.g. improved self-efficacy; physical self-worth and self-esteem; cognitive and social skills). However, the bigger policy issue of the nature of the relationship between such impacts and outcomes such as changed behaviours and a reduction in anti-social and/or criminal behaviour remains a difficult one. Here it is appropriate to finish with the conclusions about the operation of highly focused and small-scale rehabilitation programmes referred to earlier. Taylor *et al.* (1999: 50) agreed that physical activities do not by themselves reduce offending and that personal and social developments, sooner or later, might improve offending behaviour, although their impact is unpredictable and 'to expect anything more tangible is unrealistic'.

8 The economic impacts of sport

Investing in success?

The new economic realism

We noted in Chapter 2 that the high point of recreational welfare did not last long, with the ever-present pragmatism and instrumentalism reinforced by several political and economic factors. First, what Henry (2001: 72) refers to as the 'new economic realism' in the mid-1970s, under which the British Labour government reduced central government's contribution to local government revenue spending, a policy which was accelerated in the 1980s by Thatcherite neoliberal policies. Second, there was an increased investment in the urban programme and spending on 'social projects' and a redirection of spending to inner cities – skewing investment in sport (a policy reinforced by the urban riots of the early 1980s). Third, increased 'state flexibilisation and disinvestment' in public services, symbolized by the introduction of compulsory competitive tendering for local authority sport and recreation services in the late 1980s (Coalter, 1995). Fourth, the decline of manufacturing and industrial production changed the nature of cities and the strategic role of public leisure services. Henry (2001) characterizes this as a shift from Fordism to post-Fordism, signalling a shift from large-scale mass production and consumption to flexible production and market niches; from a dominant culture of welfarism to an 'enterprise culture' (see also Ravenscroft, 1993); from local government (and cities) investing in sport and recreation as a right of citizenship to seeking to use sport as a tool for economic and social regeneration as cities shifted from being units of production to units of consumption (Henry, 2001; Harvey, 1989), seeking to develop alternative economic strategies by using arts and sport to 'reposition' themselves as tourism destinations, or constructing attractive environments for the location of the new service-sector professionals. In such circumstances Henry (2001) argues that local authorities' interest in sport shifted from one of welfare to one of regeneration. In this regard, Gratton *et al.* (2005: 1) argue that:

> Investment in sporting infrastructure in cities over the past 20 years was not primarily aimed at getting the local community involved in sport, but was instead aimed at attracting tourists, encouraging inward investment and changing the image of the city.

In terms of leisure services, the new economic realism led to a clear shift in the rationale for the arts much earlier and more radically than for sport. For example, as arts came under attack from neoliberal politicians for subsidy-dependency and a 'welfare mentality', the rationale shifted from community arts and aesthetic issues to an increasing emphasis on economics. Evans (2001: 139) refers to this as the growth of the 'new cultural economy' (partly driven by the need to find strategies for the economic redevelopment of deindustrializing cities). Evans (2001) illustrates that this shift in arts policy was widespread – in addition to the UK (Myerscough, 1988), economic impact studies of the arts were undertaken in Germany, the Netherlands (Kloosterman and Elfring, 1991) and the USA (Heilbrun and Gray, 1993).

In the UK, systematic consideration of the potential economic impact of sport emerged more slowly, although in the USA regeneration strategies based on municipal investment in facilities for franchised professional sports teams began in the early 1970s. For example, Indianapolis sought to compensate for the decline of its car industry by investing $1.7 billion between 1974 and 1984 in inner-city construction, of which facilities for professional team sport and the hosting of major sports were a substantial component (Rosentraub *et al.*, 1994; Schimmel, 2001).

In the 1990s, the emphasis on sport's economic role increased substantially, reflecting broad changes in the economy, the changing nature of, and increased competition between, cities and changing priorities and increased pragmatism of government. In this chapter we will examine four broad aspects.

(i)   The presumed contribution of sport to the urban regeneration of post-industrial cities.
(ii) The nature of the economic impact of sporting events. This is related closely to (i), but with its own literature, issues and debates.
(iii) The overall economic importance of sport to the economy. This derives from the arts-related debates of the late 1980s and seeks to counteract the accusations of subsidy-dependency by illustrating that the nature and size of the 'sports economy' mean that it should be taken seriously by governments and viewed as an asset and not a cost.
(iv) The economic benefits of a more physically active population. Such data have been used to dramatize the economic cost of obesity and ill-health and to encourage investment in sport and physical activity.

Although the issues in this chapter differ from the social issues and processes discussed in earlier chapters, these areas are also characterized by similar debates: the nature of the processes, mechanisms and relationships involved, the nature of relevant evidence and the robustness of current research evidence. Given the economic and political interests involved in many of these areas (e.g. bidding for large-scale sports events, expensive regeneration projects) it is not surprising that, more than any other area of sports policy, many of the issues considered in this chapter illustrate Solesbury's (2001: 9) comment that 'there sometimes seems to be a tension between power and knowledge in the shaping of policy'. There is frequently a tension between those promoting economic and sporting interests and academics and others concerned with conceptual and methodological issues and the accuracy of evidence underpinning decision-making. Despite the use of the notion of economic 'cost benefit' in many of these analyses, aspects of this policy area provide a clear illustration of Weiss's (1993) contention that *political benefit* is often more important than cost benefit when understanding policy initiatives. For example, Schimmel (2001) uses 'urban regime' theory and the idea of 'growth coalitions' to argue that much sports event-related development reflects the interests and strategies of urban elites rather than any systematic strategic consideration of 'whole city' benefits.

Sport and urban regeneration

In the context of a decline in manufacturing industries many cities have turned to arts and sport to address issues of economic decline. Rather than produce physical commodities for others to consume, some cities have sought to turn themselves into commodities for tourists to consume (and appear more attractive for inward investment for new service industries). This has led to the adoption of strategies of reimagining and city marketing (Gratton and Henry, 2001; Fainstein and Judd, 1999). As Friedman *et al.* (2004: 121) argue, 'less interested in enhancing public welfare than attracting private capital, the post-industrial city thus emerged with the overriding aim of luring "highly mobile and flexible production, financial, and consumption flows into its space" (Harvey, 1989/2001: 359)'.

Friedman *et al.* (2004) suggest that the significance of sport in such strategies is explained partly by increasing urban homogeneity, with many cities having a broadly similar range of entertainments, restaurants and retail outlets. In this context major sporting events, new stadia and sports-related experiences are regarded as an effective means by which to construct *place identity.* Smith (2001) argues that sport has several attractions to cities seeking to reimage and reposition themselves. For example, sport has the potential to promote the impression of prestige and transition from an unattractive industrial past. Second, what people choose to perceive is related closely to what they care about and sport's widespread appeal means that sporting initiatives can be more easily accepted into a potential tourist's image of the city. Related to this is the argument that effective imaging strategies must evolve from current images and the association of sport and sports stadia with traditional industrial communities could be regarded as a natural development (e.g. Glasgow's attempts to rebrand itself as a 'city of sport' draws heavily on its long (if not unproblematic) football tradition – Rangers, Celtic, Hampden Park). Where such traditions are not present, such a strategy might prove to be more difficult. This seems broadly similar to Roche's (2000) contention that 'mega-events' permit elites to promote dominant ideologies, mark progress and progressiveness and establish continuities with the past. Smith (2001) also suggests that sports stadia are 'imageable', which refers to the quality of an object which gives it a high probability of evoking a strong image (Lynch, 1960).

As Thornley (2002) points out, stadia can become tourist attractions in their own right, such as Barcelona's Nou Camp stadium. Finally, there is the issue of 'autonomous image formation agents' (Gunn, 1998, quoted in Smith, 2001: 134), which refers to independent reports, documentaries, movies and news articles often produced by non-sporting press and media representatives attracted to the city by large-scale sporting events. The presumed importance of such information is that it is often regarded as unbiased (i.e. not reflecting deliberate promotional campaigns).

Smith (2001) admits that this analysis relates solely to the *potential* of sport for reimaging and that there may be a number of problems with this approach. For example, any image enhancement may be short-lived if there is not an ongoing programme to capitalize and reinforce it (Ritchie and Smith, 1991) – this is especially so for one-off events. Second, there is a need for cities of sport continuously to differentiate themselves from each other and occupy distinct market niches – an increasingly difficult task (especially with the rather limited number of large-scale mobile sporting events with the requisite TV coverage: Gratton *et al.*, 2005).

These rebranding and repositioning aspirations underpinned much of the early attempts in cities in the USA to use sport to redevelop, or at least stop the decline of, downtown business areas, as populations and businesses moved to suburbs (Austrian and Rosentraub, 2002). Indianapolis is generally regarded as the first significant example in the 1970s, followed by cities such as Baltimore, Dallas, Detroit, Pittsburgh (Euchner, 1993). The strategies were often based partly on the uniquely American phenomenon of franchised sports teams (baseball, American football, basketball), which are attracted to, or retained by, cities because of municipally provided stadia and various tax incentives. The scale of this is indicated by the fact that in the 1990s $21.7 billion was spent on 95 such stadia, with two-thirds of the costs being covered by public money (Siegfried and Zimbalist, 2000).

In order to compensate for the decline of its car industry Indianapolis targeted the service sector and sought to use sport as a catalyst for economic regeneration and to redevelop a dilapidated downtown area (Rosentraub, 1997; Schimmel, 2001). Between 1974 and 1984 $1.8 billion was invested in inner-city construction, of which sporting infrastructure was a major part. There was substantial capital investment in major facilities (e.g. a swimming and diving complex; a track and field stadium; a velodrome), a National Institute for Fitness and Sports, the hosting of sports organizations and major sports events. Between 1977 and 1991, 330 sports events were hosted; in 1991 18 sports organizations and nine sports facilities employed 526 people, and 35 sports events generated $97 million (Davidson, 1999, quoted in Gratton *et al.*, 2005: 990).

In an assessment of the impact of the Indianapolis strategy, Rosentraub *et al.* (1994: 225) concedes that 'it is very difficult, if not impossible to completely disentangle the sports strategy from the non-sports elements of the downtown development program'. It is also admitted that the strategy created a small number of jobs and the spin-off from attendance at sporting events 'generated a substantial number of service sector and hotel jobs' (Rosentraub *et al.*, 1994: 237). However, sports-related jobs accounted for only 0.32 percent of all jobs in the Indianapolis economy (a relatively insignificant increase of 0.03 percent) and sports-related payrolls accounted for less than 0.5 percent of the total payrolls of all Indianapolis businesses. This leads Rosenbtraub (1994: 238) to conclude:

> Without minimising the success and publicity Indianapolis has enjoyed, outcomes of this magnitude are so small that it is plausible to consider that, had the city focused on other factors, a larger economic impact would have been possible. Given how small sports is as an industry and the low pay associated with the numerous service sector jobs created by sports activities, sports is not a prudent vehicle around which a development or redevelopment effort should be organised.

In later, comparative, work Rosentraub (1997) concluded that, although Indianapolis was able to stabilize the downtown population, employment growth remained much stronger in the suburbs.

In a more general analysis of the impact of sports teams in 37 US cities, Coates and Humphreys (2003) concluded that the positive impact tends to be concentrated in particular employment sectors. Further, because some spectator expenditure is substitution (i.e. it would have been spent somewhere else in the local economy), it has a negative effect on some others (e.g. if the stadium provides catering this is likely to have a negative impact on existing food outlets – the 'WalMart effect'). Humphreys (2001: 37) offers the general conclusion that 'cities receive benefits from having professional sports teams, but job creation, higher earnings and additional tax revenues are not among these benefits'. Siegfried and Zimbalist (2000: 104) suggest that this is because:

> Sports teams are small businesses … for a medium sized city like St Louis the baseball team accounts for less than 0.3 per cent of local economic activity; for a large city like New York, a baseball team contributes less than 0.03 per cent of economic output.

Siegfried and Zimbalist (2000: 103) provide a more general and rather damning conclusion:

> Few fields of empirical economic research offer virtual unanimity of findings. Yet, independent work on the economic impact of stadiums and arenas has uniformly found that there is no statistically significant positive correlation between sports facility construction and economic development.

However, many of the findings which point to limited economic impact (e.g. slowing but not reversing the rate of inner-city decline) tend to relate solely to the impact of a single team or stadium. In this regard it is interesting to note that Baade (1996) found a positive relationship between sports teams and per capita income only for Indianapolis, but commented that it was the only city which included sports as part of a larger development strategy (others tended to build sports stadia in the suburbs, often not regarding them as economic development tools: Chema, 1996). Reflecting this analysis, Chapin (2004) argues that there has been a shift in focus of the development rationale from an emphasis on the indirect economic benefits of a new stadium (e.g. job creation) to an emphasis on their role as a catalyst for the physical redevelopment of portions of cities. Consequently, Santo (2005) questions the overly generalized view that there is no positive relationship between investment in sports facilities in US cities and economic development, illustrating that specific aspects of location, stadium type and sport are important factors influencing economic impact. Santo (2005) suggests that some of the previous, relatively negative, analyses are flawed because they used out-of-date data which did not relate to the new type of stadia built in the 1990s, which were designed to serve as architectural symbols with tourist appeal and to act as a catalyst to urban development. To test this hypothesis the author uses a cross-sectional time-series methodology, using more current data (1984–2001) and excludes older, more utilitarian stadia from the analysis. Nineteen metropolitan statistical areas are included, representing every city that either gained, or lost, an NFL or MBL team, or had a stadium construction or renovation for such a team between 1984 and 2001. The results indicate that the presence of a new baseball stadium has a significant positive impact on regional income share (they host ten times more home games than American football stadia, generating more economic activity).

Santo (2005) stresses the importance of contextual issues, such as the location (with downtown locations much more likely to have beneficial impacts than suburban locations) and the clearly positive impact of attracting new teams (which seems to lead to a realignment of leisure spending, giving a larger share of regional income to a city). Nevertheless, the author does not conclude with broadly positive conclusions on the economic merits of sport facilities and admits that the analysis ignores issues relating to the efficiency of such spending and related *opportunity costs*. The issue of opportunity costs is a consistent theme in such discussions. It relates to a concern that there is a widespread tendency to ignore the, admittedly difficult, issue of alternative uses for such investments with potentially greater benefits.

In terms of location and context, Thornley (2002) outlines three possible strategies, based on UK examples. First, the location of a stadium such as the Cardiff Millennium Stadium in a central commercial district, able to draw on good public transport and generate synergy with existing central area uses (although some interests view the related crowds as a nuisance and disruptive to business on match days: Jones, 2001). The second option is the (re)location of stadia on cheap land on the edge of a city (served by motorways and reducing congestion) and with the old stadium being sold for redevelopment. Such a move may of course be resented by traditional fans and may make little contribution to economic or social regeneration. For example, Thornley (2002) points to the attempts of the Amsterdam ArenA (home of Ajax FC) to establish links with the adjacent

Bijlmermeer district (one of the poorest in Amsterdam). The third option is to seek to make a more direct contribution by locating a stadium in an inner-city area: for example, Arsenal Football Club which has built the Emirates Stadium on local disused industrial land, with improvements to the local underground station, a new access bridge opening up the area to a main thoroughfare and the old nearby stadium being redeveloped for housing (Newman and Tual, 2002).

Austrian and Rosentraub (2002) emphasize the need for downtown stadia to be part of a much wider strategy (a sort of 'sport plus' approach). On the basis of a longitudinal analysis of sports-related developments in four US cities (Cleveland and Indianapolis with long-standing sports-related strategies and Cincinnati and Columbus, recent adopters of such strategies) they suggest that a downtown sports strategy can help to sustain the vitality of an urban centre's core area, but not as a *direct result* of tangible outcomes related to the sports investment itself. In other words, the presence of the teams and their facilities do not lead to the creation of a large number of new jobs. However, a wider focus on tourism-based facilities and experiences can lead to the creation of higher paying service-sector jobs in tourism-related industries. The focus on sports and tourism-related industries did appear to create a set of connections, or 'excitement', within downtown areas that reduced the rate of outflow of jobs to suburban locations. Consequently, they argue that the use of a downtown sports-related development strategy is a valid policy tool, but only if it is part of a broader set of business partnerships and avoids providing excessive profits for team owners (a particularly North American problem) and is not based on regressive tax financing systems (e.g. funding via lotteries which are played largely by those on low wages and who often cannot afford to buy tickets for high-priced sports facilities). Jones (2002a: 168) suggests that the issue of regressive taxation via lottery funding is even greater in the UK because, unlike the USA 'there is no mechanism via which taxpayers can force discussion of individual spending decision by politicians' or non-elected lottery distribution boards.

In this regard Friedman *et al.* (2004) offer a critical evaluation of Baltimore's attempt to use a new 'post-modern' baseball stadium (Oriole Park) as part of a strategy to differentiate itself from other cities, many of whom had copied its supposedly successful tourism-led regeneration of its old business district. However, the authors argue that, because the public purse assumed the risk of the $210 million stadium, the private sector has gained most of the rewards, with the 'stadium subsidised annually by $14 million of public money in excess of the taxes collected from economic activity and employment related to the Orieles and the ball park' (Friedman *et al.*, 2004: 129). This was accompanied by an increase in the commercial value of the baseball team from $13 million in 1979 to $173 million in 1993. Because much of the financing of the stadium and its operation came from lottery income (which was initially intended for funding of education and is disproportionately played by those from the lower socio-economic groups), Friedman *et al.* (2004) conclude that the investment effectively represented a drain on local government resources and public services. Noll and Zimbalist (1997: 5) appear to deliver a particularly damning conclusion, arguing that the evidence illustrates that 'no recent facility appears to have earned anything approaching a reasonable return on investment. No recent facility has been self-financing in terms of its impact on net tax revenues.'

These concerns are reflected in critical questions raised by others about the nature of the 'regeneration' that accompanies sports-stadia-led developments. For example, Kidd (1995), discussing the impact of the Toronto Skydome, argues that benefits may accrue unevenly (often benefiting the affluent – reinforced by increased entrance charges to new stadia: Siegfried and Peterson, 2000; Siegfried and Zimbalist, 2000) and can serve to reassert commercial control over urban areas which formerly were the territory of minority and disadvantaged groups (see also Schimmel, 2001). In a similar vein, Jones (2001) illustrates that the development of the Millennium Stadium in Cardiff led to the demolition of the Empire Pool (a low-cost public facility) and its replacement with retail and food outlets. In this regard Friedman *et al.* (2004) use Debord's (1995) concept of 'veil of appearance', to suggest that many spectacular stadia obscure the complexities and uneven development of urban life (including poverty and structural decline). More generally, Ritchie and Hall (2000: 8) argue that 'in focusing on one narrow set of commercial, economic and political interests in the pursuit of major sporting events such as the Olympics, other community and social interests, particularly those of inner-city residents, are increasingly neglected'.

Finally, some commentators suggest that, although the potential economic impacts from publicly subsidised stadia are consistently exaggerated, there are other relatively legitimate (but difficult to measure) potential *intangible benefits* (Johnson and Sack, 1996). For example, Crompton (1995, 2004) lists such benefits as increased community visibility, enhanced community image and psychic income to city residents. Crompton (2004) suggests that the contingency valuation method (i.e. willingness to pay) is one approach to the measurement of the psychic income derived from a professional sports franchise. In this regard, Humphreys (2001: 37) argues that 'the decision to finance the construction of professional sports facility should depend solely on the value that taxpayers place on the consumption benefits flowing from professional sports'.

Johnson *et al.* (2001) used the contingent valuation method in a household survey (35.6 response rate) to explore the value placed on the Pittsburgh Penguins of the National (Ice) Hockey League. They collected data on attendance at team games, TV watching, reading and discussing of team matters, levels of interest in the team, how their quality of life would change if the Penguins left and their evaluation of the team and willingness-to-pay – e.g. if keeping it in Pittsburgh was important and various tax-related options to ensure that the team remained permanently. Nearly three-quarters of respondents identified themselves as Penguins fans and just over half indicated that they would be willing to pay for hockey-related public goods rather than lose them. However, as with other researchers who deal with such issues, Johnson *et al.* (2001) are unsure if the value of such public goods generated by sports teams is large enough to justify high public subsidies.

Perhaps the key conclusion to be drawn from much of these analyses is similar to many other chapters in this book – the claims for sports-led regeneration strategies are frequently exaggerated (reflecting the interests of 'growth coalitions' and the political needs of coalition building (Weiss, 1993)); it is not possible to generalize about the economic impact of sports-led regeneration schemes, because so much depends on the context – the balance between public/private investment, location, the nature of associated business partnerships, the nature of the job opportunities, the infrequently considered opportunity costs, the ability to redistribute the benefits of regeneration and the nature and value of the so-called 'intangible benefits' (which Johnson and Sack (1996: 380) suggest policy-makers ignore 'at their peril').

Many of these arguments are also central to the debates about one-off large-scale events.

Large-scale sport events

You seem to get a lot for the money

The building of sports stadia as part of a strategy of re-imaging and regeneration is closely related to the dramatically increased interest in the staging of large-scale sports events (e.g. Olympic Games, World Cup, Commonwealth Games). Interestingly, the modern stimulus for the current intense competition to stage the Olympic Games – Los Angeles – was the only bidder for the 1984 games. Other bidders were deterred by fear of costs, terrorism (after the 1972 Munich Olympics) or long-term indebtedness (e.g. in 1976 Montreal made an estimated loss of £692 million). However, by 1992 there were 22 bidders – largely because of the commercial success of the Los Angeles Games (which, importantly, had no public money and used many refurbished rather than new facilities) (Andranovich *et al.*, 2001). Chalkley and Essex (1999: 374) suggest that this increased interest reflects 'the greatly increased international inter-urban competition for investment, business and image'. They also argue that the massive scale of media interest and associated income means that more money is available to invest in facilities and infrastructure and therefore tends to generate much more urban change. More generally, Chalkley and Essex (1999: 370) suggest that, 'for urban planners and policy-makers, the [Olympic] Games have come to represent a major opportunity for infrastructural investment and environmental improvement'. For example, Preuss (2004a; see also Preuss 2004b) suggests that the Munich Olympics (1972) accelerated urban development plans (especially those for transport) by 15 years and Barcelona's already existing extensive redevelopment plans were advanced by 10 years. Both the Rome and Tokyo Olympics led to new water-supply systems and for the Seoul Olympics the Han River was cleaned and an environmental development plan led to 389 new parks (Preuss, 2004a; see also Preuss 2004b).

However, Chalkley and Essex (1999), in a review of the history of the urban development impacts of the Olympic Games, illustrate that the effect has been variable and that some cities have made much greater, strategic, efforts than others to use the Olympics to stimulate substantial urban development. They offer a number of explanations for these differences. First, where investment is predominantly private, as in the case of Los Angeles and Atlanta Olympics, there has been little link with public sector planning and there has been minimal change. In this regard Preuss (2004a) comes to a relatively simple conclusion that the most economically successful summer Olympic Games were those with the lowest investment in infrastructure and facilities (e.g. Los Angeles Games in 1984). Second, the potential for change reflects local needs and priorities (e.g. Tokyo and Seoul). Third, political influences and aspirations often lead to substantial development, as in Barcelona's desire to express the achievements of a relatively autonomous Catalonia.

This is a policy area in which ambitious and often extravagant (non-sporting) claims are made as part of the extensive lobbying processes associated with securing national and local political and business support to bid for such events. For example, *Game Plan* (DCMS and Strategy Unit, 2002) lists wide-ranging claimed benefits, such as improved image and short- and long-term increases in tourism, urban regeneration and sporting facility legacy and rather vague wider economic benefits. For example, Madden and Crowe (1998) suggested that a successful Sydney Olympics could lead to a 0.5 percent increase in demand for Australian manufactured exports. Szymanski (2002: 1) quotes the Australian Sports Commission's view that, in addition to the benefits for Australian sport and Australian athletes, the hosting of international events provides 'commercial returns for the Commission and meets government policy and foreign relations imperatives'. In France, the hosting of major events is justified on foreign policy grounds, ensuring the recognition of France internationally. In Canada, in addition to direct benefits to sport, there are such claimed benefits as job creation, regional development, tourism, exports, infrastructure and tax revenue and the expression of Canadian identity. As Szymanski (2002) notes, many of the claimed benefits for large-scale events are either intangible, or extremely difficult to define precisely, measure and attribute directly to the events. Even claims that such events contribute to a general increase in sports participation have little support from existing research evidence (Coalter, 2004, 2007; Veal, 2003; Murphy and Bauman, 2007).

However, most bids for large-scale events are accompanied by claims which it should be possible to measure: that they produce substantial *direct and indirect economic benefits*. Here we have a substantial volume of claims and a variety of types of evidence, balanced by an equivalent amount of academic scepticism about motivations and methodologies. For example, Crompton (1995) suggests that many economic impact analyses report inaccurate results, especially those produced prior to the event as part of the bidding process (see also Kasimati's (2003) analysis of the impact studies for the summer Olympics and Matheson (2002) on the exaggerated claims for sports events in the USA). In part this is to be explained by the motives of those commissioning studies which understandably tend to produce high estimates of economic impacts in support of their political and economic interests (we will examine Crompton's (1995) more technical explanations for overestimation below). In this regard we have already noted Schimmel's (2001) use of 'urban regime theory' and the idea of 'growth coalitions' to argue that much event-related development reflects the interests and strategies of urban elites, rather than any systematic strategic consideration of whole city benefits. For example, in the case of the 1991 World Student Games the bidding city Sheffield, in its desire to develop a post-industrial strategy, rejected (and failed to publish) a pre-bid consultant's report which suggested that the Games might result in a loss. A second report was commissioned which subsequently supported the economic basis of the bid. The Games subsequently had an event deficit of £10 million and the capital costs nearly doubled (Critcher, 1992; Henry, 2001; Roche, 1992, 1994), although subsequent analysis suggests that the longer term events-led strategy has been relatively successful (Gratton *et al.*, 2005).

Horne and Manzenreiter (2004) point out that the most optimistic economic impact projections for the 2002 Japan/South Korea World Cup were provided by research agencies associated with an advertising agency involved in the promotion of world football. They also emphasize the influence of Japan's *zenekon* (general contractors) and the impact of the ideology of the 'construction state' on the bid (see also Sack and Johnston (1996) on the hosting of the 1989 Volvo International Tennis Tournament in New Haven; Searle (2002) on the Sydney Olympics). In addition to these 'internal interests', Preuss (2004a: 35) warns of 'external' ones, arguing that, although cities should bid for large sporting events, they should 'not forget the decision-makers who award the event ... give their sporting event to a city that most supports their movement, not to a city that deserves it as a tool for development'. In this regard Wildsmith and Bradfield (2007: 14–15) argue that Halifax's bid for the 2014 Commonwealth Games floundered because 'the bid was tailored to the interests of the Commonwealth Games Federation General Assembly [and not] the needs and wants of the city of Halifax ... a concept that was lost in the drive to win the bid at any cost'.

Multiplication is the name of the game

Of course the implication is not that such events cannot generate substantial sums of money. For example, the soccer tournament Euro '96, staged in England, attracted 280,000 overseas visitors who spent around £120 million. When domestic visitors not resident in host cities are taken into account, the total economic impact was £195 million, with an estimated 0.1 percent impact on British Gross Domestic Product between April and June (Gratton and Taylor, 2000). However, reflecting one of the central concerns of the book, we need to explore the nature of the processes and mechanisms via which such impacts are made and the methodologies adopted to estimate claimed impacts.

We have already noted concerns about the motivations underpinning pre-event estimates of economic impacts (Crompton, 1995; Matheson, 2002). In addition to this, Crompton (1995), on the basis of an assessment of 20 studies and a comprehensive review of published economic impact literature, identifies 11 potential sources of error, leading mostly to overestimation of the economic impact of sporting (or other) events. Before providing a broad outline of these issues it is worth noting that the key 'mechanism', the process by which large-scale events are supposed to produce economic returns, is known as the *multiplier*. Multiplier analysis is based on the notion of a chain of spending and respending. The construction of facilities and the holding of large-scale events involves spending in the local economy (e.g. wages, purchase of materials, spectator and tourism expenditure). In turn, this expenditure becomes income to others (local workers and businesses), who in turn spend their (possibly increased) wages in the local economy and this becomes someone else's income and so on. Consequently, the initial event-related increased spending is the start of a series of related increased income and spending, with the final impact on expenditures and jobs being a *multiple* of the initial injection of money into the local economy. Related to this is the issue of *leakage* – at each stage in this cycle part of the original spending is not re-spent in the local economy. For example, goods and services might have to be imported from outside the local economy (especially if it is a small area), wages might be spent outside the local economy, profits (e.g. in national or international hotels) exported and some of the increased income will go in tax and/or be saved. In such circumstances the proportion of the additional visitor spend retained in the economy may be low (e.g. Gratton and Taylor (2000) used a multiplier of 0.2 for their work on events on Sheffield, Glasgow and Birmingham – assuming that only 20 percent of the additional income was retained).

Many of the concerns of Crompton (1995) and others (Szymanski, 2002; Matheson, 2002) relate to the assumptions underpinning such *multipliers* and the associated complexities in their calculation. Because of our overall concern with issues of processes and mechanisms these are worth listing in full:

- The use of total volume of sales instead of household income multipliers. This relates to the need to take account only of the money which remains in the host community and of leakages – thereby reducing the claimed economic impact.
- Misrepresenting employment multipliers. Employment multipliers measure the direct, indirect and induced effect of an additional unit of visitor spending on the creation of employment in the relevant area. Crompton (1995) argues that too often the assumption is made that all existing employees are fully utilized and that increased visitor numbers and spending will lead to increased employment (e.g. hotel and bar staff). However, especially for short-term, one-off events, the increased demand can often be accommodated by flexible use of the existing labour force (or simply by using spare capacity).
- Using incremental instead of normal multiplier coefficients. Whereas the normal multiplier expresses the total income created as a multiple of the initial cash injection (and includes leakages), incremental multipliers express the total income created as a multiple of the direct income, providing a higher total and making a better, if misleading, case (Szymanski, 2002).
- Failing to define accurately the impacted area. To quote Crompton (1995: 25) 'conventional wisdom posits that the larger is the defined area's economic base,

then the larger is likely to be the value added from the original expenditures and the smaller the leakages that is likely to occur'. Consequently a bid for (say) games in east London might be tempted to claim economic impacts for the whole of the UK.

- Including local spectators. The true economic impact of an event relates solely to the *new money* injected into an economy by visitors. Only spectators who reside outside the relevant area and who visit for the express purpose of attending an event can be included – local residents' expenditure is a recycling of money which would have been spend elsewhere in the local economy (unless the event encouraged the spectators to forgo a holiday outside the area, or use long-term savings). Related to this are the problems associated with pre-event estimates of spectator numbers. Gratton and Taylor (2000) provide details of predicted attendances at six sporting events, of which four proved to be overestimates (two substantially so). In the two cases in which the forecasts were relatively close to the actual, both were annual events and relatively easy to predict.

- Failing to exclude *time-switchers* and *casuals*. Time-switchers are those who would have visited the city/region anyway, but visited to coincide with the event. Casuals are those who are in the area for other reasons, but visit the event. In such circumstances they do not represent new money (although there is the possibility that they may have spent more than they otherwise would: Preuss, 2005). Also related to this is the category of those who may be *crowded out* – both visitors and residents who avoid the area because of the event and possible congestion and increased prices (hotels, restaurants, bars). In this regard Preuss (2005) refers to a Utah Skier Survey which found that 50 percent of non-resident skiers said that they would not consider skiing in Utah during the 2002 Winter Games. In relation to the summer Olympics, Pyo *et al.* (1988) found that between 1964 and 1984 there was a generally negative effect on visitor numbers. Lenskji (2002) quotes a study indicating that 14 percent of Sydney residents (500,000) were planning to leave the city during the Olympics.

- Using 'fudged' multiplier coefficients. Crompton (1995) argues that, although multipliers should be calculated for each event, limited resources and/or expertise often lead to the adaptation of other frequently high and misleading multipliers. For example, research suggests that it may be misleading to make revenue projections based on *average tourist spend* as there is some evidence that sports tourists spend less (French and Disher, 1997) and are also less likely to visit popular tourist destinations (Economic Research Associates, 1984).

- Claiming the total instead of the marginal economic benefits attributable to public sector investments (i.e. ignoring the contribution of other sources of funding).

- Confusing turnover, the continuous circulation of money associated with the event, and multiplier (i.e. ignoring issues of leakages in each round of spending).

- Measuring benefits while omitting costs. Most assessments of the economic impact of events ignore such things as the negative impact of increased congestion on business and tourism (before and during games), increased accommodation and food prices, environmental damage. In other words, economic impact studies are not cost–benefit analyses.
- Omitting opportunity costs. Opportunity costs refer to possible alternative investments for the funds used to subsidize an event. For both technical (difficult) and political (sensitive) reasons this is rarely considered (in certain circumstances is also possible that the finance would not be available for alternative investments). Some commentators (Crompton, 1995; Szymanski, 2002) point to the relatively low and mostly short-term economic/tourism impacts of sporting events compared to (say) a convention centre or retail/ service developments. Also, as low-paid jobs tend to be associated with events, Baade (1987) suggests that a city focusing on sports to foster its development may find that its economy compares poorly with other development strategies (see also Jones, 2002b; Chapin, 2004). Crompton's (1995) conclusion is that those considering investing in sports events need to adopt a cost–benefit analysis rather than the limited and frequently flawed economic impact approach.

The problems of estimating costs are illustrated by Madden and Crowe's (1997) work for the New South Wales Treasury on the Sydney Olympics – a phase which can last for eight years. Such costs are influenced by a range of factors, such as labour and skill shortages (and wage inflation) in host and neighbouring communities, broader economic conditions and policies (e.g. interest rates) and increased material and energy costs. Kasimati (2003) also refers to high construction costs (e.g. a shortage of relevant skills can lead to substantial wage inflation; increased demand for steel was reported to have added £75 million to the cost of the new Wembley Stadium). In addition to the initial coalition-building pressures to underplay cost estimates (or overestimate benefits), there is also the widespread tendency of large building projects to over-run. For example, Wildsmith and Bradfield (2007) point to the cost of the Barcelona Olympics increasing fivefold over an eight-year period and the fact that the final cost of the Manchester Commonwealth Games was five times the original estimate. The initial successful London Olympic 2012 bid was based on total estimated costs of £3.4 billion, which escalated to £9.35 billion within less than two years of winning the bid. Further, there is some indication of the opportunity costs associated with this dramatic increase, as a proportion of it will be funded from the National Lottery, resulting in a decrease of £99.9 million to sport within the UK and £112.5 million to the arts.

Another much emphasised benefit is the claim that events will provide a 'sporting legacy' of newly constructed sporting facilities and associated infrastructure. However, Kasimatai (2003) highlights widespread examples of subsequently underutilized elite sporting facilities which result in long-term high revenue costs (a major problem after the South Korea/Japan World Cup (Horne and Manzenreiter, 2004) and the Montreal, Athens and Sydney Olympics). For example, in an analysis of the Sydney Olympics, Searle (2002) argues that the subsequent financial troubles of Stadium Australia and the SuperDome are explained partly because they were built in response to a 'passing opportunity', rather than rooted in a strategic approach to recreation and leisure planning for the greater Sydney area (in which there were already three municipally owned 40,000 capacity stadia with long-term contracts with the major Australian sports). However, the planning for the Manchester Commonwealth Games illustrates that such problems are not inevitable, with facilities planned within the context of a regional sports strategy, agreement reached with local government and universities about post-games ownership and management of the two 50-metre pools, the commitment of Manchester City FC to become the tenant of the new City of Manchester Stadium (plus a threshold ticket deal giving money to the City Council or associated Trust) and the location of a regional sports institute at the main venue.

There are few studies which compare pre-games projections and post-games performance. One such study was undertaken by Baade and Matheson (2004) who explored the accuracy of forecasting in relation to the 1994 World Cup in the USA. Using a balance of payment model and longitudinal data (1970–2000) on metropolitan growth they conclude that, although impacts varied substantially between cities, overall the predictions presented substantial overestimates of the real economic impacts. In fact, they estimate that there was an *overall reduction* in income: $9.26 billion, compared to projections of $4 billion increase. Although they admit that small margins of error could lead to substantial differences in the estimates, they believe that the overall negative impact is broadly accurate. They explain this because of a crowding-out effect on non-match days over a three-week period. The perception that the World Cup was an ongoing event, rather than a limited number of matches on specific days, lost convention business and televised matches kept locals at home, thereby altering residents' spending. More generally, Szymanski (2002) illustrates that long-term analysis suggests that there is no statistically significant positive macro-economic impact of the World Cup and that it should simply be regarded as expenses, or investments, in the promotion of nations or cities. In relation to the Athens Olympics it is reported that the £8 billion cost has left Greek tax payers with at least two decades of debt (Smith, 2005).

Few would wholly agree with the *Game Plan*'s (DCMS and Strategy Unit, 2002: 66) general conclusion that those investing in mega events need to 'be clear that they appear to be more about celebration than economic returns'. Nevertheless, Szymanski (2002: 12) refers to widespread academic scepticism about the economic value of many events as follows:

> All economic impact studies are capable of generating large positive benefits if the right assumptions are made. Where large estimates are arrived at the usual explanation is that possible leakages and crowded out effects have been ignored and multipliers adopted have been unreasonably large. Given

the inherent difficulties of checking the figures ex post, promoters and their consultants can to some degree 'get away with it'; even if the academic consensus is that the economic impact of major sporting events is relatively small.

Gratton *et al.* (2005: 998) provide a slightly different perspective, based on the importance of the source of funding:

> When the money for sporting infrastructure investment is provided by local taxpayers, as it was for the World Student Games in Sheffield, the question arises of whether other projects might have provided better returns to the local community. When the money for investment comes primarily from outside the local community, as it did for the Commonwealth Games in Manchester, then it is an unequivocal benefit to the local community in economic terms, but may not be the best use of the funds from a national perspective.

Different games, different results

Although questions remain about the broader and long-term economic and developmental impact of large-scale sporting events, there is an emerging body of work related to a more limited analysis of the economic value of a range of different types and scale of sporting events (taking into account some of Crompton's (1995) concerns). Based on the work of the Leisure Industries Research Unit (e.g. Gratton and Taylor, 2000; Gratton *et al.*, 2001; Shibli and Gratton, 2001), *Measuring Success 1* (UK Sport, 1999) provides a guide to the definition and measurement of the economic impacts of a range of sports events. *Measuring Success 2* (UK Sport, n.d.) extends this work and provides detailed analysis of 16 major sporting events, including the spending levels and patterns of key groups (e.g. media), a balance of payments analysis for certain international events and an evaluation of the accuracy of its forecasting model (between 64 and 79 percent for six events). These various publications serve to bring some clarity and precision to the often overly generalized debates and assertions about the economic importance of sports events. They do so by identifying four broad types of sporting events, based on the scale of the event (including media coverage) and, most importantly, the balance between spectators and competitors.

Not surprisingly, the most potentially lucrative events are the ones over which there is so much competition: irregular, one-off major international *spectator-dominated* events such as the World Cup and European Football Championships (usually based on existing or upgraded facilities), Olympic Games (usually requiring major infrastructural and facility development) and World and European championships in certain sports (e.g. athletics). For example, Dobson *et al.* (1997) estimate that the economic impact of the 280,000 visitors and media to the Euro '96 international soccer tournament held in eight English cities was approximately £120 million. This estimate was arrived at via surveys of visiting supporters to establish both the visit and expenditure patterns of each group of supporters. As several teams played in more than one city, these supporters were surveyed in two cities. Dobson *et al.* (1997) estimate that the visitors generated over 900,000 bed nights and created over 4,000 full-time equivalent job years (not necessarily new jobs, but the expenditure to sustain this level). In addition, UK residents visiting other cities generated a further £75 million additional expenditure (although the extent to which this is new money depends on the definition of the area of economic impact).

The second tier of events includes major *spectator events* that are part of an annual domestic cycle (and usually have a fixed location) – in the UK this includes the FA Cup Final, Six Nations Rugby matches, Wimbledon and cricket Test Matches. As the majority of these are held at fixed locations, their impacts are limited to these locations. This of course may simply imply a redistribution of income within the UK, with a minority of spectators being from overseas (e.g. FA Cup Final).

The third tier tend to have a more *equal mix of spectators* and (*low spending*) *competitors* – world and European Championships in a range of less popular events (e.g. gymnastics, badminton). The importance of these events is that they are the ones that most cities (or countries) are able to bid for, but are also those events whose economic impacts are most uncertain. The final tier, with limited economic activity and little media coverage, are those events which tend to be *participant dominated* (with families and friends): national/regional championships in any sport.

Mondello and Rishe (2004) present a survey-based analysis of the economic impact of a variety of amateur sporting events in several cities in the USA – broadly similar to Gratton *et al.*'s (2001) fourth tier. The authors conclude that the impacts of such events depend on a number of factors: the number and origin of non-local teams; the proximity to the event location of the teams involved; visitor spending patterns, length of visitor stay; and operational and organisational expenditures by non-local organizations. Not surprisingly the main factors were average length of visitor stay and the percentage of non-local attendees. Amateur events involving teenage competitors are likely to draw greater spending crowds than seniors' events (presumably because of the presence of parents and siblings), although this analysis is questioned by data provided about seniors' event provided by Gratton and Taylor (2000). However, the authors acknowledge that their analyses are ex ante (i.e. data collected from spectators during events) and that ex-post studies provide a more accurate measure of net economic impact, rather than the gross economic impact which they report. Nevertheless, Matheson (2006: 193–4) provides three theoretical explanations in support of Mondello and Rishe's (2004) analysis.

(i)   Crowding out is less likely, with such events getting all of the benefits of increased visitor spending without the costs of displaced visitors.

(ii) Security costs, local inconvenience, infrastructural and investment costs will be much lower.

(iii) As smaller events are less likely to cause deviations from normal business patterns, the multipliers applied are much more likely to represent an accurate estimate of indirect spending.

To return to the UK Sport/Gratton *et al.* approach: its clear value is that it provides a framework for cities seeking to compete for events to evaluate the role of various types of events in an overall strategy. For example, it might be quite rational for a city to seek to stage a number of low-cost and low-income events in an attempt to brand itself as a 'city of sport', even as a precursor to bidding for one of the major events. For example, this broadly describes the strategy adopted by Glasgow, which culminated in its bid for the 2014 Commonwealth Games.

However, the debate between proponents of the economic value of sporting events and academic sceptics remains unresolved because of the general lack of robust, longitudinal, research on the precise role of sport as a tool for regeneration (Coalter *et al.*, 2000; Gratton and Henry, 2001; Cambridge Econometrics, 2004; Gratton *et al.*, 2005). In fact, Preuss (2004a: 35) also raises questions about our ability to resolve the debate 'because each sporting event has a different impact and size and because each city has a different history, culture and structure, there is no guidance on how sporting events – whatever size – create urban development'.

Finally, in this area of sports policy, politics is clearly more important than any 'evidence', which will always be the subject of debate and qualified by claims about even more difficult to measure 'intangible benefits'. Given the political and economic interests at stake in such bids, it is probably best to remember Solesbury's (2001) warning that to emphasize the role of knowledge at the expense of power seems naïve and Weiss's (1993) comment that evaluation is a rational exercise that takes place in a political context.

The sports economy

The third major area of the economic impact (or importance) of sport relates to the *sports economy*: the economic value of sport and sports-related activities. The growing importance of this area is illustrated by the dramatic growth in such studies, with Gratton and Taylor (2000) listing studies undertaken in all countries in the UK, Netherlands, Belgium, Finland, Denmark, Germany and France (Andreff, 1994). Such exercises are frequently undertaken in order to convince government that sport is an 'industry' and should be accorded this status. For example, the Sports Industry Research Centre (2007) argues that in England sport has greater economic importance than the creative industries (video, photography, music, visual and performing arts, design, radio and TV and publishing). A second political reason for such work is to illustrate that, in aggregate, sport contributes more in the form of taxation (e.g. income tax and VAT) than it gets in terms of public subsidy. However, as in many other areas, the data on which many of these statements are made are not wholly robust. This is largely because such estimates are dependent on secondary data sources, which are frequently not compiled for these purposes, are rarely comprehensive, require a substantial degree of interpretation and are subject to substantial margins of error.

The Sports Industry Research Centre (2007) estimated that in 2003 sports-related employment in England was over 421,000 (up by 22 percent since 1998) and accounted for 1.8 percent of all employment (more than the combined employment in the radio and TV and publishing sectors); sport generated £13,531 million value-added (the difference between total income based on wages and profit and the costs of inputs used in the production process). Cambridge Econometrics (2004) estimated that in 2000, sports-related employment provided households in England with £5.8 billion in disposable income (just over 1 percent of total household disposable income) and that sport contributed £5.5 billion to central government via taxes, compared with £660 million received in direct grants (e.g. to local authorities and the voluntary sector). Similar estimates for Scotland (Leisure Industries Research Centre, 2003) indicate that sports-related expenditure (excluding gambling) accounted for 1.2 percent of total consumer spending and sports-related employment represented 1.6 percent of total employment.

As in all other areas of sports-related research there are significant issues of methodology underpinning such estimates and a range of possible methodologies (see LIRC (1997) and Gratton and Taylor (2000) for a review of the relative strengths and weaknesses of the various methodologies: National Income Accounting framework; input–output analysis; multiplier analysis; Census of Employment-based statistics). In the UK the method used is known as the *National Income Accounting framework*, which Gratton and Taylor (2000: 18), the key experts, admit is 'a rather piecemeal approach'. Such an approach is required because many of the data sources do not identify *sport* as a distinct industrial sector and a series of assumptions have to be made about the extent to which the expenditure and income are 'sports-related'. This approach uses government statistical sources to measure flows of income, expenditure and output in the economy – i.e. how expenditure in one sector flows as income to other sectors. The seven sectors are (Gratton and Taylor, 2000; Cambridge Econometrics, 2004):

- households;
- commercial sport (events, sports-related tourism, commercial sports clubs, sports departments of media companies and sports goods manufacturers and retailers);
- commercial non-sport (suppliers of goods and services to the sports sector, suppliers of household goods and services which are used in connection with sports activity and the higher education sector);
- voluntary sector (non-profit-making organizations that are run by participants, consuming the services and opportunities which they produce);
- local government (including secondary education);
- central government;
- overseas sector.

Gratton and Taylor (2000) outline two 'ad hoc add-ons' to the flow-of-funds approach. First, to move from these various sectoral accounts to estimating the economic importance of the whole sports economy it is necessary to estimate the value-added, i.e. 'the value that is added to a product at each stage of production/ retailing ... expressed via wages, salaries and profits' (Gratton and Taylor, 2000: 8). Second, although public sector employment data can be obtained from the Census of Employment, other means are required for other sectors. This is done by taking the average wage in each sector and dividing this into the total sectoral wage bill to arrive at an estimate of total sectoral employment.

Within sectors there are also several interesting judgements which need to be made to estimate sports-related expenditure. For example, the sports-related value of the TV public broadcasting annual licence fee is based on the sports-related content derived from the BBC annual report (roughly the same process is followed for satellite subscriptions). The sports-related value of bicycles is derived from Consumer Trends and the proportion of sports-related bicycle journeys from the National Travel Survey.

There are also substantial gaps in economic data relating to the voluntary sector in sport, whose economic importance is emphasized by Gratton and Taylor's (2000: 23) speculation that a true estimate of the economic value of this sector 'would add up to 50 percent to the estimate'. This weakness reflects mainly the major methodological difficulties in collecting representative and robust data from such a diverse and fluid sector, but also in estimating an appropriate 'shadow wage' for voluntary labour (Gratton and Taylor, 2000). One estimate of the scale of the voluntary sector is provided by Sport England (2003) who estimated that, in England in 2002, volunteer labour was equivalent to 720,000 full-time equivalent jobs, with an estimated value of £14 billion per annum (see Chapter 4 for a fuller discussion of the voluntary sector in sport).

Gratton and Taylor (2000) also suggest that the nature of the data available for attendance at sports events means that their true economic impact is underestimated. Although household expenditure data are available for entrance charges, this is only one component of the 'composite price' associated with attendance at such events, which also includes travel costs, food and drink and sometimes accommodation. Also, the current national data underestimate the significant regional effects of such expenditure. Sports tourism is the other major area of under-reporting (Gratton and Taylor, 2000; Cambridge Econometrics, 2004). Gratton and Taylor (2000) argue that the relatively unsystematic approach to the collection of tourism data underestimates the economic effects of sports tourism and holidays, which include active sport and recreation (which they estimate accounts for more than one-fifth of tourist trips in Europe). For example, the random sample approach to the collection of tourism statistics underestimates the highly seasonal tours by recreational sports clubs (e.g. soccer, rugby, hockey). Second, the large number of nights away from home by members of national squads for competition and training is underestimated.

Because of the deficiencies of many of the secondary data sources there is a view that such estimates are probably *underestimates*. For example, Cambridge

Econometrics (2004) also suggest that there is a lack of robust information from government departments in which sport is a secondary function (e.g. the investment in sports infrastructure by economic development agencies; sports-relevant expenditure by educational departments). Other areas identified as presenting difficulties in arriving at more accurate estimates include the problems of defining more precisely the commercial sport sector and local authorities' use of the planning system to obtain 'planning gain' via the provision of sports facilities as part of new housing or retail developments. Also Cambridge Econometrics (2004) suggest that a concentration on the impact of sport on spending, incomes, employment and value-added may underestimate the broader influence which sport has in encouraging wider infrastructure developments and its role in regeneration projects. They refer to such developments as new and enhanced sports stadia, especially English Premier League clubs, and associated investment in non-sport-related infrastructure (e.g. the upgrading of the local underground stations as a result of the new Wembley stadium and the substantial improvements in transport infrastructure brought forward as part of the preparations for such events as the 2002 Commonwealth Games in Manchester).

The economic benefits of a more physically active population

The increased concerns to promote physical activity in order to address general issues of ill-health and to reduce obesity and its negative health consequences have been accompanied by calculations of the associated economic benefits. Such calculations perform a dual purpose: they dramatize the nature of the issues and their broader, collective, consequences and also act as part of the lobbying process for greater public investment in sport. Calculations about the economic benefits of a more physically active population are based on the widespread consensus about general links between physical activity and health (US Dept of Health and Human Services, 1996; European Heart Network, 1999). It is generally accepted that regular physical activity can contribute to a reduction in the incidence of obesity and a series of related illnesses, such as cardiovascular disease, non-insulin-dependent diabetes (Krisha, 1997; Boule et al., 2002), colon cancer (Thune and Furberg, 2001) and haemorrhagic strokes (Rodriguez et al., 2002). In addition, load-bearing/resistance-based physical activity in childhood and early adolescence contributes to the reduction in the incidence of osteoporosis (Shaw and Snow, 1995; Puntila et al., 1997; Kemper et al., 2000). The premise of the economic calculations is that such diseases produce three types of costs: (i) direct costs to the health care system; (ii) indirect costs relating to days off work and lost productivity; and (iii) costs of premature deaths (e.g. earnings lost from the death of working age people). Consequently, the achievement of higher and more frequent levels of physical activity should lead to substantial economic savings. In fact *Game Plan* (DCMS and Strategy Unit, 2002: 42) concludes that health-related costs constitute the largest single argument for government promotion of increased physical activity:

We considered both the total cost of inactivity and the annual savings from a 10 per cent reduction in inactivity and estimated that the total cost to England of physical inactivity, according to this basic and conservative model, is in the order of £2bn a year. This figure comprises indirect costs of about 10,000 working days lost and 54,000 lives lost prematurely (approximately 150/day). Using this model we also calculated a 10% increase in adult activity would benefit England by around £500m pa (6,000 lives/day).

Similar figures (although rarely comparable because of differing assumptions and healthcare costs) have been produced for a number of countries – from $76.6 billion per annum in the USA (Pratt *et al.*, 2000); 1.6 billion Swiss francs per annum (Martin *et al.*, 2001); £3.5 million annual savings to the NHS resulting from a one percentage point per year increase in participation for five years in Scotland (Scottish Executive, 2002). Such calculations are based on varying combinations of existing surveys of physical activity levels (whose definitions and measurement of participation, frequency and intensity vary widely); published statistical material covering the prevalence of disease; assessment of the relative risk of particular diseases (e.g. coronary heart disease, strokes, colon cancer) occurring in the population at specific levels and intensity of physical activity and an estimate of the average costs of treating each disease.

A more direct approach was adopted by Pratt *et al.* (2000) in the USA via a cross-sectional analysis of 20,041 respondents to the 1987 National Medical Expenditures Survey (aged 15 plus; 52 percent women). Data were collected on socio-demographic factors, health status, use and expense of medical care and health-risk factors such as regular physical activity (30 minutes of moderate/ strenuous physical activity three or more times per week) and smoking (those who had smoked at least 100 cigarettes). Consistent medical cost savings were identified for regularly active men and women, smokers and non-smokers, those with and without physical limitations and young and old (fewer physician visits, fewer hospital stays, less medication). The largest difference in direct medical costs was among women 55 and older. Even among those reporting limitations in carrying out moderate physical activities, medical costs were lower among those who were regularly active (some of this may be accounted for by less severe health limitations, but may also reflect a benefit of physical activity). Although the authors admit that causality cannot be determined from a cross-sectional study, they argue that the data suggest that increasing participation in moderate physical activity among sedentary adults may reduce substantially direct medical expenditures (a saving of $76.6 billion at 2000 prices).

Although most authors accept the overall analysis that physical activity has health, and therefore economic, benefits, they admit that some of the estimates (taken from routine data sources) are somewhat crude. Inevitably such calculations are imprecise, contain substantial margins of error and are based on theoretically informed judgements (e.g. what proportion of (say) colon cancer could be reduced solely by increased physical activity). The nature of the issues involved (and the limitations of calculations based on a single variable, physical activity) is outlined as follows:

> The existing research base regarding the health impact of sedentary lifestyles is limited. Far more work in this area is required to enable evidence-based research and analysis to be carried out. Some epidemiologists refuse to undertake research that treats physical activity in isolation from dietary intake. The simple fact is that existing research has not been able to account for physical activity and the range of confounding variables that impact on an individual's health.
>
> (Dept of Health, Social Security and Public Safety (NI), 2002: 3)

The call for more policy-relevant evidence once again raises a general concern in many of the areas we have covered. There seems to be a need to consider more rigorously the assumptions about the precise nature of the relationship between different levels of exercise and various aspects of health in differing subpopulations. Nevertheless, irrespective of the level of precision of such estimates (and the nature of our understanding of mechanisms and confounding variables), it seems undoubtedly to be true that increased physical activity will serve to reduce medical costs in relation to certain diseases among certain groups.

An injury to health?

However, because many of these calculations relate to theoretically potential benefits associated with particular levels of *physical activity*, they frequently ignore potentially negative costs associated with *sports* participation: sports-related injuries. For example, *Game Plan* (DCMS and Strategy Unit, 2002) provides a conservative estimate of the cost of sports injuries as being nearly £1 billion per annum. Nicholl *et al.* (1991) found that among young adults (predominantly male, 15–44) the average annual medical care costs per person that might be incurred as a result of full participation in sport and exercise exceeded the costs that might be avoided by the disease prevention effects of exercise. However, in older adults (45 plus) the estimated medical costs avoided greatly outweighed the costs likely to be incurred. Similar conclusions are found in a Swiss study (Martin *et al.*, 2001), which estimated that about 300,000 sporting accidents per year caused 160 deaths and incurred direct treatment costs of 1.1 billion Swiss francs. Accordingly, the authors suggest that measures aimed at risk control and accident prevention in sport should be intensified.

The reason for such conclusions is the nature of the contact and high-risk sports undertaken by young people (especially young males). For example, in the UK most sports injuries involve men (70 percent) and 48 percent occur in the 16–25 age group, with 29 percent of all reported injuries accounted for by soccer (DCMS and Strategy Unit, 2002). In 2002 about 200,000 people attended accident and emergency departments with a sports injury (Dept of Trade and Industry, 2003). The general conclusion from these data is that, if increased sport and physical activity are to be encouraged on the basis of improving health and reducing health costs, there is a need to promote 'safe sports' among young people (Nicholl et al., 1991; Martin et al., 2001; DCMS and Strategy Unit, 2002). Slightly more optimistically, *Game Plan* (DCMS and Strategy Unit, 2002: 48) suggests that as 'improved coaching and refereeing start to have an impact, injury rates should reduce due to improved skill'! Such issues received official recognition in 2005 with the launching of the option for NHS doctors to train in sport and exercise medicine, not only to treat sports injuries but also to prevent them (Dept of Health, 2005).

Part of the reason for ignoring the negative consequences of sports participation is the consistent failure to distinguish systematically between physical activity and *sport*. In part, this is because much of the debate, especially in the UK, is based on the Council of Europe definition:

> Sport means all forms of physical activity which, through casual or organised participation, aim at expressing or improving physical fitness and mental well-being, forming relationships or obtaining results in competitions at all levels.
>
> (Quoted in Sport England, 2004: 3)

This all-encompassing definition serves to fudge important distinctions between physical activity, physical recreation, recreational and competitive sport. It thereby permits the sports lobby to claim to be a major contributor to the fitness and health agenda (although the concern with the costs of sports injuries would imply that we require more precise definitions in this area).

Only one part of the game?

Here it is worth noting a UK study which raises some important questions about the relationship between the clear clinical benefits of *general physical activity* compared to more traditional forms of recreational sporting participation in the context of people's everyday lives. Roberts and Brodie (1992) report on a four-year longitudinal study of 7,000 people in six UK cities, including non-participants and participants in activities provided in local authority sports and leisure centres (where most increased and/or 'life-long' participation is likely to occur). Playing sport did result in *fitness* benefits (especially increased muscular power and improved lung functions). Further, these benefits were evident in all socio-demographic groups and were additional to those experienced as a result of other lifestyle practices. Roberts and Brodie (1992: 138) conclude that 'sport participation was certainly not the sole determinant of these people's health, but however favourable or unfavourable their other circumstances and living habits, playing sport was leading to measurable gains'.

However, they also conclude that, although sports participation was improving participants' self-assessment and strength, it was not improving their cardiovascular health, or their freedom from illness (e.g. those who played sport remained just as vulnerable to self-reported illnesses, infections, accidents and injuries). A major reason for this was that, 'at low levels of sport activity, less than three times a week, only *self-assessments* showed statistically significant and consistent improvements within all socio-demographic groups' (Roberts and Brodie, 1992: 139).

They also state that, even alongside favourable lifestyle practices, participation in sport was not eliminating or reducing the health inequalities associated with age, sex and socio-economic status, i.e. all were improving, but inequalities remained. On the basis of this evidence they conclude that if the 'aim of health promotion is to draw the less healthy sections of the population towards the norm, sport will not be an effective vehicle' (Roberts and Brodie, 1992: 140). They base this conclusion on three factors. First, their data indicate that sports participation needs to be energetic and frequent to achieve changes in physical functioning – 'improving one's health through sport is hard work. Weekly swimming is not enough' (Roberts and Brodie, 1992: 140). Consequently they question if it is possible to build the required level of sport activity into a typical adult's lifestyle (when most surveys indicate that 'lack of time' constrains both participation and frequency of participation). Related to this is the fact that for many so-called sports 'participants' commitment is rather cyclical, with most dropping in and out of sport over time, with only a minority of participants taking part regularly over time. Second, they suggest that lifestyles are not the basic source of health inequalities because, 'even when economically disadvantaged groups were making the healthiest of all possible leisure choices, their well-being remained handicapped by their low incomes, relatively poor housing and working conditions and vulnerability to unemployment' (Roberts and Brodie, 1992: 141).

Third, the persistent socio-demographic differences in sports participation patterns (age, sex, social class, educational status) remain a major and significant obstacle to the development of preventative health policies based on increased participation in sport and physical recreation. Such concerns lead them to conclude:

> The balance of all the evidence and arguments ... points towards a niche rather than a foundation role for sport within health policy and promotion ... its impact is focused on a limited number of health factors and it offers no solutions to socio-economic health inequalities.
>
> (Roberts and Brodie, 1999: 141–2)

Flow with the flow?

In such circumstances the policy dilemma seems to be whether the best strategy is to seek to develop policies to change fundamental and historic patterns of sports participation, or simply 'concentrate on retaining existing players, encouraging them to persist and to participate at the frequency necessary to maximise health benefits' (Roberts and Brodie, 1992: 143). Such dilemmas are illustrated by data from the English Health Survey (Sport England, 2004) which indicate that, among the 30.4 percent of adults who met the government target of 30 minutes of moderate activity five times per week, only 8 percent did so via sport (with a further 12 percent doing so via walking). The majority (64 percent) of those who meet the basic criteria did so via occupation-related activity. More recent data from the largest sports participation survey ever undertaken in the UK (363,724 adults in England aged 16 plus) indicates that only 21 percent of the adult population took part in moderate intensity sport and physical recreation for at least 30 minutes for three days per week – three-fifths of the recommended minimum (Sport England, 2007). Such data serve to illustrate Roberts and Brodie's general point about a 'niche' role for sport in preventative health policies.

Further, the *sports category* for the most active is dominated by individual, non-competitive and flexible activities: walking, swimming, cycling, aerobics, running and exercise (press-ups/sit-ups). Again this raises significant policy issues, depending on whether the intention is to develop sport, or contribute to the preventative health agenda. Commentators (Roberts and Brodie, 1992; Coalter, 1999) have argued that, if the key policy objective is simply to increase participation as a contribution to improved fitness and health, then it is probably best to 'flow-with-the-flow' by promoting those 'sports' which reflect modern social, cultural and work factors, rather than seek to promote more traditional sports.

Irrespective of the strategy adopted – an attempted revival of traditional sports, or a concentration on new individualised, lifestyle physical recreations – research-based policy interventions face a rather confused and inconclusive body of research when attempting to move beyond standard correlations (age, sex, social class) and understand the precise *mechanisms* underlying both participation and non-participation in sport and physical recreation. For example, a review of 108 research studies of correlates of physical activity among children and adolescents (Sallis *et al.*, 2000) found 40 variables for 3–12 year olds and 48 variables for 13–18 year olds. Further, it found that 60 percent of the associations were statistically significant, with the most notable result being that there was a lack of consistency across the studies!

Studies tend to find that childhood and adolescent participation in sport and physical activity makes adult participation much more likely than non-participation (Malina, 1996). However, because of a wide range of, often unexplored, intervening variables (e.g. post-school education, social status of parents, life course changes), it cannot guarantee it. Although studies tend to find some relationship between adolescent participation and continued adult physical activity, the correlations vary because of differing methodologies, definitions and measurement of the nature and level of sport/physical activity, age at which adult measures are taken and differing cultural contexts. For example, authors variously identify the significant aspects of adolescent participation as intensive endurance sports and those which encourage diversified sports skills (Tammelin *et al.*, 2003); competitive inter-school sports (Curtis *et al.*, 1999); time spent on activities (Vanreusel *et al.*, 1997); participation in pre-teen sports and perceived experience of choice (Taylor *et al.*, 1999); high levels of adolescent participation (Perkins *et al.*, 2004); the importance of organized activity (Taylor *et al.*, 1999; Tammelin *et al.*, 2003); extra-curricular school-aged sport (Kraut *et al.*, 2003); adolescent physical characteristics and fitness scores (Beunen *et al.*, 2004). However, in most cases, because of a range of complex intervening variables, the correlations are mostly weak to moderate and consistently decline with age (Malina, 1996; Shephard and Trudeau, 2005). In relation to more general attempts to increase levels of physical activity, Blamey and Mutrie (2004: 748), quoting Buchner and Miles (2002), conclude that 'systematic reviews of physical activity have to date not uncovered a few interventions that, if prioritised and implemented, would dramatically influence population levels of physical activity'.

In a systematic review of evidence for participation and non-participation in sport, Foster *et al.* (2005: 6) concluded that there was an urgent need for policy-makers to fund 'well-conducted qualitative research into attitudes to physical activity ... in the absence of such evidence-based policy-making we are likely to continue to see well-meaning policy statements from government that are not rooted in the realities of people's lives'.

Interestingly, and reflecting the analysis in previous chapters, Foster *et al.* (2005), drawing on their backgrounds as medical researchers, suggest that such research should be conducted within a framework of *theories of behaviour change*. They suggest the use of the transtheoretical/stages of change approach (Marcus and Simkin, 1994) in which behaviour change (from non-participation to regular participation) is viewed as involving movement between the stages of pre-contemplation, contemplation, preparation, action and maintenance. This approach, which requires researchers to address issues of knowledge, meaning, priorities, context, process and socio-psychological mechanisms, has increasingly been proposed by researchers who are concerned to understand and change people's attitudes to and participation in sport and physical activity (Biddle, 1994; Biddle and Mutrie, 2001; Loughlan and Mutrie, 1997; Bailey *et al.*, 2007; Blamey and Mutrie, 2004).

An economy of solutions?

In this wide-ranging chapter we have illustrated the increased interest in the contribution which sport can make to some of the economic priorities of government: economic (and social) regeneration, employment and reduction of healthcare costs. The new policy prominence of sport reflects two broad sets of influences. First are the increased political demands being made of all areas of public investment to contribute to cross-cutting agendas and parallel pressures to illustrate the efficiency and effectiveness of public investment – to quote Richard Caborn (2003): 'we will not accept simplistic assertions that sport is good as sufficient reason to back sport'. The second set of influences consists of various combinations of growth coalitions and the sports lobby who have sought to promote the broader economic value of sports-related activities in order to increase policy status, political support and public investment. It is clear that there is political benefit to be had for some in pursuing such arguments, but the precise nature of the economic cost–benefits is less clear. The point is *not* to suggest that various aspects of sport do not have economic significance, but to illustrate that there are substantial methodological disputes about how such impacts should be defined and measured, the mechanisms by which some of these impacts are achieved and the nature and scale of the impacts – including the argument of last resort, the difficult to define and measure intangible benefits (which, of course, can also include 'disbenefits').

As we have seen in other chapters, there is a substantial gap between the apparent confidence of the political rhetoric and the more complex processes of obtaining valid and reliable evidence. In the area of economic impacts, the apparent ignoring of the general weakness of much of the evidence base reminds us that objective evidence has to compete with a range of more powerful influences, alliances and imperatives in the policy process (Chapter 3). For example, many commentators suggest that the choice of particular methodologies (e.g. versions of the multiplier and economic impact or cost–benefit analysis) reflects political rather than research needs. Further, the nature of methodologies (e.g. in calculating the nature and size of the sports economy) are a matter of legitimate academic and policy debate. Similarly, although there is a general agreement that increased physical activity will make some contribution to health improvement, its precise contribution within broader lifestyles is not wholly understood and the relationship between sport and physical activity remains a matter of policy debate.

In other chapters we have argued that, to be effective, sport often has to work in conjunction with a range of other processes and interventions – 'sport plus' – even if it can sometimes be viewed as a catalyst. This seems an even more important conclusion in this chapter, where various types of sporting interventions are seeking to address issues of deindustrialization and economic decline, globalization and increased competition between cities for 'the tourist dollar' and widespread sedentary and unhealthy lifestyles. It seems that Pawson's (2006: 31) comment that 'all interventions are conditioned by the action of layer upon layer of contextual influences ... such contingencies represent the greatest challenge to evidence-based policy' is highly relevant to these areas of sport policy.

9 From methods to logic of inquiry

Who is listening?

In Chapter 2 we outlined the various reasons why sport has found a higher profile place on political and policy agendas. These ranged from a new emphasis on joined-up government and cross-cutting agendas (requiring all areas of public investment to contribute to the multifaceted social inclusion agenda), to the increasing emphasis on the rebranding and repositioning of cities in a new globalized market for tourism and jobs. For many in sport these developments were viewed wholly positively – as an opportunity to 'get money into sport' and/or 'to get sport on the agenda' – perhaps to become more of a policy-maker than a policy-taker (Houlihan and White, 2002).

However, these opportunities were also accompanied by a much more instrumental and pragmatic approach to public funding, based on target-driven, objective-led management and an increased emphasis on outcomes, accountability and effectiveness. Accompanying this was a new emphasis on *evidence-based policy-making*, with government demanding a 'willingness to question inherited ways of doing things, better use of evidence and research in policy making and better focus on policies that will deliver long term goals' (Cabinet Office, 1999: 16). It is this second element of strategic policy change which could be viewed as less of an opportunity and more of a threat to sport. As several policy-driven narrative reviews (Collins *et al.*, 1999; Coalter *et al.*, 2000) illustrated, there was a widespread lack of empirical research on outcomes to inform policy and practice, with the government policy document *Game Plan* (DCMS and Strategy Unit, 2002: 79) concluding that 'the evidence base needs to be strengthened to enable policy makers to construct and target effective interventions'.

However, it is essential to acknowledge that the evidence-based approach also exposed limitations in other areas of social research, including those with a much longer and better funded research tradition than sport. For example, Oakley *et al.* (2005: 17), commenting on 22 systematic reviews in various areas of social science research, all of which used flexible criteria for inclusion, stated that 'of the 291 studies reviewed in depth, a minority – 22 percent (63) – were assessed by review groups as yielding "high quality" overall weight of evidence … a considerable indictment of the state of social science research'. They also refer to the fact that 'applicability and generalisability were limited by scant information' (Oakley *et al.*, 2005: 12). Consequently, the general inability of sports research to contribute to the new evidence-based interventions partly reflects more general limitations of social research methodology (we will return to this below).

Of course, one might also express some scepticism about the real changes heralded by the ideology of evidence-based policy-making. For example, Solesbury (2001: 6) suggests that the approach had as much to do with politics and power as it had to do with knowledge, expressing New Labour's suspicions about 'many established influences on policy, particularly within the civil service, and anxious to open up policy thinking to outsiders'. One presumes that weak or marginal areas were less likely to be subjected to the full rigours of the evidence-based stick than large spending areas, with strong professional groupings. In the case of sport, the new emphasis on evidence was often cloaked in the mist of its mythopoeic nature in which positive outcomes are taken for granted. For example, in *Game Plan* (DCMS and Strategy Unit, 2002: 6), which concluded that there was a need for more evidence to enable more effective interventions, Tessa Jowell (Secretary of State for Culture Media and Sport) nevertheless states that:

> Sport defines us as a nation. It teaches us about life. We learn self discipline and teamwork from it. We learn how to win with grace and lose with dignity. It gets us fit. It keeps us healthy. It forms a central part of the cultural and recreational parts of our lives.

Given politicians' great desire for seemingly simple and relatively cheap solutions to complex social and economic problems, it is not clear what type, quality and volume of information is required to influence policy. Jowells's statement reminds us of Keynes's comment (quoted in Solesbury, 2001: 7) that 'there is nothing a government hates more than to be well-informed; for it makes the process of arriving at decisions much more complicated and difficult'. Further, issues of power, access and 'professional repertoires' remain. As Oakley *et al.* (2005: 23) suggest:

> Where policy makers and practitioners often rely on the opinions of a small circle of professionals rather than published information about effectiveness, either because of their attitudes to the type of knowledge or lack of easy access, there is little demand for systematic research synthesis.

In addition, Weiss (1993: 96) reminds of us of realpolitik by arguing that 'a considerable amount of ineffectiveness may be tolerated if a program fits well with prevailing values, if it satisfies voters, or if it pays off political debts'.

Consequently the question arises as to who the audience is for such policy-informing research. Weiss and Bucuvalas (1980a) argue that policy-makers tend to be concerned with broad purposes and not specifics and very rarely with the content of specific research studies. The experience of most researchers in the UK (Long and Sanderson, 2001; Pawson, 2006) is that the key policy-makers are rarely interested in 'evidence' and are concerned largely with organizational advantage, status, alliances and partnerships and resources – complex research findings distilled into oversimplified sound bites tends to be their fare. As one ascends the intervention hierarchy, 'the capacity to absorb complex information dwindles by the bullet point' (Pawson, 2006: 175). Given that, as Weiss (1997) argues, there are no 'killer facts', it is unlikely that senior policy-makers are the key audience. Experience suggests that we need to look lower down the intervention hierarchy and possibly find a more receptive audience among programme planners and managers – those with direct responsibility for delivering the inflated and often intellectually incoherent promises. Of course it could be argued that, in order to expose such inflated promises, it is necessary to engage with those who formulate them. However, where policy-making is dominated by political processes of opportunism, persuasion, negotiation, partnership building, the seeking of organizational and interest-group advantage and deeply embedded professional repertoires, entry is often difficult and usually confined to the 'chosen few'.

The issue of the 'entry point' for research is even more difficult in the rather diffuse and under-professionalized world of sports policy. For example, many of the issues explored in this book relate to policies implemented at local level, often in one-off projects which are not part of any overall strategy. This is unlike the situation of, for example, the Health Development Agency (HDA) which seeks to promote 'evidence into practice' by producing guidance on public health, health technologies and clinical practice, using the expertise of the NHS, healthcare professionals and academics. Of course such a system is not necessarily wholly effective (see Shergold and Grant (2006) for criticism of the dissemination and use of evidence), it is clear that medicine (and education) are characterized by reasonably coherent professional groupings and relatively effective networks for the dissemination of practice-relevant information (even if it is ineffective, it indicates the existence of research/knowledge-sensitive professional cultures). This is not the case in the much looser, fragmented and under-professionalised world of sports policy and practice.

Several writers (Weiss and Bucuvalas, 1980a; Weiss, 1997; Solesbury, 2001) suggest that because of the political, bureaucratic and interest-ridden nature of organizational decision-making processes, there are few examples of direct and immediate influence of research on decisions. Research results tend to reach policy-makers and practitioners in diverse ways and the diffusion of research into practice is a rather hit and miss affair. However, this is especially so in non-clinical and under-professionalised areas, such as sport.

More generally it is suggested that, in the absence of killer facts, there is a long, gradual, cumulative process, vividly summarized in the title of a Weiss (1980) article – 'knowledge creep and decision accretion'. Weiss and Bucuvalas (1980b: 156; quoted in Pawson and Tilley, 2000: 13) found that there was a

> Diffuse and undirected infiltration of research ideas into [decision-makers'] understanding of the world ... they absorbed the concepts and generalisations from many studies over extended periods of time and they integrated

research ideas ... into their interpretation of events ... [there was a] gradual sensitisation to the perspectives of social science.

This not only raises questions about the point of entry, but also about the nature of the research required, the dialogue between policy-makers/practitioners and researchers and the available time frame for knowledge creep – especially in sports policy, where many talk about the urgent need to capitalize on a 'window of opportunity' and status anxiety frequently precludes open discussion of complex issues and assumptions.

Nevertheless, there seems to be a sort of consensus emerging, as researchers consider how to improve the robustness and policy-relevance of research. The proposed way forward is still somewhat embryonic (although some policy-oriented researchers have been proposing it for some time: Weiss, 1980) and its attraction seems to be that it necessarily entails a 'conversation' between researchers, policy-makers and practitioners. This conversation is based on theory-based approaches to understanding and evaluating interventions and programmes. Interestingly, Weiss (1997: 520) suggests that one of the clearest arguments for theory-based evaluation is 'when prior evaluations show inconsistent results' – a common situation in most research into the various impacts of sport. Consequently, it is not surprising that this approach is emerging within sports research. We will return to the issue of conversations below, but first we need to explore the topic of these conversations.

From fuzzy snapshots to clear videos

In the previous chapters we have noted limitations in the research evidence about the broader impacts of sport (further limited by much research being related to the more diffuse category of physical activity). However, we have also noted a growing concern that traditional 'scientific' methods have limited value in an era of aspirations to evidence-based policy-making – even where they seem to indicate positive relationships between participation in sport, certain desired intermediate impacts and (less so) outcomes. In particular, there is a widespread discontent with the 'black box' approach to sports research, in which the 'treatment' and its 'magical properties' (Papacharisis and Goudas, 2005) are taken as given and impacts and (some) outcomes are measured and certain 'input factors' (e.g. age, sex, education, social class, race) are irregularly and inconsistently controlled for.

For example, Fox (2000), commenting on the relationship between physical activity and self-esteem, conjectures that factors such as the qualities of the leader, the exercise setting and relationships with other participants are probably more important than the activity or the physiological impacts. Discussing the limitations of research into the relationship between sport and educational performance, Grissom (2005) admits that the understanding of these issues will probably not be achieved via experimental or correlational designs and suggests that there is an urgent need for 'naturalistic' research to understand mechanisms and contribute to the building of theory. Reviewing work by Almond and Harris (1998) on the effectiveness of interventions based on PE curricula, Biddle *et al.* (2004: 689) state that the 'authors concluded that the extant literature did little to improve understanding of what kinds of programmes or what aspects of programmes bring about health gains or valued outcomes'.

In the material on social cohesion and sport-in-development there is a clear concern as to the nature of the processes involved in the formation and sustaining of different types of social capital, in different types of circumstances (with Bourdieu, Coleman and Putnam offering differing approaches) and the extent to which such processes are amenable to policy intervention (Long and Sanderson, 2001; Portes and Landolt, 2000; Leisure Industries Research Centre, 2003). In the material on the potential role of sport in reducing anti-social behaviour or recidivism there is almost a consensus that process is all – the type of activity (e.g. task versus ego orientation), the nature of the relationships and the role of leadership and various 'protective factors'. For example, Sandford *et al.* (2006: 262), in a review of research on the role of physical education programmes in re-engaging 'disaffected youth', state that 'it has been argued that the social relationships experienced during involvement in physical activity programmes are the most significant factor in effecting behavioural change'. Bailey (2006: 399) in a review of the benefits of physical education and sport in schools, concludes that although many of the desired physical, affective, social and cognitive outcomes are possible, they are not automatic because 'the actions and interactions of teachers and coaches largely determine whether or not children and young people experience these positive aspects of PES and whether or not they realize its great potential'. Even in the more technical and statistical area of the economic importance of sport there is a debate about the precise role of sport in urban regeneration, the nature and extent of tangible and intangible impacts of sporting events and the nature of the 'mechanism' via which events produce positive economic outcomes (the multiplier). In fact Preuss (2004a: 35) questions if it is possible to resolve some of these debates in any generalizable manner, 'because each sporting event has a different impact and size and because each city has a different history, culture and structure, there is no guidance on how sporting events – whatever size – create urban development'.

Offering a more general comment on sports research, Coakley (2003: 99) suggests that most of the findings on:

> [t]he causes and benefits of playing sports have tended to be superficial, and they have told us little about sport socialisation as an ongoing process in people's lives. They have given us fuzzy snapshots, rather than clear videos, of socialisation.

Like the various writers quoted above, Coakley (1998: 2) concludes that the way forward is to regard 'sports as *sites* for socialisation experiences, not *causes* of socialisation outcomes'. This reflects others' arguments that we need to 'decentre' (Crabbe, 2000), or 'de-mythologize', sport in order to understand what sports work for what subjects, in what conditions.

It's all about families

Such perspectives serve to shift our focus from families *of programmes* (sport and crime; education; social cohesion) to *families of mechanisms* (or programme theories), with apparently diverse interventions sharing common components. For example, Pawson (2006: 174) suggests:

> There are probably some common processes (e.g. how people react to change) and thus generic theories (about human volition) that feed their way into all interventions. If synthesis were to concentrate on these middle-range mechanisms, then the opportunities for the utilisation of reviews would be much expanded.

The research examined in the previous chapters indicates that many apparently disparate programme areas – sport-in-development, sport and crime reduction, sport and education – are often trying to achieve the same *intermediate impacts*, although in pursuit of slightly different outcomes. Leaving aside the more complex issues about the precise relationship between certain intermediate impacts (e.g. increased self-efficacy, physical self-worth, self-confidence, self-esteem, acceptance of certain values, development of forms of social capital) and subsequent behavioural outcomes, it is clear that many sports programmes are seeking to achieve the same basic impacts on participants. Further, other non-sporting programmes are also seeking to address the same issues, via broadly similar mechanisms. For example, Tacon (2007) argues that football-based social inclusion projects have much in common with social work and health work practice, as they seek to promote tolerance, reduce youth offending and drug use. Consequently, he suggests the need for 'cross-fertilisation between sports-based projects, social work and nursing, through information-sharing, staffing and skills development' (Tacon, 2007: 13). Biddle's (2006) stress on 'social climates', intrinsic motivational approaches, task and mastery orientation (Chapter 5) and Witt and Crompton's (1997) concept of 'protective factors' (Chapter 6) refer to *generic* mechanisms, with sport being a site for, but not cause of, socialization experiences (Coakley, 1998).

Consequently, the implication of such an approach is that there is a need to understand the nature of such 'middle range mechanisms'. This relates to Merton's (1968: 39) concept of 'middle-range theories that lie between the minor but necessary working hypotheses that evolve in abundance during day-to-day research and the all-inclusive systematic efforts to develop a unified theory that will explain all observed social behaviour'. For example, in programme design and daily practice across a range of seemingly different programmes, certain mechanisms or processes will result in the development of (say) self-efficacy by certain participants and not others. The identification of the communalities of such mechanisms across a range of interventions can lead to the development of, or linking with, broader analytical frameworks, providing a much more robust and potentially generalizable version of 'what works', in what circumstances, for whom and why.

In such an approach, the world of evidence, the sense-making, the teaching and learning interactions, the conversations, usefully go beyond the world of sport (or at least specific sports programmes such as sport and crime reduction). Clearly, such a concentration on middle-range mechanisms would enable programme designers to adopt a broader view of the world of evidence and draw on a wide range of generic research and practice. It should also lead to conceptual clarification and improved programme design and, probably, increased ability to achieve the desired intermediate impacts. In a sense, such work has already influenced programmes which, having identified the absence or weakness of such mechanisms in sports programmes and have adopted a 'sport plus' approach. For example, *Playing for Success* (Sharp *et al.*, 2003) uses sport partly as a 'fly paper' to attract children to other more traditional educational programmes and associated mechanisms; crime reduction programmes such as Midnight Basketball (Wilkins, 1997; Hartmann and Depro, 2006) combine sport with a range of programmes addressing issues of personal development; sport-in-development programmes are embedded in a set of other social and organizational relationships (Chapter 5); commentators argue that in terms of social cohesion sports programmes need to be complemented by other measures to stimulate social regeneration (Skidmore *et al.*, 2006; Delaney and Keaney, 2005).

The above provides a broad outline of the assessment of the limitations of much current research and the type of issues which need to be addressed in the 'conversations' between researchers, practitioners and policy-makers. We now turn to consider this shift from methods to more inclusive approaches to the world of evidence and the understanding of the programme theories held by policy-makers and practitioners.

From methods to logic of inquiry

Oakley *et al.* (2005: 19), referring to the general lack of availability of social science evidence to inform the implementation of effective interventions, suggest two possible responses: 'improve the standards of effectiveness research, or synthesise the evidence for "promising" interventions that may ultimately be shown to be effective'. With regard to the latter they propose:

> [a]n innovative model in which the findings of well-designed intervention research are set alongside data from 'qualitative' studies that are more likely to represent the views of target populations ... Policy makers' 'what works' questions are thus set in the much broader social context of public expectations and experiences.
>
> (Oakley *et al.*, 2005: 19)

This approach is broadly similar to Faulkner *et al.*'s (2006) attempt to capture the full complexity of the world of evidence via a *better practices* approach

(Comprehensive School Health Research, 2005). This 'provides one framework for integrating critical reviews of existing empirical evidence with contextual and practical considerations relevant to organisations, focused on the translation of the results' (Faulkner *et al.*, 2006: 124). This approach attempts to use, but move beyond, standard literature searches and reviews by assembling a broad-based team of researchers, practitioners, decision-makers and participants and seeking to obtain unpublished materials. Material is assessed on the basis of effectiveness according to positive and negative outcomes; associated study designs and a set of 'plausibility criteria' (approach to evaluation, content attributes); whether formative or process evaluation is available; whether appropriate theoretical foundations have been applied and a range of precise attributes (e.g. collaborative approach, sustainability). Faulkner *et al.* (2006: 119) state:

> The core principle of this approach is that scientific evidence about what is effective is inherently limited – the ultimate determination must be made by the practitioners and decision-makers who understand the scientific evidence, the specific needs of a given population and situation, and the resources available to them at the time.
>
> (Maule *et al.*, 2003: S134)

This reflects a more general shift from an emphasis on methodological rigour and purity to 'a logic of inquiry' (Pawson, 2006: 178) and via an increased embracing of a loose amalgam of theories of behaviour change (Foster *et al.*, 2005; Bailey *et al.*, in press), realist evaluation (Pawson and Tilley, 2000; Pawson, 2006; Nichols and Crow, 2004; Tacon, 2007) and theory-based evaluations to seek to understand the assumptions underpinning interventions, the policy-makers' and practitioners' understanding of the presumed 'mechanisms' and consequently to provide a framework for their evaluation. For example, Blamey and Mutrie (2004: 751), commenting on research on the promotion of physical activity (a necessary, but not sufficient condition to obtain benefits) suggest that 'process information, such as the rationale and theories driving programmes, is increasingly being seen as important to understanding why and how programmes work for certain populations sub-groups'.

However, although these new approaches are being considered as a result of the limitations of current research approaches and findings, there is also a 'political' element to their adoption. As we have already noted, a major attraction of theory-based approaches to evaluation is that they provide an opportunity to close the distance between academic research and policy-makers. In fact, it requires what Pawson and Tilley (2000: 201) refer to as mutual 'teaching and learning interactions'. The attraction is clear for Bailey *et al.* (in press: 31) who suggest:

> One of the key tasks for researchers is to work with programme developers and sponsors to analyse the outcomes for which they are hoping. More importantly, the analysis reveals assumptions (and micro-assumptions) that have been made about the ways in which programme activities will lead to

intended outcomes. A theory of change approach to evaluation argues that this clarification process is valuable for all parties, particularly in making explicit powerful assumptions that may or may not be widely shared, understood or agreed.

As outlined in Chapter 3, a theory-based approach requires what Pawson (2006: 169) refers to as 'sense-making'. Researchers and practitioners have to explore and make explicit their *programme theories* (Weiss, 1997), the nature of their assumptions about sports programmes; the nature of the properties and processes of the programmes that are expected to lead to specific outcomes (although in terms of programme theories, the easier questions relate to intermediate impacts, i.e. individuals' changed attitudes and competences, rather than the more difficult issue of changed behaviours). Weiss (1997) argues that this approach can serve to identify and resolve different theories (often in the same organization) about how shared desired outcomes are to be achieved. More radically, as we saw in Chapter 5, such an approach can lead to 'a direct assault on hegemonic knowledge' (Elabor-Idemudia, 2002: 232) and, depending on who is involved in this process, issues of cultural diversity and local solutions can be addressed (Nicholls, 2007). In this regard Weiss (1997: 517–18) provides a broad outline of the advantages of theory-based evaluation (or evaluation based on theories of change) for a range of interest groups.

Programme designers

They are encouraged to think harder and deeper about their assumptions and the programmes they design. Such evaluation indicates not only the kinds of activities that produce good outcomes, but also suggests the mechanisms by which those activities work.

Practitioners

It may be that members of the same organization or programme have different theories about how the programme works. If they can work through their differences and agree on a common set of assumptions about what they are doing and why, they can increase the force of the intervention.

Programme managers

A major advantage for them is that the evaluation provides feedback about which chain of reasoning breaks down and where it breaks down.

Managers and funders of similar programmes elsewhere

If they understand the what, how and why of programme success (and failure), they can undertake new ventures better prepared to reproduce those elements of the programme that are associated with the successful transition to the next link in the chain of assumptions and to rethink and rework those elements that do not lead to the next interim marker.

Policy-makers and the public

Theory-based evaluation provides explanations – stories of means and ends – that communicate readily to policy-makers and the public.

Programme evaluator

The theory-base evaluation approach helps evaluators to focus the study on key questions. It provides information on short-term and intermediate outcomes, which are linked, according to the best available knowledge, to the long-term outcomes of interest.

The value of such an approach lies not only in strengthening the relationship between researchers and practitioners, but it can also lead to improved coherence and effectiveness in policy and organizational processes. As suggested in Chapters 3 and 5, it has the potential to contribute to capacity-building, develop a greater sense of ownership, understanding and integration and develop an organizational ability to reflect on and analyse attitudes, beliefs and behaviour (Shah *et al.*, 2004; Coalter, 2006).

This approach returns us to an issue raised in the Introduction about the relationship between 'engineering' and 'enlightenment' approaches to the relationship between research and policy. Both Weiss (1980) and Pawson (2006) argue that the theory-based approach moves beyond simple 'political arithmetic' and 'partisan support' and embraces the philosophy underpinning an 'enlightenment' approach to research, in which the 'influence of research on policy occurs through the medium of ideas rather than of data' (Pawson, 2006: 169). This approach and the more pragmatic turn in widening the definition of relevant evidence seem to reflect Hammersley's (1995: 19) argument that 'philosophy must not be seen as superordinate to empirical research … research is a practical activity and cannot be governed in any strict way by methodological theory'.

Further, perhaps this approach can go some way to assisting sceptics such as Long and Sanderson (2001). A mixture of valuing professionals' experience and a desire not to undermine the efforts of community activists, leads them into a methodologically ambivalent position (Long and Sanderson, 2001: 201–2).

> More precise evidence … might provide the basis for more effective arguments in support of sport and leisure policies and programmes at the local level. It would help to clarify realistic objectives and priorities; and it would help in the design of effective local initiatives which can play an appropriate role in community development … Nevertheless, scarred by experience of community initiatives that are justified on the basis that they process people at a lower per capita cost we are wary of the siren call of quantitative measures

... which almost inevitably place consideration of service delivery and social control above those of elusive social dynamics.

Perhaps accepting and exploring the methodological and evidential implications of Pawson's (2006: 35) assertion that all 'social interventions are always complex systems thrust amidst complex systems' may help to reconcile the views of Richard Caborn and Long and Sanderson. Who knows?

A social vaccine?

However, a big problem remains. Even if all of the above was achieved and we developed a better understanding of what *processes* produce what *outcomes* for which *participants* and in what *circumstances*, we are still left with a more fundamental issue – are the 'solutions' (i.e. intermediate impacts) that sport is offering relevant to the problems which it seeks to address? This is also a major component of a theory-based approach: the need to understand the *causes* of the behaviour which sports programmes wish to change (e.g. crime, educational underachievement, weak social capital). We have noted researchers' comments that many programmes tend to be based on the presumed properties of sport, rather than a diagnosis of the causes of the behaviour they wish to change – somehow what sport offers is a sort of all-purpose 'social vaccine' for a range of social problems (the term is borrowed from Emler's (2001b) critical analysis of the centrality of self-esteem in many policy interventions).

Improving our understanding of the mechanisms involved to improve the effectiveness of sports programmes' ability to achieve desired *intermediate impacts* may be of little use if the initial diagnosis of the causes of problems (and therefore the solutions) is incorrect. For example, in Chapter 4 it was not clear that policies aimed at increasing social cohesion and social capital through sport are based on any coherent understanding of the social and cultural basis of these two desired outcomes (and the implication was that sport might have a very minor role). In Chapter 7 we noted the often overly simplistic understanding of the causes of anti-social behaviour and crime that underpins some sports programmes. In Chapter 6 we noted that many of the discussions about sport's potential contribution to educational performance are devoid of analyses of the complex causes of educational underachievement.

The shift from developing sports in the community to the 'development of the community through sport' has required new understanding. Some have questioned the traditional, sports-centred, 'product-led' approaches and proposed 'needs-based' approaches. In this regard McDonald and Tungatt (1992: 33) argue that if sport is to be used to address broader issues of social inclusion, then sport may have to change because 'there is a danger that aims and objectives may incorporate many of the values that traditional sports provision stood for'.

Consequently, there has been a tendency for a lack of in-depth consideration of the relationship between causes and programme content and process, or the extent to which there is evidence that what they are offering can contribute to a solution (Crabbe, 2000; West and Crompton, 2001; Williams and Strean, 2006). As Pawson (2006: 9) comments, in general, programme design is frequently 'a research free zone'.

The frequent failure to address such issues is reflected in Weiss's (1993: 103) concerns that many social interventions fail because they are 'fragmented, one-service-at-a-time programs, dissociated from people's total patterns of living' and her quotation of Daniel Moynihan's argument that 'integrated policies that reach deeper into the social fabric will have to be developed'. In part this is because of the frequently individualistic assumptions that underpin many sports programmes, with a strong emphasis placed on aspects of individual character-building, self-efficacy, self-control, self-esteem, self-discipline and self-confidence. Consequently, it is suggested that there is a need to recognize that actions and choices take place within the material, economic and cultural realities within which the 'empowered' live (Mwaanga, 2003; Morris *et al.*, 2003). Or, as Weiss (1993: 105) puts it:

> We mount limited-focus programs to cope with broad-gauge problems. We devote limited resources to long-standing and stubborn problems. Above all we concentrate attention on changing the attitudes and behaviour of target groups without concomitant attention to the institutional structures and social arrangements that tend to keep them 'target groups'.

For example, in Chapter 6 we noted Grissom's (2005) comment that, because it is very difficult to raise student achievement, beyond what might be expected, an intervention that seeks to do it indirectly (via sport and PE) might be expected to encounter even more difficulty.

In part, the growth of 'sport plus' programmes indicates a growing awareness of some of these issues and the need to examine more closely the strengths and limitations of sports programmes. Fox (1992) speaks for many others in related fields when he argues that 'it would be a political mistake for physical education to build its case on self-esteem promotion, because this fails to identify its unique contribution ... the physical self and physical competence, fitness and physical appearance' (see Tinning (2005) for similar sentiments about the relationship between sport and PE and active lifestyles). Such concerns have also been gradually reflected in sports policy rhetoric, where there has been a retreat from the heady early days of New Labour to slightly more circumspect claims that sport can 'contribute' to the solution of some social problems – a rhetorical fudge that seems to keep policy-makers, practitioners and some researchers happy. In part, this book has been concerned to examine the vague concept of 'contribution' and to suggest that we need to re-examine our approaches to evidence in support of this assertion.

Not proven

Most of this book has been concerned to illustrate the limitations of much research evidence for the wider impacts of sport, or in the case of economic impacts that they may be less than presumed. In most areas there is an increasing acknowledgement of such limitations and the associated lack of robust evidence for many of the claims about sport which underpin sports-related policy. However, in many cases this cannot simply be taken as 'disproof' – i.e. that sport does *not* have its claimed impacts (outcomes are more difficult). As I am writing this as a member of staff of a Scottish university, it is appropriate that we offer a Scottish legal verdict on the evidence before us – *not proven*. The not proven verdict is used when a jury does not believe the case has been proven against the defendant, but is not sufficiently convinced of their innocence to bring in a 'not guilty' verdict.

Rather, as many commentators have emphasized, much of the research is characterized by methodological shortcomings – in some cases the chosen methods had little chance of providing robust evidence (often admitted in caveats in the final paragraphs of long academic articles in the world of 'publish or perish' – although, as we have noted, such deficiencies are not confined to sports-related research: Oakley *et al.*, 2005). However, the most fundamental deficiency, admitted by a wide variety of researchers and commentators, has been a widespread failure to address issues of process, or in Pawson's (2006) terms the 'mechanisms' which inform the programme theories of policy-makers and practitioners.

It is appropriate to finish with one rather long and one very short quotation. The long quotation is from the President's Council on Physical Fitness and Sports (2006: 4) which, although concerned with the character-building potential of sport, has a much more general relevance:

> Taken together, the results from these studies underscore the importance of not lumping all sports or sport participants together. For several reasons, broad generalizations about 'sports' are unlikely to be helpful. For one, the rule structures of the various sports promote different types of social interaction. The developmental stimuli provided by a boxing match are likely to differ from those of a golf tournament. In addition, each sport tends to have its own subculture and implicit moral norms. The culture of rugby is quite different from that of competitive swimming. There are also differences based on age and competitive level. Major league baseball and Little League provide quite different social experiences. Even within a single sport area and developmental level, individual sport teams are different because each team develops its own unique moral microculture through the influence of particular coaches, athletes, fans, parents, and programs. Moreover, even within a single team, participants' own appraisals of the experience may vary substantially.

The short quotation is provided by Taylor *et al.* (1999: 50), summing up their evaluation of programmes using sport to reduce recidivism.

> All programmes agree that physical activities do not by themselves reduce offending. All agree that there are personal and social development objectives

that form part of a matrix of outcomes. These developments may, sooner or later, improve offending behaviour, but their impact is unpredictable in scale and timing. To expect anything more tangible is unrealistic.

References

6, P (1997) *Social Exclusion: Time to be Optimistic*, Demos Collection 12 3–9c, London: Demos.

Aaron, H.J. (1978) *Politics and the Professors: The Great Society in Perspective*, Washington, DC: Brookings Institution.

Advisory Sports Council (1966) *Annual Report*, London: HMSO.

Aitchison, C. (1992) 'Women and the Implications of Compulsory Competitive Tendering in the UK Local Authority Leisure Services', in D. Leslie (ed.) *Perspectives on Provision*, LSA Publication No. 52, Eastbourne: Leisure Studies Association, pp. 37–47.

Almond, L. and Harris, J. (1998) 'Interventions to promote health-related physical education', in S.J.H. Biddle, J.F. Sallis and N. Cavill (eds) *Young and Active? Young People and Health-Enhancing Physical Activity: Evidence and Implications*, London: Heath Education Authority, pp. 133–49.

American Association of University Women (AAUW) Educational Foundation (1998) *Separated by Sex: A Critical Look at Single-sex Education for Girls*, Washington, DC: AAUW Educational Foundation.

Andranovich, G., Burbank, M.J. and Heying, C.H. (2001) 'Olympic Cities: Lessons Learned from Mega-Event Politics', *Journal of Urban Affairs* 23(2): 113–31.

Andreff, W. (1994) *The Economic Importance of Sport in Europe: Financing Economic Impact*, Strasbourg: Committee for the Development of Sport, Council for Europe.

Andrew, B. (2004) 'Social Capital in Sport in South London', unpublished MSc thesis, Loughborough: Loughborough University.

Andrews, J.P. and Andrews, G.J. (2003) 'Life in a Secure Unit: The Rehabilitations of Young People through the Use of Sport', *Social Science and Medicine* 56: 531–50.

Armstrong, G. and Giulianotti, R. (eds) (2004) *Football in Africa: Conflict Conciliation and Community*, Basingstoke: Palgrave Macmillan.

Asquith, S., Buist, M., Loughran, N., MacAuley, C. and Montgomery, M. (1998) *Children, Young People and Offending in Scotland: A Research Review*, Edinburgh: Scottish Office.

Atkins, H. (n.d.) *Mathare United: A Model CECAFA Club*: www.toolkitsportdevelopment. org.

Attwood, C., Singh, G., Prime, D., Rebecca, C. *et al.* (2003) *Home Office Citizenship Survey: People, Families and Communities*, London: Home Office.

Audit Commission (1989) *Sport for Whom? Clarifying the Local Authority Role in Sport and Recreation*, London: HMSO.

Australian Sports Commission (2006) *The Case for Sport in Australia*, Canberra: Australian Sports Commission.

Austrian, Z. and Rosentraub, M.S. (2002) 'Cities, Sports and Economic Changes: A Retrospective Assessment', *Journal of Urban Affairs* 24(5): 549–63.

Baade, R. (1987) *Is there a Rationale for Subsidizing Sports Stadiums?*, Heartland Policy Study, 13, Chicago, IL: Heartland Institute.

Baade, R. (1996) 'Professional Sports as Catalysts for Metropolitan Development', *Journal of Urban Affairs* 18(1): 1–17.

Baade, R. and Matheson, V.A. (2004) 'The Quest for the Cup: Assessing the Economic Impact of the World Cup', *Regional Studies* 38(4): 343–54.

Bailey, P. (1978) *Leisure and Class in Victorian England*, London: Routledge & Kegan Paul.

Bailey, R. (2006) 'Physical Education and Sport in Schools: A Review of Benefits and Outcomes', *Journal of School Health* 76(8): 397–401.

Bailey, R. (2005) 'Evaluating the Relationship between Physical Education, Sport and Social Inclusion', *Education Review* 57(1): 71–90.

Bailey, R., Armour, K., Kirk, D., Jess, M., Pickup, I., Sandford, R. and the BERA Physical Education and Sport Pedagogy Special Interest Group (in press) 'The Educational Benefits Claimed for Physical Education and School Sport: An Academic Review', *Research Papers in Education*, submitted for publication.

Bale, J. and Cronin, M. (2003) *Sport and Post-colonialism*, Oxford: Berg.

Bandura, A. (1962) *Social Learning through Imitation*, Lincoln, NE: University of Nebraska Press.

Bandura, A. (1975) *Social Learning and Personality Development*, New York: Holt, Rinehart & Winston.

Bandura, A. (1986) *Social Foundations of Thought and Action: A Social Cognitive Theory*, Englewood Cliffs, NJ: Prentice-Hall.

Bandura, A. (1998) 'Self-Efficacy', in V.S. Ramachaudran (ed.) *Encyclopaedia of Human Behavior*, New York: Academic Press, vol. 4, pp. 71–81.

Bandura, A. and Ribes-Inesta, E. (1976) *Analysis of Delinquency and Aggression*, Hillsdale, NJ: Lawrence Erlbaum Associates.

Begg, D., Langley, J., Moffitt, T. and Marshall, S. (1996) 'Sport and Delinquency: An Examination of the Deterrence Hypothesis in a Longitudinal Study', *British Journal of Sports Medicine* 30: 335–41.

Beunen, G.P., Lefevre, J., Philippaerts, R.M., Delvaux, K., Thomis, M., Claessens, A.L., Vanreusel, B., Lysens, R., Eynde, B.V. and Renson, R. (2004) 'Adolescent Correlates of Adult Physical Activity: A 26 Year Follow-up', *Medicine and Science in Sport and Exercise* 36(11): 1930–6.

Bianchini, F. (1992) 'Cultural Policy and the Development of Citizenship', a paper presented at the ELRA Conference, Leisure and the New Citizenship, Bilbao, June.

Biddle, S. (1994) 'What Helps and Hinders People Becoming More Physically Active?', in A.J. Killoran, P. Fentem and C. Caspersen (eds) *Moving on: International Perspectives on Promoting Physical Activity*, London: Health Education Authority, pp. 110–48.

Biddle, S. (2006) 'Defining and Measuring Indicators of Psycho-social Well-Being in Youth Sport and Physical Activity', in Y. Vanden Auweele, C. Malcolm and B. Meulders (eds) *Sports and Development*, Leuven: Lannoo Campus, pp. 163–84.

Biddle, S. and Mutrie, N. (2001) *Psychology of Physical Activity*, London: Routledge.

Biddle, S., Coalter, F., O'Donovan, T., MacBeth, J., Nevill, M. and Whitehead, S. (2005) *Increasing Demand for Sport and Physical Activity by Girls*, Research Report, 100, Edinburgh: sportscotland.

Biddle, S., Gorley, T. and Stensel, D.J. (2004) 'Health-Enhancing Physical Activity and Sedentary Behaviour in Children and Adolescents', *Journal of Sports Sciences* 22: 679–701.

Blackie, J., Coppock, T. and Duffield, B. (1979) *The Leisure Planning Process*, London: Social Sciences Research Council/Sports Council.

Blackshaw, T. and Long, J. (2005) 'What's the Big Idea? A Critical Exploration of the Concept of Social Capital and its Incorporation into Leisure Policy Discourse', *Leisure Studies* 24(3): 239–58.

Blair, T. (1999) *Speech to the International Convention on Sikhism*, London: 10 Downing Street.

Blamey, A.S. and Mutrie, N. (2004) 'Changing the Individual to Promote Health-Enhancing Physical Activity: The Difficulties of Producing Evidence and Translating it into Practice', *Journal of Sports Sciences* 22: 741–54.

Bloom, M., Grant, M. and Watt, D. (2005) *Strengthening Canada: The Socio-Economic Benefits of Sport Participation in Canada*, Ottawa: Conference Board of Canada.

Blunkett, D. (2001) *Politics and Progress: Renewing Democracy and Civil Society*, London: Demos.

Bonner, L. (2003) 'Using Theory-Based Evaluation to Build Evidence-Based Health and Social Care Policy and Practice', *Critical Public Health* 13: 77–92.

Boonstra, N., Krouwel, A., Veldboer, L. and Duyvendak, J. (2005) 'A Good Sport? Research into the Capacity of Recreational Sport to Integrate Dutch Minorities', paper presented at International Conference on Sport and Urban Development, Rotterdam, 9–11 November.

Botcheva, L. and Huffman, M.D. (2004) *Grassroot Soccer Foundation HIV/AIDS Education Program: An Intervention in Zimbabwe*, White River Junction, VT: Grassroot Soccer Foundation.

Boule, N.G., Hadded, E., Kenny G.P., Wells, G.A. and Sigal, R.J. (2002) 'Effects of Exercise on Glycemic Control and Body Mass in Type 2 Diabetes Mellitus: A Meta-analysis of Controlled Clinical Trials', *Scandinavian Journal of Medicine and Science in Sports* 12(1): 60–1.

Bourdieu, P. (1986) *Distinction: A Social Critique of the Judgement of Taste*, London: Routledge.

Bourdieu, P. (1997a) 'The Forms of Capital', in A.H. Halsey, H. Launder, P. Brown and A. Stuart Wells (eds) *Education, Culture, Economy and Society*, Oxford: Oxford University Press.

Bourdieu, P. (1997b) 'Cultural Reproduction and Social Reproduction', in J. Harabel and A.H. Halsey (eds) *Power and Ideology in Education*, New York: Oxford University Press.

Bovaird, A. (1992) 'Evaluation, Performance Assessment and Objective-led Management in Public Sector Leisure Services', in J. Sugden and C. Knox (eds) *Leisure in the 1990s: Rolling Back the Welfare State*, Leisure Studies Association, Publication No 46, Brighton: Leisure Studies Association.

Bovaird, T., Nicols, G. and Taylor, P. (1997) *Approaches to Estimating the Wider Economic and Social Benefits Resulting from Sports Participation*, Birmingham: Aston Business School Research Institute.

Bowker, A., Gadbois, S. and Cornock, B. (2003) 'Sport Participation and Self-Esteem: Variations as a Function of Gender and Role Orientation', *Sex Roles* 49(1/2): 47–58.

Brady, M. and Kahn, A.B. (2002) *Letting Girls Play: The Mathare Youth Sports Association's Football Program for Girls*, New York: Population Council.

Bramham, P., Henry, I., Mommas, H. and van der Poel, H. (eds) (1993) *Leisure Policies in Europe*, Wallingford: CAB International.

Buchner, D. and Miles, R. (2002) 'Seeking Contemporary Understanding of Factors that Influence Physical Activity', *American Journal of Preventive Medicine* 18: 35–43.

Bulmer, M. (1982) *The Uses of Social Research*, London: Allen & Unwin.

Burnett, C. (2001) 'Social Impact Assessment and Sport Development: Social Spin-offs of the Australia–South Africa Junior Sport Programme', *International Review for the Sociology of Sport* 36(1): 41–57.

Cabinet Office (1999) *Modernising Government*, London: Cabinet Office.

Caborn, R. (2003) *Transcript of Richard Caborn's Opening Speech at CCPR 20*, Department of Culture Media and Sport, May 2003: http://www.culture.gov.uk/Reference_library/Minister_Speeches/Richard_Caborn/Richard_Caborn_Speech03.htm.

Calfas, K.J. and Taylor, W.C. (1994) 'Effects of Physical Activity on Psychological Variables in Adolescents', *Pediatric Exercise Science* 6(4): 406–23.

California Task Force to Promote Self-Esteem and Personal and Social Responsibility (1990) *Toward a State of Esteem: The Final Report of the California Task Force to Promote Self-Esteem and Personal and Social Responsibility*, Sacramento, CA: Bureau of Publications, California State Department of Education.

Cambridge Econometrics (2004) *The Value of the Sports Economy in England in 2000*, Cambridge: Sport England.

Canadian Policy Research Initiative (2005) *Social Capital as a Public Policy Tool*: www.policyresearch.gc.ca.

Cap Gemini Ernst and Young (2003) *Splash 2002: Final Report*, London: Youth Justice Board.

Carlson, B.R. and Petti, K. (1989) 'Health Locus of Control and Participation in Physical Activity', *American Journal of Health Promotion* 3: 32–7.

Chalkley, B. and Essex, S. (1999) 'Urban Development through Hosting International Events: A History of the Olympic Games', *Planning Perspectives* 14: 369–94.

Chapin, T.S. (2004) 'Sports Facilities as Urban Redevelopment Catalysts', *Journal of the American Planning Association* 70(2): 193–209.

Chema, T. (1996) 'When Professional Sports Justify the Subsidy, a Reply to Robert A. Baade', *Journal of Urban Affairs* 18(1): 19–22.

Clarke, A. (1992) 'Citizens and Consumers', in J. Sugden and C. Knox (eds) *Leisure in the 1990s: Rolling Back the Welfare State*, Leisure Studies Association Publication, 46, Eastbourne: Leisure Studies Association, pp. 109–20.

Coakley, J. (1997) *Sport in Society: Issues and Controversies*, Boston, MA: McGraw Hill.

Coakley, J. (1998) *Sport in Society: Issues and Controversies*, 6th edn, Boston, MA: McGraw Hill.

Coakley, J. (2004) *Sport in Society: Issues and Controversies*, 8th edn, Boston, MA: McGraw Hill.

Coalter, F. (1988) *Sport and Anti-Social Behaviour: A Literature Review*, Research Report, 2, Edinburgh: Scottish Sports Council.

Coalter, F. (1993) 'Sports Participation: Price or Priorities?', *Leisure Studies* 12(3): 171–82.

Coalter, F. (1995) 'Compulsory Competitive Tendering for Sport and Leisure Management: A Lost Opportunity', *Managing Leisure: An International Journal* 1(1): 3–15.

Coalter, F. (1998) 'Leisure Studies, Leisure Policy and Social Citizenship: The Failure of Welfare of or the Limits of Welfare?', *Leisure Studies* 17: 21–36.

Coalter, F. (1999) 'Sport and Recreation in the UK: Flow with the Flow or Buck the Trends?', *Managing Leisure: An International Journal* 4(1): 24–39.

Coalter, F. (2002) *Sport and Community Development: A Manual*, Research Report, 86, Edinburgh: sportscotland.

Coalter, F. (2004) 'Stuck in the Blocks? A Sustainable Sporting Legacy?', in *After the Goldrush: The London Olympics*, London: Institute for Public Policy Research/DEMOS.

Coalter, F. (2005) *The Social Benefits of Sport: An Overview to Inform the Community Planning Process*, Research Report, 98, Edinburgh: sportscotland.

Coalter, F. (2006) *Sport-in-Development: A Monitoring and Evaluation Manual*, London: UK Sport.

Coalter, F. (2007) 'London Olympics 2012: The Catalyst that Inspires People to Lead More Active Lives', *Journal of the Royal Society for the Promotion of Health* 127(3): 109–10.

Coalter, F. and Allison, M. (1996) *Sport and Community Development*, Research Digest, 42, Edinburgh: Scottish Sports Council.

Coalter, F., Allison, M. and Taylor, J. (2000) *The Role of Sport in Regenerating Deprived Urban Areas*, Edinburgh: Scottish Executive.

Coalter, F., Dowers, S. and Baxter, M. (1995) 'The Impact of Social Class and Education on Sports Participation: Some Evidence from the General Household Survey', in K. Roberts (ed.) *Leisure and Social Stratification*, Eastbourne: Leisure Studies Association, pp. 59–71.

Coalter, F., Long, J. and Duffield, B. (1988) *Recreational Welfare: The Rationale for Public Sector Investment in Leisure*, Aldershot: Gower/Avebury.

Coates, D. and Humphreys, B.R. (2003) 'The Effect of Professional Sports on Earnings and Employment in the Services and Retail Sectors in US Cities', *Regional Science and Urban Economics* 33: 175–98.

Coe, D.P., Pivarnik, J.M., Womack, C.J. and Reeves, M.J. (2006) 'The Effects of Physical Education on Activity Levels on Academic Achievement in Children', *Medicine and Science in Sport and Exercise* 38(8): 1515–19.

Coleman, J. (1988–9) 'Social Capital in the Creation of Human Capital', *American Journal of Sociology* 94: 95–120.

Coleman, J.S. (1961) *Adolescent Society: The Social Life of the Teenager and its Impact on Education*, New York: Free Press.

Coleman, J.S. (1994) *Foundations of Social Theory*, Cambridge, MA: Belknap Press.

Collins, M. and Kay, T. (2003) *Sport and Social Inclusion*, London: Routledge.

Collins, M., Henry, I., Houlihan, B. and Buller, J. (1999) *Sport and Social Inclusion: A Report to the Department of Culture, Media and Sport, Institute of Sport and Leisure Policy*, Loughborough: Loughborough University.

Comaroff, J. and Comaroff, J. (eds) (1999) *Civil Society and the Political Imagination in Africa: Critical Perspectives*, Chicago, IL: University of Chicago Press.

Comprehensive School Health Research (2005) *The Better Practices Model Resource Guide: Informing Researchers, Policy Makers and Organizations*, Prince Edward Island, Canada: Comprehensive School Health Research.

Crabbe, T. (2000) 'A Sporting Chance? Using Sport to Tackle Drug Use and Crime', *Drug Education, Prevention and Policy* 7(4): 381–91.

Critcher, C. (1992) 'Sporting Civic Prides: Sheffield and the World Student Games of 1991', in J. Sugden and C. Knox (eds) *Leisure in the 1990s: Rolling Back the Welfare State*, Leisure Studies Association Publication No 46, Brighton: Leisure Studies Association, pp. 193–204.

Crompton, J.L. (1995) 'Economic Impact Analysis of Sports Facilities and Events: Eleven Sources of Misapplication', *Journal of Sport Management* 9(1): 14–35.

Crompton, J.L. (2000) 'Repositioning Leisure Services', *Managing Leisure* 5(2): 65–75.

Crompton, J.L. (2004) 'Beyond Economic Impact: An Alternative Rationale for the Public Subsidy of Major League Sports Facilities', *Journal of Sport Management* 18: 40–58.

Crompton, J.L. and Witt, P.A. (1997) 'Programs that Work: The Roving Leader Program in San Antonio', *Journal of Park and Recreation Administration* 15(2): 84–92.

Curtis, J., McTeer, W. and White, P. (1999) 'Exploring Effects of School Sport Experiences on Sport Participation in Later Life', *Sociology of Sport Journal* 16: 348–65.

Danish, S.J. and Nellen, V.C. (1997) 'New Roles for Sport Psychologists: Teaching Life Skills through Sport to At Risk Youth', *Quest* 49: 100–13.

Davidson, L. (1999) 'Choice of a proper methodology to measure quantitative and qualitative effects of the impact of sort', in C. Jeanreaud (ed.) *The Economic Impact of Sport Events*, Neuchatel: Centre International d'Etude du Sport (CIES).

Deane, J. (1998) 'Community Sports Initiatives: An Evaluation of UK Policy Attempts to Involve the Young Unemployed. The 1980's Action Sport Scheme', in *Sport in the City: Conference Proceedings*, Loughborough and Sheffield: Loughborough University, Sheffield Hallam University and University of Sheffield, vol. 1, Sheffield, 2–4 July, pp. 140–59.

Debord, G. (1995) *The Society of the Spectacle*, tr. D. Nicholson-Smith, New York: Zone Books; 1st published 1967.

DeFilippis, J. (2001) 'The Myth of Social Capital in Community Development', *Housing Policy Debate* 12(4): 781–806.

Delaney, L. and Keaney, E. (2005) *Sport and Social Capital in the United Kingdom: Statistical Evidence from National and International Survey Data*, London: Department of Culture, Media and Sport.

Department for International Development (2005) *Guidance on Evaluation and Review for DFID Staff Evaluation Department*, London: Department for International Development.

Department of Culture, Media and Sport (1999) *Policy Action Team 10: Report to the Social Exclusion Unit – Arts and Sport*, London: HMSO.

Department of Culture, Media and Sport and the Home Office (2004) *Bringing Communities Together Through Sport and Culture*, London: Home Office.

Department of Culture, Media and Sport and the Home Office (2006) *Bringing Communities Together Through Sport and Culture*, London: Home Office.

Department of Culture, Media and Sport and the Strategy Unit (2002) *Game Plan: A Strategy for Delivering Government's Sport and Physical Activity Objectives*, London: Cabinet Office.

Department of Health (1999) *NHS R&D Strategic Review Primary Care: A Report of Topic Working Group*, London: The Stationery Office.

Department of Health (2005) *Sports Injuries Shown the Red Card*: www.dh.gov.uk/publicationAnd Statistics/PressReleases.

Department of Health, Social Security and Public Safety (NI) (2002) *A Health Economics Model: The Cost Benefits of the Physical Activity Strategy for Northern Ireland – A Summary of Key Findings*, Belfast: Economics Branch, Department of Health, Social Services and Public Safety for the Northern Ireland Physical Activity Strategy Implementation Group.

Department of National Heritage (1995) *Sport: Raising the Game*, London: Department of National Heritage.

Department of Social Security (1998) *A New Contract for Welfare: New Ambitions for our Country*, Cm 3805, London: Stationery Office.

Department of the Environment (1975) *Sport and Recreation: White Paper*, Cmnd 6200, London: HMSO.

Department of the Environment (1977a) *Leisure and the Quality of Life Experiments*, London: HMSO.

Department of the Environment (1977b) *Recreation and Deprivation in Inner Urban Areas*, London: HMSO.

Department of Trade and Industry (2003) *Home and Leisure Accident Surveillance Systems*, London: Department of Trade and Industry.

Diawara, M. (2000) 'Globalization, Development Politics and Local Knowledge', *International Sociology* 15(2): 361–71.

Dobson, N., Gratton, C. and Holliday, S. (1997) *Football Came Home: The Economic Impact of Euro96*, Sheffield: Leisure Industries Research Centre.

Donnison, D.V. and Chapman, V. (1965) *Social Policy and Administration*, London: Allen & Unwin.

Driscoll, K. and Wood, L. (1999) *Sporting Capital: Changes and Challenges for Rural Communities in Victoria*, Melbourne: Victoria Centre for Applied Social Research, RMIT University.

Dwyer, T., Coonan, W.E., Leitch, R., Hetzel, B.S. and Baghurst, P.A. (1983) 'An Investigation of the Effects of Daily Physical Activity on the Health of Primary School Students in South Australia', *International Journal of Epidemiology* 12: 308–13.

Dwyer, T., Sallis, J.F., Blizzard, L., Lazarus, R. and Dean, K. (2001) 'Relation of Academic Performance to Physical Activity and Fitness in Children', *Pediatric Exercise Science* 13: 225–37.

Dyerson, M. (2001) 'Maybe it's Better to Bowl Alone: Sport, Community and Democracy in American Thought', *Culture, Sport and Society* 4(1): 19–30.

Economics Research Associates (ERA) (1984) 'Community Economic Impact of the 1984 Summer Olympic Games in Los Angeles', Los Angeles: typescript.

Edwards, H. (1986) 'The Collegiate Athletics Arms Race', in R.A. Lapchick (ed.) *Fractured Focus*, Lexington, MA: Lexington Books.

Eichberg, H. (2006) 'From Sport Export to Politics of Recognition: Experiences from the Cooperation between Denmark and Tanzania', paper presented at the international seminar 'Sport, Poverty and Africa' at the University of Stirling, 5 May 2006.

Eitle, T.M. (2005) 'Do Gender and Race Matter? Explaining the Relationship between Sports Participation and Achievement', *Sociological Spectrum* 25: 177–95.

Eitle, T.M. and Eitle, D.J. (2002) 'Race, Cultural Capital, and the Educational Effects of Participation in Sports', *Sociology of Education* 75(April): 123–46.

Ekeland, E., Heian, F. and Hagen, K.B. (2005) 'Can Exercise Improve Self-Esteem in Children and Young People? A Systematic Review of Randomised Control Trials', *British Journal of Sports Medicine* 39: 792–8.

Elabor-Idemudia, P. (2002) 'Participatory Research: A Tool in the Production of Knowledge in Development Discourse', in K. Saunders (ed.) *Feminist Post-Development Research*, London: Zed Books.

Elliot, D.S. and Voss, H.L. (1974) *Delinquency and Dropout*, Lexington, MA: D.C. Heath & Co.

Emler, N. (2001a) *Commonly-Held Beliefs about Self-Esteem are Myths, Warns New Research Review*: http://www.jrf.org.uk/pressroom/releases/281101.asp.

Emler, N. (2001b) *Self-Esteem: The Costs and Causes of Low Self-Worth*, York: Joseph Rowntree Foundation.

Endersen, I.M. and Olwens, D. (2005) 'Participation in Power Sports and Antisocial Involvement in Preadolescent and Adolescent Boys', *Journal of Child Psychology and Psychiatry* 46(5): 468–78.

Etnier, J.L., Nowell, P.M., Landers, D.M. and Sibley, B.A. (2006) 'A Meta-regression to Examine the Relationship between Aerobic Fitness and Cognitive Performance', *Brain Research Reviews* 52: 119–30.

Etnier, J.L., Salazar, W., Landers, D.M., Petruzzello, S.J., Han, M. and Nowell, P. (1997) 'The Influence of Physical Fitness and Exercise upon Cognitive Functioning: A Meta-analysis', *Journal of Sport and Exercise Psychology* 19: 249–77.

Etzioni, A. (1993) *The Spirit of Community: Rights, Responsibilities and the Communitarian Agenda*, London: Fontana.

Euchner, C.C. (1993) *Playing the Field: Why Sports Teams Move and Why Cities Fight to Keep Them*, Baltimore, MD: Johns Hopkins University Press.

European Heart Network (1999) *Physical Activity and Cardiovascular Disease Prevention in the European Union*, Brussels: European Heart Network.

Evans, G.L. (2001) *Cultural Planning: An Urban Renaissance?*, London: Routledge.

Evans, J. and Roberts, G.C. (1987) 'Physical Competence and the Development of Children's Peer Relations', *Quest* 39: 23–35.

Fainstein, S. and Judd, D.R. (eds) (1999) *The Tourist City*, New Haven, CT: Yale University Press.

Farr, J. (2004) 'Social Capital: A Conceptual History', *Political Theory* 32(1): 6–33.

Farrell, W., Johnson, R., Sapp, M., Pumphrey, R. and Freeman, S. (1995) 'Redirecting the Lives of Urban Black Males: An Assessment of Milwaukees's Midnight Basketball League', *Journal of Community Practice* 2(4): 91–107.

Faulkner, G., Taylor, A., Ferrence, R., Munro, S. and Selby, P. (2006) 'Exercise Science and the Development of Evidence-Based Practice: A "Better Practices" Framework', *European Journal of Sports Science* 6(2): 117–26.

Ferron, C. (1997) 'Body Image in Adolescence: Cross-Cultural Research-Results of the Preliminary Phase of a Quantitative Survey', *Adolescence* 32: 735–45.

Field, J. (2003) *Social Capital*, London: Routledge.

Finn, J.D. (1989) 'Withdrawing from School', *Review of Educational Research* 59: 117–42.

Fitzpatrick, S., Hastings, A. and Kintrea, K. (1998) *Including Young People in Urban Regeneration: A Lot to Learn?* Bristol: Policy Press. Available at: www.ehnheart.org/pdf/activity.pdf.

Forrest, R. and Kearns, A. (1999) *Joined-up Places? Social Cohesion and Neighbourhood Regeneration*, York: YPS for the Joseph Rowntree Foundation.

Foster, C., Hillsdon, M., Cavillo, N., Allender, S. and Cowburn, G. (2005) *Understanding Participation in Sport: A Systematic Review*, London: Sport England.

Fox, K.R. (1990) *The Physical Self-Perception Profile Manual*, Bristol: University of Bristol.

Fox, K.R. (1992) 'Physical Education and the Development of Self-Esteem in Children', in N. Armstrong (ed.) *New Directions in Physical Education*, vol. 2, *Towards a National Curriculum*, Leeds: Human Kinetics.

Fox, K.R. (1999) 'The Influence of Physical Activity on Mental Well-Being', *Public Health Nutrition* 2(3a): 411–18.

Fox, K.R. (2000) 'The Influence of Exercise on Self-Perceptions and Self-Esteem', in S.J.H. Biddle, K.R. Fox and S.H. Boutcher (eds) *Physical Activity and Psychological Well-Being*, London: Routledge, pp. 88–117.

Fox, K.R. and Corbin, C.B. (1989) 'The Physical Self Perception Profile: Development and Preliminary Validation', *Journal of Sport and Exercise Psychology* 11: 408–30.

French, S. and Disher, M. (1997) 'Atlanta and the Olympics: A One-Year Retrospective', *Journal of the American Planning Association* 63(3): 379–92.

Friedman, M.T., Andrews, D.L. and Silk, M.L. (2004) 'Sport and the Facade of Redevelopment in the Postindustrial City', *Sociology of Sport Journal* 21: 119–39.

Fukuyama, F. (2001) 'Social Capital, Civil Society and Development', *Third World Quarterly* 22(1): 7–20.

Gaskin, K. and Smith, D. (1995) *A New Civic Europe? A Study of the Extent and Role of Volunteering*, London: Volunteer Centre UK.

Giddens, A. (1998) *The Third Way*, Cambridge: Polity Press.

Giulianotti, R. (2004) 'Human Rights, Globalization and Sentimental Education: The Case of Sport', *Sport in Society* 7(3): 355–69.

Giulianotti, R. and Armstrong, G. (2004) 'Drama, Fields and Metaphors: An Introduction to Football in Africa', in G. Armstrong and R. Giulianotti (eds) *Football in Africa: Conflict Conciliation and Community*, Basingstoke: Palgrave Macmillan, pp. 1–26.

Glasner, P.E. (1977) *The Sociology of Secularisation*, London: Routledge & Kegan Paul.

Glyptis, S. (1989) *Leisure and Unemployment*, Milton Keynes: Open University Press.

Grabe, M. (1981) 'School Size and the Importance of School Activities', *Adolescence* 16(61): 21–31.

Granger, R.C. (1998) 'Establishing Causality in Evaluations of Comprehensive Community Initiatives', in K. Fulbright-Anderson, A.C. Kubisch and J.P. Connell (eds) *New Approaches to Community Initiatives*, vol. 2, *Theory, Measurement and Analysis*, Washington, DC: Aspen Institute: www.aspenroundtable.org/vol2/granger.htm.

Gratton, C. and Henry, I. (eds) (2001) *Sport in the City: The Role of Sport in Economic and Social Regeneration*, London: Routledge.

Gratton, C. and Taylor, P. (1985) *Sport and Recreation: An Economic Analysis*, London: E. & F.N. Spon.

Gratton, C. and Taylor, P. (2000) *Economics of Sport and Recreation*, London: E. & F.N. Spon.

Gratton, C., Dobson, N. and Shibli, S. (2001) 'The Role of Major Sports Events in the Economic Regeneration of Cities: Lessons from Six World or European Championships', in C. Gratton and I.P. Henry (eds) *Sport in the City: The Role of Sport in Economic and Social Regeneration*, London: Routledge, pp. 35–45.

Gratton, C., Shibli, S. and Coleman, R. (2005) 'Sport and Economic Regeneration in Cities', *Urban Studies* 42(5/6): 1–15.

Green, M. (2004) 'Changing Policy Priorities for Sport in England: The Emergence of Elite Sport Development as a Key Policy Concern', *Leisure Studies* 23(4): 365–85.

Grissom, J.B. (2005) 'Physical Fitness and Academic Achievement', *Journal of Exercise Physiologyonline* (JEPonline) 8(1) (Feb.).

Gruber, J. (1986) 'Physical Activity and Self-Esteem Development in Children: A Meta-analysis', *American Academy of Physical Education Papers* 19: 30–48.

Gunn, C. (1998) *Vacationscape*, New York: Van Nostrand-Reinhold.

Hall, P.A. (1999) 'Social Capital in Britain', *British Journal of Political Science* 29: 417–61.

Halpern, D. and Mikosz, D. (eds) (1998) 'The Third Way': summary of the NEXUS on-line discussion, 1998: www.netnexus.org.

Hammersley, M. (1995) *The Politics of Social Research*, London: Sage.

Hanson, S.L. and Kraus, R. (1998) 'Women, Sports and Science: Do Female Athletes Have an Advantage?', *Sociology of Education* 71(2): 93–110.

Hantrais, L. (1984) 'Leisure Policy in France', *Leisure Studies* 3(2): 129–46.

Hantrais, L. (1989) 'Central Government Policy in France under the Socialist Administration 1981–86', in P. Bramham, I. Henry, H. Mommas and H. van der Poel (eds) *Leisure and Urban Processes*, London: Routledge, pp. 69–89.

Harrison, B. (1973) 'State Intervention and Moral Reform in 19th Century England', in P. Hollis (ed.) *Pressure from Without in Victorian England*, London: Edward Arnold.

Harter, S. (1982) 'The Perceived Competence Scale for Children', *Child Development* 53: 87–97.

Harter, S. (1988) 'Developmental Processes in the Construction of the Self', in T.D. Yawkey and J.E. Johnson (eds) *Integrative Processes and Socialisation: Early to Middle Childhood*, Hillsdale, NJ: Erlbaum, pp. 45–78.

Harter, S. (1990) 'Self and Identity Development', in S. Feldman and G.R. Elliott (eds) *At the Threshold: The Developing Adolescent*, Cambridge, MA: Harvard University Press, pp. 352–88.

Harter, S. (1999) *The Construction of the Self: A Developmental Perspective*, New York, Guildford Press.

Hartmann, D. and Depro, B. (2006) 'Rethinking Sports-Based Community Crime Prevention: A Preliminary Analysis of the Relationship between Midnight Basketball and Urban Crime Rates', *Journal of Sport and Social Issues* 30(2): 180–96.

Harvey, D. (1989) 'Reinventing Geography: An Interview with the Editors of *New Left Review*', in D. Harvey (ed.) (2001) *Spaces of Capital: Towards a Critical Geography*, Edinburgh: Edinburgh University Press, pp. 3–26.

Hastad, D.N., Segrave, J.O., Pangrazi, R. and Petersen, G. (1984) 'Youth Sport Participation and Deviant Behavior', *Sociology of Sport Journal* 1: 366–73.

Heal, K. and Laycock, G. (1987) *Preventing Juvenile Delinquency: The Staffordshire Experience*, Crime Prevention Unit Paper, 8, London: Home Office.

Heilbrun, J. and Gray, C.M. (1993) *The Economics of Art and Culture: An American Perspective*, Cambridge: Cambridge University Press.

Hendry, L.B., Shucksmith, J., Love, J.G. and Glendinning, A. (1993) *Young People's Leisure and Lifestyles*, London: Routledge.

Henry, I.P. (2001) *The Politics of Leisure Policy*, 2nd edn, Basingstoke: Palgrave.

Hillman, C.H., Castelli, D.M. and Buck, S.M. (2005) 'Aerobic Fitness and Neurocognitive Function in Healthy Preadolescent Children', *Medicine and Science in Sport and Exercise* 37(11): 1967–74.

Hognestad, H. (2005) 'Norwegian Strategies on Culture – and Sports Development with Southern Countries', a presentation to the Sports Research Forum, Australian Sports Commission, Canberra, 13–15 April.

Hognestad, H. and Tollisen, A. (2004) 'Playing Against Deprivation: Football and Development in Nairobi, Kenya', in G. Armstrong and R. Giulianotti (eds) *Football in Africa: Conflict Conciliation and Community*, Basingstoke: Palgrave Macmillan, pp. 210–28.

Holland, A. and Andre, T. (1987) 'Participation in Extracurricular Activities in Secondary School: What is Known, What Needs to be Known?', *Review of Educational Research* 57(4): 437–66.

Holtham, G. (1998) *The Third Way: The Left's Long March*, London: Nexus Library.

Home Office (2005) *Positive Futures Impact Report: Staying in Touch*, London: Home Office.

Horch, H. (1998) 'Self-Destroying Processes of Sports Clubs in Germany', *European Journal of Sports Management* 5(1): 46–58.

Horne, J. and Manzenreiter, W. (2004) 'Accounting for Mega-events: Forecast and Actual Impacts of the 2002 Football World Cup Finals on the Host Countries Japan/Korea', *International Review for the Sociology of Sport* 39(2): 187–203.

Houlihan, B. and White, A. (2002) *The Politics of Sports Development: Development of Sport or Development through Sport?*, London: Routledge.

Humphreys, B.R. (2001) 'The Myth of Sports-Led Economic Development', *Commentary* (spring): 34–7.

Hutton, W. (1995) *The State We're In*, London: Vintage.

Ibsen, B. (1999) 'Structure and Development of Sports Organisations in Denmark', in K. Heinemann (ed.) *Sports Clubs in Various European Countries*, vol. 1, *Series Club of Cologne*, Cologne: Hofmann & Schattaur, pp. 241–68.

Jackson, N.W., Howes, F.S., Gupta, S., Doyle, J.L. and Waters, E. (2005) 'Interventions Implemented through Sporting Organisations for Increasing Participation in Sport', *Cochrane Database of Systematic Reviews*, Issue 2.

Janowitz, M. (1972) *Sociological Models and Social Policy*, Morristown, NJ: General Learning Systems.

Jarvie, G. (2003) 'Communitarianism, Sport and Social Capital', *International Review for the Sociology of Sport* 38(2): 139–53.

Jesson, D. and Crossley, D. (2005) *Educational Outcomes and Value Added by Specialist Schools*, London: Specialist Schools and Academies Trust.

Johnson, A.T. and Sack, A. (1996) 'Assessing the Value of Sports Facilities: The Importance of Noneconomic Factors', *Economic Development Quarterly* 10(4): 369–81.

Johnson, B.K., Groothuis, P.A. and Whitehead, J.C. (2001) 'The Value of Public Goods Generated by a Major League Sports Team: The CVM Approach', *Journal of Sports Economics* 2(1): 6–21.

Johnston, G. and Percy-Smith, J. (2003) 'In Search of Social Capital', *Policy and Politics* 31(3): 321–34.

Jones, C. (2001) 'Mega-events and Host-Region Impacts: Determining the True Worth of the 1999 Rugby World Cup', *International Journal of Tourism Research* 3(3): 241–51.

Jones, C. (2002a) 'Public Cost for Private Gain? Recent and Proposed "National" Stadium Developments in the UK, and Commonalities with North America', *Area* 34(2): 160–70.

Jones, C. (2002b) 'The Stadium and Economic Development: Cardiff and the Millennium Stadium', *European Planning Studies* 10(7): 819–29.

Judkins, M. and Rudd, P. (2005) 'Evaluation of High-Performing Specialist Schools', paper presented at the British Educational Research Association Annual Conference, University of Glamorgan, Pontypridd, 15–17 September.

Kahn, E.B., Ramsey, L.T., Brownson, R.C., Heath, G.W., Howze, E.H., Powell, K.E., Stone, E.J., Rajab, M.W., Corso, P. and the Task Force on Community Preventive Services (2002) 'The Effectiveness of Interventions to Increase Physical Activity: A Systematic Review', *American Journal of Preventive Medicine*, 22(4S): 73–107.

Kasimati, E. (2003) 'Economic Aspects and the Summer Olympics: A Review of Related Research', *International Journal of Tourism Research* 5(6): 433–44.

Keaney, E. and Gavelin, K. (n.d.) *Sport, Physical Activity and Civil Renewal: Literature Review*, London: Institute of Public Policy Research.

Kearns, A. (2004) *Social Capital, Regeneration and Urban Policy*, CRN Paper, 15, ESRC Centre for Neighbourhood Research: http://www.bristol.ac.uk/sps/cnrpaperspdf/cnr15pap.pdf.

Keays, J.J. and Allison, K.R. (1995) 'The Effects of Regular Moderate to Vigorous Physical Activity on Student Outcomes: A Review', *Canadian Journal of Public Health* 86(1): 62–5.

Keck, M. and Sikkick, K. (1998) *Activists Beyond Borders*, Ithaca, NY: Cornell University Press.

Keller, H., Lamprocht, M. and Stamm, H. (1998) *Social Cohesion through Sport*, Strasbourg: Committee for the Development of Sport, Council of Europe.

Kemper, H.C.G., Twisk, J.W.R., Van Mechelen, W., Post, G.B., Ross, J.C. and Lips, P. (2000) 'A Fifteen-Year Longitudinal Study in Young Adults on the Relation of Physical Activity and Fitness with the Development of the Bone Mass: The Amsterdam Growth and Health Longitudinal Study', *Bone* 27(6): 847–953.

Kerrigan, D. (1999) *Peer Education and HIV/AIDS: Concepts, Uses and Challenges*, Washington, DC: Horizons/Population Council.

Kidd, B. (1995) 'Toronto's Skydome: The World's Greatest Entertainment Centre', in J. Bale and O. Moen (eds) *The Stadium and the City*, Keele: Keele University Press, pp. 175–96.

Kloosterman, R.C. and Elfring, T. (1991) *Werken in Nederland*, Schoonhoven: Academic Service.

Kotze, J.C. (1993) *In their Shoes*, Kenwyn, Johannesburg: Juta & Co.

Kraut, A., Melamed, S., Gofer, D. and Froom, P. (2003) 'Effect of School Age Sports on Leisure Time Physical Activity in Adults: The CORDIS Study', *Medicine and Science in Sport Exercise* 35(12): 2038–42.

Krisha, A. (1997) 'Physical Activity and the Prevention of Type II (Non-Insulin Dependent) Diabetes', *President's Council on Physical Fitness and Sports: Research Digest* (June) 2(10). Available at: fitness.gov/diabetes.pdf.

Kruse, S.-E. (2006) 'Review of Kicking AIDS Out: Is Sport an Effective Tool in the Fight Against HIV/AIDS?', draft report to NORAD, unpublished.

Langbein, L. and Bess, R. (2002) 'Sports in School: Source of Amity or Antipathy?', *Social Science Quarterly* 83(2): 436–54.

Leisure Futures (2002) *Positive Futures: A Review of Impact and Good Practice*, London: Sport England: www.sportengland.org.

Leisure Industries Research Centre (1997) *A Review of the Economic Impact of Sport: A Report to the Sports Council*, London: Sports Council.

Leisure Industries Research Centre (2003) *Sports Volunteering in England in 2002*, London: Sport England.

Leith, L.M. (1994) *Foundations of Exercise and Mental Health*, Morganstown, WV: Fitness Information Technology.

Lengkeek, J. (1993) 'Collective and Private Interest in Recreation and Tourism: The Dutch Case. Concerning Consequences of a Shift from Citizen Role to Consumer Role', *Leisure Studies* 12(1): 7–33.

Lenskji, H.J. (2002) *The Best Olympics Ever? Social Impacts of Sydney 2000*, Albany, NY: State University of New York Press.

Leonard, M. (2004) 'Bonding and Bridging Social Capital: Reflections from Belfast', *Sociology* 38(5): 927–44.

Le Roux, N., Camy, J., Chantelat, P., Froberg, K. and Madella, A. (2000) *Sports Employment in Europe*, Lyon: European Observatoire of Sports Employment.

Levacic, R. and Jenkins, A. (2004) *Evaluating the Effectiveness of Specialist Schools*, London: Centre for the Economics of Education, London School of Economics.

Levitas, R. (1996) 'The Concept of Social Exclusion and the New Durkheimian Hegemony', *Critical Social Policy* 16(1): 5–20.

Lillbacka, R. (2006) 'Measuring Social Capital', *Acta Sociologica* 49(2): 201–20.

Lindner, K.J. (1999) 'Sport Participation and Perceived Academic Performance of School Children and Youth', *Pediatric Exercise Science* 11: 129–43.

Lipsky, R. (1981) *How we Play the Game*, Boston, MA: Beacon.

Long, J. and Sanderson, I. (2001) 'The Social Benefits of Sport: Where's the Proof?', in C. Gratton and I. Henry (eds) *Sport in the City*, London: Routledge, pp. 187–203.

Long, J., Welch, M., Bramham, P., Butterfield, J., Hylton, K., and Lloyd, E. (2002) *Count me in: The Dimensions of Social Inclusion through Culture and Sport*, Leeds: Centre for Leisure and Sport Research.

Loughlan, C. and Mutrie, N. (1997) 'An Evaluation of the Effectiveness of Three Interventions in Promoting Physical Activity in a Sedentary Population', *Health Education Journal* 56: 154–65.

Lowndes, V. (2000) 'Notes and Comments, Women and Social Capital: A Comment on Hall's Social Capital in Britain', *British Journal of Political Science* 30(3): 533–7.

Loxley, C., Curtin, L. and Brown, R. (2002) *Summer Splash Schemes 2000: Findings from Six Case Studies*, Crime Reduction Research Series Paper, 12, London: Home Office. Available at: http://www.homeoffice.gov.uk/rds/pdfs2/crrs12.pdf.

Lynch, K. (1960) *Image of the City*, Cambridge, MA: MIT Press.

McDermott, L. (2000) 'A Qualitative Assessment of Significance of Body Perception to Women's Physical Activity Experiences: Revisiting Discussions of Physicalities', *Sociology of Sport Journal* 17: 331–63.

McDonald, D. and Tungatt, M. (1992) *Community Development and Sport*, London: Sports Council.

McGiboney, G.W. and Carter, C. (1988) 'Boredom Proneness and Adolescents' Personalities', *Psychological Reports* 63: 741–2.

McIntosh, P. and Charlton, V. (1985) *The Impact of Sport for All Policy, 1966–1984 and a Way Forward*, London: Sports Council.

McKenzie, D.L. (1997) 'Criminal Justice and Crime Prevention', in L.W. Sherman, D. Gottfredson, D. MacKenzie, J. Eck, P. Reuter and S. Bushway (eds) *Preventing Crime: What Works, What Doesn't, What's Promising?* Office of Justice Program Research Report, Baltimore, MD: Department of Criminology and Criminal Justice, University of Maryland, ch. 9.

MacMahon, J.R. (1990) 'The Psychological Benefits of Exercise and the Treatment of Delinquent Adolescents', *Sports Medicine* 9(6): 344–51.

MacMahon, J.R. and Gross, R.T. (1988) 'Physical and Psychological Effects of Aerobic Exercise in Delinquent Adolescent Males', *American Journal of Diseases of Children* 142(12): 1361–6.

McNeal, R.B. (1999) 'Participation in High School Extracurricular Activities: Investigating School Effects', *Social Science Quarterly* 80: 291–309.

Madden, J.R. and Crowe, M. (1998) 'Estimating the Economic Impact of the Sydney Olympic Games', paper presented to 38th European Regional Science Association Congress, Vienna, 28 August–1 September.

Malina, R.M. (1996) 'Tracking of Physical Activity and Physical Fitness across the Lifespan', *Research Quarterly for Exercise and Sport* 67, suppl. 3: 48–57.

Marcus, B.H. and Simkin, L.R. (1994) 'The Transtheoretical Model: Applications to Exercise Behaviour', *Medicine and Science in Sports and Exercise* 26: 1400–4.

Marsh, H.W. (1993) 'The Effects of Participation in Sport during the Last Two Years of High School', *Sociology of Sport Journal* 10: 18–43.

Marsh, H.W. and Kleitman, S. (2003) 'School Athletic Participation: Mostly Gain with Little Pain', *Journal of Sport and Exercise Psychology* 25: 205–28.

Martin, B.W., Beeler, I., Szucs, T., Smala, A.M., Brugger, O., Casparis, C., Allenbach, R., Raeber, P.-A. and Marti, B. (2001) 'Economic Benefits of Health-Enhancing Effects of Physical Activity: First Estimates for Switzerland', *Sportmedizin und Sporttraumatologie* 49(3): 131–3.

Mason, V. (1995) *Young People and Sport in England, 1994: A National Survey*, London: Sports Council.

Matarasso, F. (1998) *Beyond Book Issues: The Social Potential of Library Projects*, Stroud: Comedia.

Matheson, V.A. (2002) 'Upon Further Review: An Examination of Sporting Event Economic Impacts Analysis', *Sports Journal* 15(1): 2.

Matheson, V.A. (2006) 'Is Smaller Better? A Comment on "Comparative Economic Analyses" by Michael Mondello and Patrick Rishe', *Economic Development Quarterly* 20(2): 192–5.

Maugham, M. and Ellis, G.D. (1991) 'Effect of Efficacy Information During Recreation Participation on Efficacy Judgements of Depressed Adolescents', *Therapeutic Recreation Journal* 25(1): 50–9.

Maule, C.O., Moyer, C.A. and Lovato, C.Y. (2003) 'Application of a Better Practices Framework to Review Youth Tobacco Use Cessation', *American Journal of Health Behavior*, 27: S132–S143.

Mennell, S. (1979) 'Theoretical Considerations on Cultural Needs', *Sociology* 13(2): 235–57.

Merton, R.K. (1968) *Social Theory and Social Structure*, 3rd edn, New York: Free Press.

Miller, K.E., Melnick, M.J., Barnes, G.M., Farrell, M.P. and Saho, D. (2005) 'Untangling the Links among Athletic Involvement, Gender, Race and Adolescent Academic Outcomes', *Sociology of Sport Journal* 22: 178–93.

Miracle, A.W. and Rees, C.R. (1994) *Lessons of the Locker Room: The Myth of School Sports*, Amherst, NY: Prometheus Books.

Mondello, M.J. and Rishe, P. (2004) 'Comparative Economic Impact Analyses: Differences across Cities, Events and Demographics', *Economic Development Quarterly* 18(4): 331–42.

Morgan, D. (1998) 'Sport off the Streets: A Preliminary Analysis of the Need for "Reczones" in the 3Ds Area of Bolton', paper presented at Sport v Youth Crime Conference, Reebok Stadium, Bolton.

Morris, L., Sallybanks, J., Willis, K. and Makkai, T. (2003) *Sport, Physical Activity and Anti-Social Behaviour*, Research and Public Policy Series, 49, Canberra: Australian Institute of Criminology.

Mukoma, M. and Flisher, A. (2004) 'Evaluations of Health Promoting Schools: A Review of Nine Studies', *Health Promotion International* 19(3): 357–68.

Munro, B. (2005) 'Role Models: Is Anything More Important for Future Development?', Role Models Retreat, Laureus Sport for Good Foundation, 23–24 November, Pretoria, South Africa.

Munro, B. (2006) 'Greed vs Good Governance: The Fight for Corruption-Free Football in Kenya', a paper presented at Play the Game 2005 – Governance in Sport: The Good, The Bad and The Ugly, Copenhagen: http://www.playthegame.org.

Murphy, N.M. and Bauman, A. (2007) 'Mass Sporting and Physical Activity Events: Are they "Bread and Circuses" or Public Health Interventions to Increase Population Levels of Physical Activity?', *Journal of Physical Activity and Health* 4(2): 193–202.

Mwaanga, O. (2003) 'HIV/AIDS At-Risk Adolescent Girls' Empowerment through Participation in Top Level Football and Edusport in Zambia', MSc thesis submitted to the Institute of Social Science at the Norwegian University of Sport and PE, Oslo.

Mwaanga, O. (n.d.) *Kicking Aids out through Movement Games and Sports Activities*, Norwegian Agency for Development Cooperation, www.kickingaidsout.net/0/OscarMwangaManual.pdf.

Myerscough, J. (1988) *Economic Importance of the Arts in Britain*, London: Policy Studies Institute.

Nahrstedt, W. (1993) 'Leisure Policy in Germany', in P. Bramham, I. Henry, H. Mommas and H. van der Poel (eds) *Leisure Policies in Europe*, Wallingford: CAB International, pp. 129–48.

Najam, A. (1999) 'Citizen Organisations as Policy Entrepreneurs', in D. Lewis (ed.) *International Perspectives in Voluntary Action: Reshaping the Third Sector*, London: Earthscan.

Newman, P. and Tual, M. (2002) 'The Stade de France: The Last Expression of French Centralism?', *European Planning Studies* 10(7): 831–43.

Nicholl, J.P., Coleman, P. and Williams, B.T. (1991) 'Injuries in Sport and Exercise: Main Report. A National Study of the Epidemiology of Exercise-related Injury and Illness', Medical Care Research Unit, Department of Public Health Medicine, Sheffield University Medical School: A report to the Sports Council.

Nicholls, S. (2007) 'On the Backs of Peer Educators', a paper presented to the International Studies Association Congress, Chicago, IL, February.

Nichols, G. (2003) *Citizenship in Action: Voluntary Sector Sport and Recreation*, London: CCPR.

Nichols, G. and Crow, I. (2004) 'Measuring the Impact of Crime Reduction Interventions Involving Sports Activities for Young People', *Howard Journal of Criminal Justice* 43(3): 267–83.

Nichols, G. and Taylor, P. (1996) *West Yorkshire Sports Counselling: Final Evaluation Report*, Sheffield: University of Sheffield, Management Unit.

Noll, R.G. and Zimbalist, A. (1997) 'Sports, Jobs, and Taxes: Are New Stadiums Worth the Cost?', *Brookings Review* 15(3): 35–9.

NORAD (2002) *Study of Future Norwegian Support to Civil Society in Mozambique*, Oslo: NORAD: http://www.norad.no/default.asp?V_ITEM_ID=1137.

Norwegian Government (2003) 'Action Plan for the Eradication of Poverty in the South 2015', *Stortingsmelding* 35 (2003–4, Oslo).

Oakley, A., Gough, D., Oliver, S. and Thoms, J. (2005) 'The Politics of Evidence and Methodology: Lessons from the EPPI-Centre', *Evidence and Policy* 1(1): 5–31.

Office of National Statistics (2001) *Social Capital: A Review of Literature*, London: Social Analysis and Reporting Division.

Office of the Deputy Prime Minister (2004) *Research Report 9: Joint Working in Sport and Neighbourhood Renewal*, London: Neighbourhood Renewal Unit.

Orcutt, J.D. (1984) 'Contrasting Effects of Two Kinds of Boredom on Alcohol Use', *Journal of Drug Issues* 161–73.

Papacharisis, V., Goudas, M., Danish, S.J. and Theodorakis, Y. (2005) 'The Effectiveness of Teaching a Life Skills Program in a Sport Context', *Journal of Applied Sports Psychology* 17: 247–54.

Patriksson, M. (1995) 'Scientific Review Part 2', in *The Significance of Sport for Society – Health, Socialisation, Economy: A Scientific Review*, prepared for the 8th Conference of European Ministers responsible for Sport, Lisbon, 17–18 May 1995, Strasbourg: Council of Europe Press.

Pawson, R. (2001a) *Evidence Based Policy*, vol. 1, *In Search of a Method*, ESRC UK Centre for Evidence Based Policy and Practice, Working Paper, 3, London: Queen Mary University of London.

Pawson, R. (2001b) *Evidence Based Policy*, vol. 2, *The Promise of 'Realist Synthesis'*, ESRC UK Centre for Evidence Based Policy and Practice, Working Paper, 4, London: Queen Mary University of London.

Pawson, R. (2004) 'Evaluating Ill-Defined Interventions with Hard-to-Follow Outcomes', paper presented to ESRC seminar Understanding and evaluating the impact of sport and culture on society, Leeds Metropolitan University, Jan.

Pawson, R. (2006) *Evidence-Based Policy: A Realist Perspective*, London: Sage.

Pawson, R. and Tilley, N. (2000) *Realistic Evaluation*, London, Sage.

Payne, W., Reynolds, M., Brown, S. and Fleming, A. (2003) *Sports Role Models and their Impact on Participation in Physical Activity: A Literature Review*, Victoria: VicHealth.

Pelak, C.F. (2006) 'Local–Global Processes: Linking Globalisation, Democratisation and the Development of Women's Football in South Africa', *Afrika Spectrum* 41(3): 371–92.

Performance and Innovation Unit (2002) *Social Capital: A Discussion Paper*, London: Cabinet Office, Performance and Innovation Unit.

Perkins, D., Jacobs, J.E., Barber, B.L. and Eccles, J.S. (2004) 'Child and Adolescent Sports Participation as Predictors of Participation in Sports and Physical Fitness Activities During Young Adulthood', *Youth and Society* 35(4): 495–520.

Petitpas, A.J., Van Raalte, J.L., Cornelius, A.E. and Presbrey, J. (2004) 'A Life Skills Development Program for High School Student-Athletes', *Journal of Primary Prevention* 24(3): 325–34.

Pollard, A. and Court, J. (2005) *How Civil Society Organisations Use Evidence to Influence Policy Processes: A Literature Review*, Working Paper, 249, London: Overseas Development Institute.

Portes, A. (1998) 'Social Capital: Its Origins and Applications in Modern Sociology', *Annual Review of Sociology* 24: 1–24.

Portes, A. and Landolt, P. (2000) 'Social Capital: Promise and Pitfalls of its Role in Development', *Journal of Latin American Studies* 32: 529–47.

Poujol, G. (1993) 'Leisure Politics and Policies in France', in P. Bramham, I. Henry, H. Mommas and H. van der Poel (eds) *Leisure Policies in Europe*, Wallingford: CAB International, pp. 13–40.

Pratt, M., Macera, C.A. and Wang, G. (2000) 'Higher Direct Medical Costs Associated with Physical Inactivity', *Physician and Sportsmedicine* 28(10): 63–70.

President's Council on Physical Fitness and Sports (2006) *Sports and Character Development* Research Digest Series, 7/1, Washington, DC: President's Council on Physical Fitness and Sports.

Preuss, H. (2004a) 'Being a Good Host', *Sports Management* 18(3): 31–5.

Preuss, H. (2004b) *The Economics of Staging an Olympics: A Comparison of the Games 1972–2008*, Cheltenham: Edward Elgar.

Preuss, H. (2005) 'The Economic Impact of Visitors at Major Multi-Sport Events', *European Sport Management Quarterly* 5(3): 281–301.

Puntila, E., Kroger, H., Lakka, T., Honkanen, R. and Tuppurainen, M. (1997) 'Physical Activity in Adolescence and Bone Density in Peri- and Postmenopausal Women: A Population-Based Study', *Bone* 21(4): 363–7.

Purdy, D.A. and Richards, S.F. (1983) 'Sport and Juvenile Delinquency: An Examination and Assessment of Four Major Theories', *Journal of Sport Behaviour* 6(4): 179–93.

Putnam, R. (1993) 'The Prosperous Community: Social Capital and Public Life', *American Prospect* 13: 35–42.

Putnam, R. (2000) *Bowling Alone: The Collapse and Revival of the American Community*, New York: Simon & Schuster.

Pyo, S., Cook, R. and Howell, R. (1988) 'Summer Olympic Tourist Market: Learning from the Past', *Tourism Management* 9(2): 137–44.

Raglin, J.S. (1990) 'Exercise and Mental Health: Beneficial and Detrimental Effects', *Sports Medicine* 9(6): 323–9.

Rapoport, R. and Rapoport, R.N. (1975) *Leisure and the Family Life-Cycle*, London: Routledge.

Ravenscroft, N. (1993) 'Public Sector Provision and the Good Citizen', *Leisure Studies* 12(1): 33–44.

Ravenscroft, N. and Tolley, J. (1993) 'Ideological Dominance in Recreation Provision: The Response of Local Authorities in Britain to CCT', paper presented at the 3rd International Conference of the Leisure Studies Association, Leisure in Different Worlds, Loughborough University, July.

Reid, I., Tremblay, M., Pelletier, R. and MacKay, S. (1994) *Canadian Youth: Does Activity Reduce Risk?*: www.lin.ca/resource/html/documant.htm.

Rigg, M. (1986) *Action Sport: Community Sports Leadership in the Inner Cities*, London: Sports Council.

Rijpma, S. and Meiburg, H. (1989) 'Sports Policy Initiatives in Rotterdam: Targeting Disadvantaged Groups', in P. Bramham, I. Henry, H. Mommas and H. van der Poel (eds) *Leisure and Urban Processes: Critical Studies of Leisure Policy in Western European Cities*, London: Routledge, pp. 141–55.

Ritchie, B. and Hall, C.M. (2000) 'Mega Events and Human Rights', unpublished paper, University of Canberra and University of Otago.

Ritchie, J.R.B. and Smith, B.H. (1991) 'The Impact of Mega-Event on Host Region Awareness: A Longitudinal Study', *Journal of Travel Research* (Summer): 3–9.

Roberts, K. and Brodie, D.A. (1992) *Inner-City Sport: Who Plays, and What are the Benefits?* Culembourg: Giordano Bruno.

Robins, D. (1990) *Sport as Prevention: The Role of Sport in Crime Prevention Programmes Aimed at Young People*, University of Oxford, Centre for Criminological Research, occasional paper, 12, Oxford: CCR.

Roche, M. (1992) *Rethinking Citizenship: Welfare, Ideology and Change in Modern Society*, Cambridge: Polity Press.

Roche, M. (1994) 'Mega-Events & Urban Policy', *Annals of Tourism Research* 21: 1–19.

Roche, M. (2000) *Mega-Events and Modernity: Olympics and Expos in the Growth of Global Culture*, London: Routledge.

Rodriguez, C.J., Sacco, R.L., Sciacca, R.R., Boden-Albala, B., Homma, S. and Di Tullio, M.R. (2002) 'Physical Activity Attenuates the Effect of Increased Left Ventricular Mass on the Risk of Ischemic Stroke: The Northern Manhattan Stroke Study', *Journal of the American College of Cardiology* 39(9): 1482–8.

Room, G. (1995) *Beyond the Threshold: The Measurement and Analysis of Social Exclusion*, Bristol: Policy Press.

Rosentraub, M.S. (1997) 'Sports Facilities and the Use of Urban Space: Indianapolis's Quest to Underscore its Centrality', in R.G. Noll and A. Zimbalist (eds) *Sports, Jobs and Taxes: The Economic Impact of Sports Teams and Stadiums*, Washington, DC: The Brookings Institute, pp. 178–207.

Rosentraub, M.S., Swindell, D., Przybylski, M. and Mullins, D.R. (1994) 'Sport and Downtown Development Strategy: If you Build it, Will Jobs Come?', *Journal of Urban Affairs* 16(3): 221–39.

Rossi, P.H., Lipsey, M.W. and Freeman, H.E. (2004) *Evaluation: A Systematic Approach*, 7th edn, Thousand Oaks, CA: Sage.

Roth, A.D. and Parry, G. (1997) 'The Implications of Psychotherapy Research for Clinical Practice and Service Development: Lessons and Limitations', *Journal of Mental Health* 6: 367–80.

Rudd, P., Aiston, S., Davies, D., Rickinson, M. and Dartnall, L. (2002) *High Performing Specialist Schools: What Makes the Difference?*, Slough: National Foundation for Educational Research.

Rutter, M. and Giller, H. (1983) *Juvenile Delinquency: Trends and Perspectives*, London: Penguin.

Saavedra, M. (2005) *Women, Sport and Development*, Sport and Development International Platform: http://www.sportanddev.org/data/document/document/148.pdf.

Saavedra, M. (2007) *Some Dilemmas and Opportunities in Gender, Sport and Development*, Chicago, IL: International Studies Association.

Sabo, D., Menick, M.J. and Vanfossen, B.E. (1993) 'High School Athletic Participation and Postsecondary Educational and Occupational Mobility: A Focus on Race and Gender', *Sociology of Sport Journal* 10: 44–56.

Sack, A.L. and Johnson, A.T. (1996) 'Politics, Economic Development and the Volvo International Tennis Tournament', *Journal of Sports Management* 10(1): 1–14.

Sallis, J., McKenzie, T., Kolody, B., Lewis, B., Marshall, S. and Rosengard, P. (1999) 'Effects of Health-Related Physical Education on Academic Achievement: Project SPARK', *Research Quarterly for Exercise and Sport* 70(2): 127–34.

Sallis, J.F., Prochaska, J.J. and Taylor, W.C. (2000) 'A Review of Correlates of Physical Activity of Children and Adolescents', *Medical Science of Sports and Exercise* 32(5): 963–75.

Sandford, R.A., Armour, K.M. and Warmington, P.C. (2006) 'Re-engaging Disaffected Youth through Physical Activity Programmes', *British Educational Research Journal* 32(2): 251–71.

Santo, C. (2005) 'The Economic Impact of Sports Stadiums: Recasting the Analysis in Context', *Journal of Urban Affairs* 27(2): 177–91.

Schafer, W. (1969) 'Some Social Sources and Consequences of Inter-Scholastic Athletics: The Case of Participation and Delinquency', *International Review of Sport Sociology* 4: 63–81.

Scheff, T.J., Retzinger, S.M. and Ryan, M.T. (1989) 'Crime, Violence and Self-Esteem: Review and Proposals', in A.M. Mecca, N.J. Smelser and J. Vasconcellos (eds) *The Social Importance of Self Esteem*, Berkeley, CA: University of California Press.

Schimmel, K. (2001) 'Sport Matters: Urban Regime Theory and Urban Regeneration in the Late Capitalist Era', in C. Gratton and I. Henry (eds) *Sport in the City*, London: Routledge.

Scottish Executive Health Department (2002) *Let's Make Scotland More Active*, Edinburgh: Stationery Office Bookshop.

Scottish Office (1999) *Social Inclusion: Opening the Door to a Better Scotland*, Edinburgh: Scottish Office: www.scotland.gov.uk/library/documents-w7/sima-00.htm.

Scraton, S. (1989) 'Boys Muscle in Where Angels Fear to Tread: The Relationship between Physical Education and Young Women's Subcultures', in F. Coalter (ed.) *Freedom and Constraint: The Paradoxes of Leisure*, London: A Comedia book published by Routledge, pp. 149–74.

Scriven, M. (1994) 'The Fine Line between Evaluation and Explanation', *Evaluation Practice* 15: 75–7.

Searle, G. (2002) 'Uncertain Legacy: Sydney's Olympic Stadiums', *European Planning Studies* 10(7): 845–60.

Segrave, J. and Hastad, D.N. (1984) 'Interscholastic Athletic Participation and Delinquency Behaviour: An Empirical Assessment of Relevant Variables', *Sociology of Sport Journal* 1: 117–37.

Seippel, O. (2006) 'Sport and Social Capital', *Acta Sociologica* 49(2): 169–83.

Serok, S. (1975) 'Difference in Game Preference between Delinquent and Non-Delinquent Children', unpublished doctoral dissertation, Case Western Reserve University.

Shadish, W.R., Cook, T. and Leviton, L. (1991) *Foundations of Program Evaluation*, Beverly Hills, CA: Sage.

Shah, M.K., Kambou, S., Goparaju, L., Adams, M.K. and Matarazzo, J.M. (eds) (2004) *Participatory Monitoring and Evaluation of Community- and Faith-Based Programs: A Step-by-Step Guide for People Who Want to Make HIV and AIDS Services and Activities More Effective in their Community*, Core Initiative.

Sharp, C., Blackmore, J., Kendall, L., Greene, K., Keys, W., Macauley, A., Schagen, I. and Yeshanew, T. (2003) *Playing for Success: An Evaluation of the Fourth Year*, Research Report, 402, Slough: National Foundation for Educational Research.

Sharp, C., Mawson, C., Pocklington, K., Kendal, L. and Morrison, J. (1999) *Playing for Success National Evaluation (Final Draft)*, Slough: National Foundation for Educational Research.

Shaw, J.M. and Snow, C. (1995) 'Osteoporosis and Physical Activity', *President's Council on Physical Fitness and Sports: Research Digest* (Sept.) 2(3): http://www.fitness.gov/osteoporosis.pdf.

Shephard, R.J. (1997) 'Curricular Physical Activity and Academic Performance', *Pediatric Exercise Science* 9: 113–26.

Shephard, R.J. and Trudeau, F. (2005) 'Lessons Learned from the Trois-Rivieres Physical Education Study: A Retrospective', *Pediatric Exercise Science* 17: 112–23.

Shergold, M. and Grant, J. (2006) *Evolution of the R&D Strategy of the Department of Health*: RAND.

Shibli, S. and Gratton, C. (2001) 'The Economic Impact of Two Major Sporting Events in Two of the UK's "National Cities of Sport"', in C. Gratton and I. Henry (eds) *Sport in the City: The Role of Sport in Economic and Social Regeneration*, London: Routledge, pp. 78–89.

Shields, D.L.L. and Bredemeier, B.J.L. (1995) *Character Development and Physical Activity*, Champaign, IL: Human Kinetics.

Sibley, B.A. and Etnier, J.L. (2003) 'The Relationship between Physical Activity and Cognition in Children: A Meta-analysis', *Pediatric Exercise Science* 15: 243–56.

Siegfried, J.J. and Peterson, T. (2000) 'Who is Sitting in the Stands? The Income Levels of Sports Fans', in W.S. Kern (ed.) *The Economics of Sports*, Kalamazoo, MI: Upjohn Institute, pp. 51–73.

Siegfried, J. and Zimbalist, A. (2000) 'The Economics of Sports Facilities and their Communities', *Journal of Economic Perspectives* 14(3): 95–114.

Sillitoe, K.K. (1969) *Planning Leisure*, London: HMSO.

Simmonds, B. (1994) *Developing Partnerships in Sport and Leisure: A Practical Guide*, Harlow: Longman.

Skidmore, P., Bound, K. and Lownsborough, H. (2006) *Community Participation: Who Benefits?* York: Joseph Rowntree Foundation.

Smith, A. (2001) 'Sporting a New Image? Sport-Based Regeneration Strategies as a Means of Enhancing the Image of the City Tourist Destination', in C. Gratton and I.P. Henry (eds) *Sport in the City: The Role of Sport in Economic and Social Regeneration*, London: Routledge.

Smith, A. and Waddington, I. (2004) 'Using "Sport in the Community Schemes" to Tackle Crime and Drug Use Among Young People: Some Policy Issues and Problems', *European Physical Education Review*, 10(3): 279–98.

Smith, H. (2005) 'Greek Smokers to Pay for Olympics', *Guardian* (30 March).

Snyder, E.E. and Spreitzer, E. (1990) 'High School Athletic Participation as Related to College Attendance among Black, Hispanic and White Males: A Research Note', *Youth and Society* 21(3): 390–8.

Social Exclusion Unit (1998) *Bringing Britain Together*, London: Cabinet Office.

Social Exclusion Unit (2000) *National Strategy for Neighbourhood Renewal: A Framework for Consultation*, London: Cabinet Office.

Solesbury, W. (2001) *Evidence Based Policy: Whence it Came and Where it's Going*, ESRC UK Centre for Evidence Based Policy and Practice, Working Paper, 1, London: University of London.

Sonstroem, R.J. (1984) 'Exercise and Self-Esteem', *Exercise and Sports Sciences Reviews* 12: 123–55.

Sonstroem, R.J. and Morgan W.P. (1989) 'Exercise and Self-Esteem: Rationale and Model', *Medicine and Science in Sport and Exercise* 21(3): 329–37.

Spady, W. (1970) 'Lament for the Letterman: Effects of Peer Status and Extracurricular Activities on Goals and Achievement', *American Journal of Sociology* (Jan.): 680–702.

Spence, J.C., McGannon, K.R. and Poon, P. (2005) 'The Effect of Exercise on Global Self-Esteem: A Quantitative Review', *Journal of Sport and Exercise Psychology* 27(3): 311–34.

Sport and Recreation Victoria (1994) *Competitive Tendering Leisure Services: A Guide for Local Government*, Melbourne: Sport and Recreation Victoria.

Sport Coaches' Outreach (2005) 'Partnership in Practice: Assessing our Capacity to Deliver Sustainable Sport and Development', unpublished workshop report.

Sport England (1999) *Active Communities and Bringing Communities together through Sport and Culture*, London: Sport England.

Sport England (2001) *Sport Action Zones: Report on the Establishment of the First 12 Zones*, London: Sport England.

Sport England (2003) *Sports Volunteers in England in 2002*, London: Sport England.

Sport England (2004) *The Framework for Sport in England*, London: Sport England.

Sport England (2005) *Participation in Sport in England: 2002*, London: Sport England.

Sport England and the Local Government Association (1999) *Best Value through Sport: The Value of Sport to Local Authorities*, London: Sport England.

Sport England (2007) *The Active People Survey*, London: Sport England: http://www.sportengland.org/index/get_resources/research/active_people.htm.

Sports Council (1982) *Sports Council Annual Report 1981/82*, London: Sports Council.

Sports Council (1990) *Managing Sport and Recreation under CCT: The Future Client-Side Role. Factfile 1 Recreation Management*, London: Sports Council.

Sports Council Research Unit NW (1990) *Scunthorpe Ethnic Minorities Recreation Project: Phase One Monitoring Report*, Manchester: Sports Council, North West Region.

Sports Industry Research Centre (2007) *Economic Importance of Sport: England 2003*, London: Sport England.

Steptoe, A. (1992) 'Physical Activity and Well-Being', in N.G. Norgan (ed.) *Physical Activity and Health*, Cambridge: Cambridge University Press, pp. 207–29.

Stolle, D. (1998) 'Bowling Together, Bowling Alone: The Development of Generalized Trust in Voluntary Associations', *Political Psychology* 19(3): 497–525.

Sugden, J. and Yiannakis, A. (1982) 'Sport and Juvenile Delinquency: A Theoretical Base', *Journal of Sport and Social Issues* 6(1): 22–30.

Svoboda, B. (1994) *Sport and Physical Activity as a Socialisation Environment, Scientific Review Part 1*, Strasbourg: Council of Europe, Committee for the Development of Sport (CDDS).

Swiss Agency for Development and Cooperation (2005) *Sport for Development and Peace*, Berne: Swiss Agency for Development and Cooperation.

Szreter, S. (1998) *A New Political Economy for New Labour: The Importance of Social Capital*, Policy Paper, 15, Sheffield: Political Economy Research Centre.

Szymanski, S. (2002) 'The Ecomomic Impact of Large-Scale Sports Events', unpublished paper, London, Tanaka Business School, Imperial College.

Tacon, R. (2005) *Football and Social Inclusion: Evaluating Social Policy*, Research Paper, 5, London: Football Governance Research Centre, Birkbeck College.

Tacon, R. (2007) 'Football and Social Inclusion: Evaluating Social Policy', *Managing Leisure: An International Journal* 12(1): 1–23.

Tammelin, T., Nayha, S., Hills, A.P. and Jarvelin, M. (2003) 'Adolescent Participation in Sports and Adult Physical Activity', *American Journal of Preventive Medicine* 24(1): 22–8.

Taras, H. (2005) 'Physical Activity and Student Performance at School', *Journal of School Health* 75(6): 214–18.

Taylor, P. (1999) 'External Benefits of Leisure: Measurement and Policy Implications', presentation to Tolern Seminar DCMS, London.

Taylor, P., Crow, I., Irvine, D. and Nichols, G. (1999) *Demanding Physical Activity Programmes for Young Offenders under Probation Supervision*, London: Home Office.

Taylor, W.C., Blair, S.N., Cummings, S.S., Chuan Wun, C. and Malina, R.M. (1999) 'Childhood and Adolescent Physical Activity Patterns and Adult Physical Activity', *Medicine and Science in Sports and Exercise* 31(1): 118–23.

Thomas, D.N. (1995) *Community Development at Work: A Case of Obscurity in Accomplishment*, London: CDF Publications.

Thornley, A. (2002) 'Urban Regeneration and Sports Stadia', *European Planning Studies* 10(7): 813–18.

Thornton, A. and Lee, P. (2000) 'Publication Bias in Meta-analysis: Its Causes and Consequences', *Journal of Clinical Epidemiology* 53: 207–16.

Thune, I. and Furberg, A.S. (2001) 'Physical Activity and Cancer Risks: Dose-Response and Cancer, All Sites and Site-Specific', *Medicine and Science in Sports and Exercise* 33(6): S530–50; discussion S609–10.

Tinning, R. (2005) 'Active Lifestyles and the Paradoxical Impact of Education and Sport'. Keynote Address to the AIESEP Congress, Lisbon, Portugal, November.

Tomporowski, P.D. (2003) 'Cognitive and Behavioral Responses to Acute Exercise in Youths: A Review', *Pediatric Exercise Science* 15: 348–59.

Trembaly, M.S., Inman, J.W. and Willms, J.D. (2000) 'The Relationship between Physical Activity, Self-Esteem, and Academic Achievement in 12-Year-Old Children', *Pediatric Exercise Science* 12: 312–23.

UK Sport (n.d.) *Measuring Success 2*, London: UK Sport.

UK Sport (1999) *Major Events: The Economics Measuring Success. A 'Blueprint' for Success*, London: UK Sport.

UNICEF (2006) *Monitoring and Evaluation for Sport-Based Programming for Development: Sport Recreation and Play*, Workshop Report, New York: UNICEF.

United Nations (2005a) *Business Plan International Year of Sport and Physical Education*, New York: United Nations.

United Nations (2005b) *Sport for Development and Peace: Towards Achieving the Millennium Development Goals*, New York: United Nations.

United Nations (2005c) *International Year of Sport and Physical Education*, United Nations: www.un.org/sport2005.

US Department of Health and Human Services (1996) *Physical Activity and Health: A Report of the Surgeon General*, Atlanta, GA: US Department of Health and Human Services, Centers for Disease Control and Prevention, National Center for Chronic Disease Prevention and Health Promotion.

US Department of Health and Human Services (1999) *Framework for Program Evaluation in Public Health*, Atlanta, GA: US Department of Health and Human Services, Centers for Disease Control and Prevention (CDC).

Utting, D. (1996) *Reducing Criminality among Young People: A Sample of Relevant Programmes in the United Kingdom*, London: Home Office Research and Statistics Directorate.

van Bottenburg, M., Rijnen, B. and van Sterkenburgh, J. (2005) *Sports Participation in the European Union: Trends and Differences*, Nieuwegein: Arko Sports Media.

Vance, D.E., Wadley, V.G., Ball, K.K., Roenker, D.L. and Rizzo, M. (2005) 'The Effects of Physical Activity and Sedentary Behavior on Cognitive Health in Older Adults', *Journal of Aging and Physical Activity* 13(3): 294–313.

van der Poel, H. (1993) 'Leisure Policy and the Netherlands', in P. Bramham, I. Henry, H. Mommas and H. van der Poel (eds) *Leisure Policies in Europe*, Wallingford: CAB International, pp. 41–70.

Vanreusel, B., Renson, R., Beunen, G., Claessens, A.L., Lefevre, J., Lysens, R. and Eynde, B.V. (1997) 'A Longitudinal Study of Youth Sport Participation and Adherence to Sport in Adulthood', *International Review for the Sociology of Sport* 32(4): 373–87.

Van Rooy, A. (1998) *Civil Society and the Aid Industry*, London: Earthscan.

Van Rooy, A. (ed.) (2004) *Global Legitimacy Game: Civil Society, Globalisation and Protest*, London: Palgrave Macmillan.

Veal, A.J. (1982) *Planning for Leisure: Alternative Approaches*, Papers in Leisure Studies, 5, May, London: Department of Extension Studies, Polytechnic of North London.

Veal, A.J. (2003) 'Tracking Change: Leisure Participation and Policy in Australia, 1985–2002', *Annals of Leisure Research* 6(3): 245–77.

Videon, T.M. (2002) 'Who Plays and Who Benefits: Gender, Interscholastic Athletes, and Academic Outcomes', *Sociological Perspectives* 45(4): 415–44.

Walsh, K. (1991) *Competitive Tendering for Local Authority Services: Initial Experiences*, London: HMSO.

Wang, C.K.J., Chatzisarantis, N.L.D., Spray, C.M. and Biddle, S.J.H. (2002) 'Achievement Goal Profiles in School Physical Education: Differences in Self-Determination, Sport

Ability Beliefs, and Physical Activity', *British Journal of Educational Psychology* 72(3): 433–45.

Wankel, L.M. and Sefton, J.M. (1994) *Physical Activity, Fitness and Health*, Champaign, IL: Human Kinetics Publishers, pp. 530–54.

Warde, A. and Tampubolon, G. (2001) *Social Capital, Networks and Leisure Consumption*, CRIC Discussion Paper, 42, Manchester: Centre for Research on Innovation and Competition, University of Manchester.

Warde, A., Tampubolon, G., Longhurst, B., Ray, K., Savage, M. and Tomlinson, M. (2003) 'Trends in Social Capital: Membership of Associations in Great Britain 1991–1998', *British Journal of Political Science* 33: 515–34.

Wasson, A.S. (1988) 'Susceptibility to Boredom and Deviant Behavior at School', *Psychological Reports* 48: 267–74.

Weiss, C.H. (1980) 'Knowledge Creep and Decision Accretion', *Knowledge: Creation, Diffusion, Utilisation* 1(3): 381–404.

Weiss, C.H. (1993) 'Where Politics and Evaluation Research Meet', *Evaluation Practice* 14(1): 93–106.

Weiss, C.H. (1997) 'How Can Theory-based Evaluation Make Greater Headway?', *Evaluation Review* 21(4): 501–24.

Weiss, C.H. and Bucuvalas, M. (1980a) 'Truth Tests and Utility Tests: Decision-Makers' Frames of Reference for Social Science Research', *American Sociological Review* 45: 302–13.

Weiss, C.H. and Bucuvalas, M. (1980b) *Social Science Research and Decision Making*, New York: Columbia University Press.

West, S.T. and Crompton, J.L. (2001) 'A Review of the Impact of Adventure Programs on At-Risk Youth', *Journal of Park and Recreation Administration* 19(2): 113–40.

White, S. (1998) *Interpreting the 'Third Way': Not One Route, But Many*, Cambridge, MA: Department of Political Science, MIT.

Wildsmith, J. and Bradfield, M. (2007) *Halifax Commonwealth Games Bid: Were the Costs and Benefits Assessed?*, Halifax: Canadian Centre for Policy Alternatives.

Wilkins, N.O. (1997) 'Overtime is Better than Sudden Death', *Parks and Recreation* (March).

Williams, D.J. and Strean, W.B. (2006) 'Physical Activity as a Helpful Adjunct to Substance Abuse Treatment', *Journal of Social Work Practice in the Addictions* 4(3): 83–100.

Willis, O. (2000) 'Sport and Development: The Significance of Mathare Youth Sports Association', *Canadian Journal of Development Studies* 21(3): 825–49.

Witt, P.A. and Crompton, J.L. (eds) (1996a) *Recreation Programs that Work for At-Risk Youth*, State College, PA: Venture Publishing.

Witt, P.A. and Crompton, J.L. (1996b) 'The At-Risk Youth Recreation Project', *Journal of Parks and Recreation Administration* 14(3): 1–9.

Witt, P.A. and Crompton, J.L. (1997) 'The Protective Factors Framework: A Key to Programming for Benefits and Evaluating Results', *Journal of Parks and Recreation Administration* 15(3): 1–18.

Woolcock, M. (2001) 'The Place of Social Capital in Understanding Social and Economic Outcomes', ISUMA *Canadian Journal of Policy Research* 2(1): 11–17.

World Bank (2004) *Monitoring and Evaluation: Some Tools, Methods and Approaches*, Washington, DC: World Bank.

World Bank (n.d.) *Social Capital and Civil Society*: http://web.worldbank.org/wbsite/external/topics/extsocialdevlopment.

World Commission on Culture and Development (1995) *Our Creative Diversity: A Report of the World Commission for Culture and Development*, UNESCO: http://www.unesco.org/culture/policies/ocd/index.shtml.

YouthNet (2005) *From Theory to Practice in Peer Education*, New York: United Nations Population Fund and Youth Peer Education Network.

Zaharopoulos, E. and Hodge, K.P. (1991) 'Self-Concept and Sport Participation', *New Zealand Journal of Psychology* 20: 12–16.

Zimmerman, M. (1990) 'Taking Aim on Empowerment Research: On the Distinction between Individual and Psychological Conceptions', *American Journal of Community Psychology* 18(1): 169–77.

Zuzanek, J., Cushman, G. and Veal, A.J. (eds) (2005) *Free Time and Leisure Participation: International Perspectives*, Wallingford: CAB International.

Index

Aaron, H.J. 45
Action Plan for the Eradication of Poverty in the South 2015 71
Action Sport 11, 65, 115, 126
active citizens 8–9, 17; and crime prevention 116; and sport participation 48–9; and sports volunteers 55–7; and the Third Way 47
adolescents 128–30
Aitchison, C. 12
Allison, K.R. 93
Allison, M. 65, 129
Almond, L. 164
Andranovich, G. 141
Andre, T. 112
Andreff, W. 150
Andrew, B. 64
Andrews, G.J. 127
Andrews, J.P. 127
Annan, K. 68
anti-social behaviour 117–19, *see also* crime
Armstrong, G. 73
Asquith, S. 119, 120, 130
Association of Directors of Social Services 25
Audit Commission 12
Australia 12, 14, 18, 26, 108, 109
Australian Sports Commission 18, 26, 29, 72
Austrian, Z. 139

Baade, R. 137, 147
Bailey, P. 8
Bailey, R. 103, 113, 115, 159, 165, 168
Bale, J. 73
Bandura, A. 76, 98, 122
Bauman, A. 142
Begg, D. 119, 123
The Benefits of Sport (2005) 26
Best Value 25
Beunen, G.P. 159
Bianchini, F. 8
Biddle, S. 30, 98, 99, 101, 102, 110, 124, 159, 166
Blackie, J. 9
Blackshaw, T. 51, 53
Blair, T. 14, 47

Blamey, A.S. 21, 28–9, 31, 33, 159, 168
Bloom, M. 18, 21, 26
Blunkett, D. 16, 47
bonding capital 53, 58, 59–60, 79
Bonner, L. 38
Boonstra, N. 60, 67
Botcheva, L. 86
Boule, N.G. 153
Bourdieu, P. 50–1, 52, 66
Bovaird, A. 13
Bowker, A. 100, 102
Bradfield, M. 143, 146
Brady, M. 77, 81, 82
Bramham, P. 12
Bredemeier, B.J.L. 132
bridging capital 53, 58, 60–2, 105
British Academy of Sport 14
Brodie, D.A. 129, 156–7, 158
Buchner, D. 159
Bucuvalas, M. 42–3, 44, 45, 162, 163
Burnett, C. 75, 88, 91

Cabinet Office 22
Caborn, R. 18, 43, 159
Calfas, K.J. 125
Canada 18, 21–2, 26, 108
CARE 72
Carlson, B.R. 125
Carter, C. 120
The Case for Sport Australia 18
Central Council for Physical Recreation (CCPR) 18, 56
Centre for Evidence-informed Education Policy and Practice (EPPI Centre) 25
Chalkley, B. 141
Chapin, T.S. 138, 146
Chapman, V. 10, 17
Charlton, V. 10
Chema, T. 138
civil society 69–70; concept 71–2; and external aid 72–3; and social capital 52–4, 58, 66–7, 72
Clarke, A. 12
Coakley, J. 34, 95, 165, 166

Coalter, F. 10, 11, 12, 13, 18, 20, 22, 23, 26, 29, 33, 38, 48, 49, 54, 65, 76, 88, 116, 117, 118, 121, 129, 133, 142, 150, 158, 161
Coates, D. 137
Coe, D.P. 97
Coleman, J. 50, 51–2, 58, 66, 89, 105
Collins, M. 16, 19, 20, 21, 22, 25, 29, 31, 32, 33, 38, 161
Commonwealth Games 143
Commonwealth Games Association of Canada 69, 72
communities, and bonding capital 59–60, 61; and bridging capital 60–2; contribution of sports clubs to 65, 66; development of 65, 171–2; effect of social capital on 67; indigenous/immigrant groups in 60–1; regeneration of 5; social capital/efficiency of 52–4, 58, 61
Compulsory Competitive Tendering (CCT) 12–13, 25
Consumer Trends 151
Convention on the Rights of the Child 69
Corbin, C.B. 101
CORE Initiative 88
Court, J. 72, 87
Crabbe, T. 127, 129, 165, 172
crime 6, 16, 17, 25, 28, 165; and achievement/self-esteem 125–8; and active citizenship 116; and adolescent development needs 128–30; advantages/liabilities of sport involvement 132; anti-social behaviour 117–19; and antidote to boredom 120–1; and autonomy/ownership 127; and blocked aspirations 125–8; community safety agenda 116; and crime prevention 115; and delivery of sport programmes 131–2; and differential association 122–5; diversionary programmes 116, 118; and drop in approach 126–7; effectiveness of programmes 121; and experiences of participation 131–2; and leadership provision 123–4, 126; mediating variables 126; and motivational climate 126; and police harassment 119; predictions of 123; and primary/secondary programmes 121; and rehabilitation programmes 115, 118; and reinforcement programmes 125, 126; relationship with sport 115–17; and respect agenda 116; and role models 124; and social inclusion agenda 116; and social interventions/processes 132; and social process of participation 124; and social relationships 131–2; social theory perspective 122–3; and sport initiatives 116–17; and sport plus 121, 130–1; and sports counselling programmes 123; and tailoring of programmes 127; theories of 119–30; and youth workers 123
Critcher, C. 143
Crompton, J.L. 18, 21, 30, 31, 38, 76, 102, 116, 117, 123, 124, 125, 126, 127, 128, 129, 130, 132, 140, 142, 143, 144, 145, 146, 148, 172
Cronin, M. 73
Crow, I. 38, 116, 117, 121, 168
Crowe, M. 142, 146
Curtis, J. 158

Danish, S.J. 110
Davidson, L. 136
Deane, J. 11, 76, 129, 131
DeFilippis, J. 51
Delaney, L. 48, 49, 62–4, 167
Denmark 56
Department of Culture, Media and Sport 22
Department for Education and Skills (DfES) 111
Department of the Environment (DoE) 115
Department for International Development 89
Department of National Heritage 14
Department of Social Security 16
Depro, B. 117, 131, 167
Diawara, M. 91
Disher, M. 145
Dobson, N. 148–9
Donnison, D.V. 10, 17
Driscoll, K. 18, 59
Dwyer, T. 97, 109
Dyerson, M. 59

economics 6; and benefits of physically active population 153–9; and decline in manufacturing/industrial production 133; disputes concerning 160; and growth coalitions/sport lobby 159–60; impact on sport 134; and increased political demands 159; and large-scale sport events 141–50; and leisure services 134; nature of data 150–3; and new economic realism 133–5; and social projects 133; and sport/urban regeneration 135–41; and sports economy 150–3; and state flexibilisation/disinvestment in public services 133
educational performance 5–6, 164; and cardiovascular fitness/cognitive performance link 94–7; and cause/effect relationship 93, 94; and eligibility to take part in sport 106; and exam results 112–14; and expectation of participation in sport 107; identification/commitment model 107–8; and increased attention from coaches, teachers, parents 106; and learning environment 112; and membership of elite groups 106; methodological/conceptual issues 93–4; and mixed evidential results 108–10; and nature of sport relationship 94; and New Labour 92; and participation in school sports/PE 93; participation-identification model 106, 107; and physical fitness 97–8; and social capital 50; and socio-psychological/self-concept aspects 98–104, 106; and specialist schools 92–3, 109; and sport effects 112–14; and

sport plus 110–12; and sport-in-development 76–7; and type/choice of sport 104–5; zero sum approach 93
EduSport Foundation 69, 82
Edwards, H. 105
Eichberg, H. 73
Eitle, D.J. 104, 105, 106, 113
Eitle, T.M. 94, 104, 105, 106, 113
Ekeland, E. 98, 103
Elabor-Idemudia, P. 90, 91, 169
Elfring, T. 134
Elliot, D.S. 125
Ellis, G.D. 125, 126, 128
Emler, N. 104, 113, 125, 127–8, 171
Endersen, I.M. 122, 127
Essex, S. 141
Etnier, J.L. 27, 30, 94, 95, 96, 102, 103, 110, 113, 114
Etzioni, A. 15
Euchner, C.C. 136
European Football Championships 148
European Social Survey 62
Evans, G.L. 134
Evans, J. 106
evidence-based policy-making 1–2, 5, 6, 19, 20, 21–3, 24, 161; and answering how/why questions 36–8; degree of rigour/evidence required 41–5; and enlightenment approach 45; and generalization 37; generative approach 36–7; and government/public organization reviews 25–6; hierarchy of approaches 36; and identification of exemplary programmes 30; and impact/outcome measurement 27–8, 33–5; and information extraction 30; and lack of precision 38–41; and learning from failure 30; limitations 161–2; logical model 32–5; medical model 28; and meta-analysis 27–9; and narrative reviews 29–30, 31–2, 36; and New Labour pragmatism 25; and process monitoring 40; and process/content 28–9; and programme theory 37–8, 40; as rational exercise in political context 41–5; realist synthesis 36–7, 39; and scepticism concerning change 162; and social intervention/hard-to-follow outcomes 30, 31–2; and social science research 43; and theory of change 39–40; theory/practice contrast 26, *see also* public policy

FA Cup Final 149
Fainstein, S. 135
Farr, J. 50
Faulkner, G. 2, 28, 167, 168
Ferron, C. 99
Field, J. 50, 51, 52, 65
Finland 56
Finn, J.D. 107
Fitzpatrick, S. 119, 122, 129
Flisher, A. 40

Football Association (FA) 111
Football Foundation 116
Forrest, R. 47, 48, 49, 59, 62–4, 65, 167
Foster, C. 20, 21, 159, 168
Fox, K.R. 29, 94, 99, 100, 101, 103, 108, 124, 125, 126, 127, 164, 172
France 12, 56, 108
Fréchette, L. 68
French, S. 145
Friedman, M.T. 135, 139, 140
Fukuyama, F. 65
Furberg, A.S. 153

Game Plan (2002) 22–3, 26, 142, 147, 153, 155, 156, 162
Gaskin, K. 48, 57
Gavelin, K. 15
gender 69, 74–5; and empowerment of women 81–4; and health of women 154; and self-esteem 100, 102–3
Germany 12, 56, 60
Giddens, A. 15, 16, 47
Giller, H. 125
Giulianotti, R. 72, 73, 91
Glasner, P.E. 9
Glyptis, S. 22
Go Sisters programme (Zambia) 5; aims of 82–4; and development of self-esteem/self-development 84; and empowerment of women 82; and HIV/AIDS education 84; success of 85; and use of abstract games/discussions 84–5
Going for the Goal programme (USA) 110
Goudas, M. 164
Granger, R.C. 39, 119
Gratton, C. 10, 13, 133, 135, 136, 143, 144, 145, 148, 148–9, 150, 151–2
Gray, C.M. 134
Green, M. 14
Grissom, J.B. 97, 98, 103, 114, 172
Gross, R.T. 103, 127
Gunn, C. 136

Hall, C.M. 140
Hall, P.A. 54–5
Halpern, D. 47
Hammersley, M. 2, 44, 170
Hanson, S.L. 103
Hantrais, L. 10
Harris, J. 164
Harrison, B. 8, 23
Harter, S. 98, 99
Hartmann, D. 117, 131, 167
Harvey, D. 133, 135
Hastad, D.N. 34, 122, 132
Heal, K. 121
health, and childhood/adolescent activity 158–9; data on 154–5; economics benefits of physically active population 153–9; and individual/non-competitive sport 158; and

inequalities 157; and lifestyle 157; and self-assessment discrepancies 156–7; and participation/non-participation review 159; policy dilemma 157–8; and socio-demographic differences 157; and sports-related injuries 155–6; and women 154
Health Development Agency (HDA) 163
Heilbrun, J. 134
Hendry, L.B. 128, 129
Henry, I.P. 10, 11, 14, 133, 135, 143, 150
High School and Beyond survey (USA) 107
Hillman, C.H. 95
HIV/AIDS 5, 19, 69, 70–1, 72, 73, 74, 82, 86, 87–90, 111
Hodge, K.P. 100
Hognestad, H. 69, 71, 73
Holland, A. 112
Holtham, G. 16, 55
Home Office 56
Home Office Drugs Strategy Directorate 116
Horch, H. 59, 65
Horne, J. 143, 146–7
Houlihan, B. 17, 18, 24, 30, 43, 161
Howell, D. 18
Huffman, M.D. 86
Humphreys, B.R. 137, 140
Hutton, W. 15

Ibsen, B. 64, 65
International Conference on Sport and Development (2003) 70
International Monetary Fund (IMF) 10
Interventions Implemented through Sporting Organizations for Increasing Participation in Sport 27

Jackson, N.W. 27–8
Janowitz, M. 45
Jenkins, A. 92
Job Seekers' Allowance 16
Johnson, A.T. 140, 141
Johnston, G. 50, 51, 53
Jones, C. 139, 140, 146
Judd, D.R. 135
Judkins, M. 93

Kahn, A.B. 77, 81, 82
Kahn, E.B. 21
Kasimatai, E. 142, 146
Kay, T. 16, 20
Keaney, E. 15, 48, 49, 62–4, 167
Kearns, A. 15, 17, 47, 50, 59, 65
Keays, J.J. 93
Keck, M. 73
Keller, H. 19, 35
Kemper, H.C.G. 153
Kenya 77–82
Kenya Football Federation (KFF) 78
Kerrigan, D. 76, 77
Kicking AIDS Out! (KAO) 69, 70, 85–6

Kidd, B. 140
Kleitman, S. 94, 107, 113
Kloosterman, R.C. 134
Kraus, R. 103
Kraut, A. 158
Krisha, A. 153
Kruse, S.-E. 70, 77, 85, 86, 90, 91

Landolt, P. 58, 59, 67
Laycock, G. 121
Le Grand, 16
Le Roux, N. 56
Learning Communities Project 38–9
Lee, P. 30
Leisure Industries Research Unit 148, 165
Leisure and the Quality of Life Experiments (DoE, 1977) 10
Leith, L.M. 99
Lengcheek, J. 12
Lenskji, H.J. 145
Leonard, M. 52, 61, 67
Levacic, R. 92
Levitas, R. 16, 21
Lillbacka, R. 67
Lindner, K.J. 93, 94, 97, 98, 110, 114
Lipsky, R. 106
Local Government Association 55, 63
Long, J. 22, 38, 51, 53, 162, 165, 170
Lottery 14
Loughlan, C. 159
Lowndes, V. 49
Loxley, C. 121, 129
Lynch, K. 135

McDermott, L. 99
McDonald, D. 45, 48, 65, 126, 171
McGiboney, G.W. 120
McIntosh, P. 10
McKenzie, D.L. 119, 128, 130
MacMahon, J.R. 103, 125, 127
McNeal, R.B. 105
Madden, J.R. 142, 146
Magglingen Declaration (2003) 70
Major, J. 14
Malina, R.M. 159
Manzenreiter, W. 143, 146–7
Marcus, B.H. 159
Marsh, H.W. 4, 103, 106, 107, 110, 113
Martin, B.W. 154, 155, 156
Mason, V. 100, 102, 129
Matarasso, F. 41
Mathare Youth Sport Association (MYSA) 5, 69, 73; achievements of 80–1; background 77–8; and commitment to community service 80; and empowerment of women 81–2; and establishment of Girls' Task Force 82; involvement in 79–81; key elements 78–9; and overseas travel 80; producing citizens 78–9
Matheson, V.A. 143, 144, 147, 148–9

Maugham, M. 125, 126, 128
Maule, C.O. 168
Meiburg, H. 102, 126
Mennell, S. 10
Merton, R.K. 166
Midnight Basketball initiative (USA) 111
Mikosz, D. 47
Miles, R. 159
Millennium Development Goals 69
Miller, K.E. 93, 100, 112
Miracle, A.W. 102
Modernising Government White Paper (1999) 25
Mondello, M.J. 148–9
Morgan, D. 117, 129
Morgan, W.P. 99, 101, 104
Morris, L. 117, 119, 125, 130, 172
Mukoma, M. 40
Munro, B. 76, 78, 79, 80, 81
Murphy, N.M. 142
Mutrie, N. 21, 28–9, 31, 33, 98, 99, 101, 159, 168
Mwaanga, O. 82, 83, 85, 86, 172
Myerscough, J. 134

Nahrstedt, W. 10, 12
Namibia 69
National Education Longitudinal Study (USA) 104–5, 107
National Football Foundation (USA) 110
National Institute for Clinical Excellence (NICE) 25
National Medical Expenditure Survey 154
National Travel Survey 151
Nationwide League 111
Nellen, V.C. 110
Netherlands 12, 60
Newman, P. 139
NHS Centre for Reviews and Dissemination 25
Nicholl, J.P. 155, 156
Nicholls, S. 76, 77, 89, 90, 91, 169
Nichols, G. 30, 38, 49, 56, 116, 117, 121, 123, 124, 127, 168
NIF 72
Noll, R.G. 139
non-governmental organizations (NGOs) 72–3, 82, 87
Norway 63
Norwegian Agency for Development Cooperation (NORAD) 69, 72
Norwegian Olympic Committee and Confederation of Sports (NIF) 69

Oakley, A. 2, 21, 28, 30, 161–2, 167, 173
Olwens, D. 122, 127
Olympic Aid Roundtable Forum 68
Olympic Games 141–3, 148
Orcutt, J.D. 120
Our Creative Diversity (1995) 71

Papacharisis, V. 29, 164

Parry, G. 28
Patriksson, M. 23, 26, 29, 34, 36, 37, 90, 122
Pawson, R. 2–4, 7, 26–31, 34–7, 40, 44, 45, 66, 88, 90, 91, 117, 119, 120, 132, 160, 162, 163, 166, 168–73
Payne, W. 76, 124
Pelak, C.F. 73, 74
Percy-Smith, J. 50, 51, 53
Perkins, D. 158
Petitpas, A.J. 110
Petti, K. 125
physical education (PE) 29, 98, 165
physical education and school sport (PESS) 113
physical education in schools (PES) 165
Physical Self-Perception Profile (PSPP) 101
Play it Smart programme (USA) 110
Playing for Success (UK) 111
Policy Action Group 10 15, 17, 116; *Report to the Social Exclusion Unit Arts and Sport* (1999) 25–6
politics 5, 161; and evidence-based research 41–5; Major government 14; New Labour/ Third Way 14–19, 24, 47, 92; and sports club participation 63; Thatcher government 11–13, 14, *see also* public policy
Pollard, A. 72, 87
Portes, A. 50, 51, 53, 58, 59, 67
Positive Futures programme 116, 130–1
Poujol, G. 12
Pratt, M. 154
Premier League 111
President's Council on Physical Fitness and Sports 8
Preuss, H. 141, 142, 145, 150, 165
public policy, and active/responsible citizen 8–9, 16, 17; ambiguity/duality of 3–4, 10; and consumer rights 12; cross-cutting concepts 17–18, 161; and development of communities through sport 18; economic/ political critiques of 11–13; equity-oriented/sport for good shift 18; information provision 162–3; and introduction of CCT 12–13; and leisure activities 9; and local authority failures 13; as a lottery 14; and neighbourhood renewal 15; and New Labour/Third Way politics 14–19, 24; and objective-led management 13; presumed outcomes 19–23; proactive approach 1; and recreation as welfare 11; and social capital 17; and social exclusion/inclusion 15–18, 19, 20; and social interventions 172; and socio-economic benefits 21–2; and sports development projects 11; urban concerns 10–11; and welfare services 9–10, 16; world-wide comparisons 18–19, *see also* evidence-based policy-making
Puntila, E. 153
Purdy, D.A. 119
Putnam, R. 15, 50, 52–4, 58, 60, 67, 105, 131

Raglin, J.S. 125
Rapoport, R. 10
Rapoport, R.N. 10
Ravenscroft, N. 12, 133
Recreation and Deprivation in the Inner City (DoE, 1977) 10
Rees, C.R. 102
Reid, I. 19, 125
research, conceptual weaknesses in 1; and families of programmes/families of mechanisms 166–7; influence of 163; and intermediate impacts 171; and knowledge creep/decision accretion 163–4; limitations in 2, 164–5, 167, 168, 172–4; and logic of inquiry 167–71; and managers/funders of similar programmes 169–70; and methodological rigour 168; methodological weaknesses of 1–2; point of entry 163–4; and policy-makers/the public 170; and practitioners 169; problems concerning 171–2; and programme designers 169; and programme evaluator 170–1; and programme managers 169; realist approaches to 2–3; and sufficiency conditions 2, 7, 23; and theory-based evaluation 2–4
Ribes-Inesta, E. 122
Richards, S.F. 119
Rigg, M. 11, 126
Right to Play (Canada) 69, 72
Rijpma, S. 102, 126
Rishe, P. 148–9
Ritchie, B. 140
Roberts, G.C. 106
Roberts, K. 129, 156–7, 158
Robins, D. 118, 120, 126
Roche, M. 8, 9, 11, 135, 143
Rodriguez, C.J. 153
The Role of Sport in Regenerating Deprived Urban Areas (2000) 26
Room, G. 15
Rosentraub, M.S. 134, 136, 137, 139
Rossi, P.H. 39, 40, 42
Roth, A.D. 28
Rudd, P. 92, 93
Rutter, M. 125

Saavedra, M. 73, 74, 76, 81
Sabo, D. 104, 105
Sack, A. 140, 141
Sallis, J. 20, 93, 94, 109, 110, 113, 114, 158
Sanderson, I. 22, 38, 162, 165, 170
Sandford, R.A. 124, 165
Santo, C. 138
Schafer, W. 119, 120, 122, 125, 128
Schimmel, K. 134, 135, 136, 143
Schools and Police Liaison Activities for the Summer Holidays (Splash) programme 120–1
Scottish Executive 26
Scottish Office 15, 17, 116, 120

Searle, G. 143, 147
Sefton, J.M. 19
Segrave, J. 122, 132
Seippel, O. 63–4, 66
self-esteem 112–14, 164; and academic performance 103–4; and autonomy/control 102; and benefits of exercise 101–2; and competitive environments 102–3; and crime 125–8; gender differences 100; global 99, 113; hierarchical/competence-based model 99–100; motivational/self-development approach 99; and PE programmes 98; and Physical Self-Perception Profile 101; and pupil identity 100–1; and task/mastery orientation 102
Serok, S. 102, 126
Shadish, W.R. 30
Shah, M.K. 87, 88, 170
Sharp, C. 111–12, 167
Shaw, J.M. 153
Shephard, R.J. 93, 94, 98, 108, 109, 110, 112, 114, 159
Shibli, S. 148
Shields, D.L.L. 132
Sibley, B.A. 30, 94, 95, 96, 103, 110, 114
Siegfried, J.J. 136, 137
Sikkik, K. 73
Sillitoe, K.K. 9
Simkin, L.R. 159
Simmonds, B. 116
Six Nations Rugby matches 149
Skidmore, P. 48, 58, 61, 63, 65, 66
Smith, A. 9, 135, 136
Smith, D. 48, 57
Smith, H. 147
Snow, C. 153
Snyder, E.E. 106
social capital 17, 165; and access to resources 50, 55; and bonding/bridging 53, 58, 59–62, 79, 105; and changing nature of sport 54–5; civic effects 52–4, 58, 66–7, 72; and class difference 50–1, 55; as closure, stability, social control 52; concept 49–50; and contribution of sports volunteering 55; and distribution of power 50; and economic/cultural capital 50, 51; and educational achievement 50; evidence-based policy questions 66–7; forming/sustaining 66–7; and human capital 105; and increase in social/sports participation 55; linking 58; as neutral resource 52–4; as positional good 51; and quality of relationships 55; relative stability of 55; and sports clubs 57–64, 66; as ubiquitous resource 51–2; use of term 50–4
Social Exclusion Unit 15, 58
social regeneration 71–2
Solesbury, W. 25, 41, 42, 43, 44, 134, 150, 162, 163
Sonstroem, R.J. 99, 101, 104
South Africa 69, 74

Spady, W. 106, 128, 132
Spence, J.C. 99, 100, 101
sport, centrality of 14; global role for 68–70; and government involvement/investment in 8–24; health/social benefits of 8; and inequalities of participation 10; institutional/ organizational location 71; metaphors associated with 9; mythopoeic nature of 9, 24, 70, 90; and need to decentre/de-mythologize 165; as neither good nor bad 122; as neutral social space 9; opportunities/ threats connected with 1–2; positive outcomes perspective 92; post-colonial 73; potential benefits of 19–23; psychological/ ecological factors 20–1; public investment in 4–5; and reconstruction of civil society 71–2; and social regeneration 71–2; traditional development 20
Sport Canada 18
Sport for Development and Peace 71
Sport England 1, 13, 26, 34, 49, 55, 56, 57, 63, 64, 65, 116, 157
sport events 165; academic scepticism concerning 147–8; benefit/costs discrepancies 146; and building of stadia 136, 138–40; confusing figures 145; and different games/different results 148–50; economic effects 141–50; and idea of sporting legacy 146–7; inclusions/exclusions 145; large-scale 141–50; and local needs/ priorities 142; motivations behind 141–2, 143; multiplier problem 143–8; omissions/ misrepresentations 144; and overestimation of benefits 143–4; and political influences/ aspirations 142; and pre-/post-game projection/performance 147; and private investment 142
Sport Industry Research Centre 150
sport plus 110–12, 172; and crime prevention 121, 130–1; or plus sport 5, 37, 70–1; and urban regeneration 139
Sport and Recreation Victoria 12
Sport and Recreation White Paper (1975) 10
Sport and Social Exclusion (1999) 25
sport-for-good programmes 46
sport-in-development 5, 19, 69, 165; accountability/development difference 87–9; case studies 77–85; developing people/creating citizens 75–7, 89–90; and education/learning 76–7; evaluation of 87–9; hitting the mark 85–7; and monitoring and evaluation (M&E) 87–9, 90–1; programmes 75–6; reasons why programmes work 90–1; success of 111; and youth peer leaders 75–7
sports clubs 111; bonding/playing with mates 59–60, 61; bridging/bowling with acquaintances 60–2; and civil behaviours 62; contribution to social/community regeneration 65, 66; and interest in politics 63; membership of 57; size/types of 66; and

social capital 57–62; and state intervention 64–5; survey evidence 62–4; and trust 62–4; volunteers in 56–7, 64–5
Sports Coaches Outreach (SCORE) 69, 89
Sports Council 11, 13
Sports Council Research Unit NW 30
Sports United to Promote Education and Recreation (SUPER) programme 110
Spreitzer, E. 106
Steptoe, A. 125
Stolle, D. 60
Strean, W.B. 130, 172
Stromme Foundation (Norway) 77
Sugden, J. 30, 102, 126
Svoboda, B. 19, 23, 30, 33, 34, 123, 125
Sweden 60
Swiss Agency for Development and Cooperation 69
Szreter, S. 55, 67
Szymanski, S. 142, 144, 146, 147

Tacon, R. 36, 38, 39, 166
Tammelin, T. 158
Tampubolon, G. 48
Tanzania 69
Taras, H. 103, 105, 106, 114
Taylor, P. 10, 13, 22, 30, 35, 102, 116, 117, 118, 123, 124, 127, 132, 143, 144, 145, 150, 151–2, 158, 173
Taylor, W.C. 125
Thatcher, M. 11, 14
theory-based evaluation (TBE), and absence of understanding of processes/mechanisms 2–3; as developmental 4; and research/policy relationship 3–4
Thornley, A. 136, 138
Thornton, A. 30
Thune, I. 153
Tilley, N. 36, 44, 163, 168
Tinning, R. 172
Tolley, J. 12
Tollisen, A. 69, 73
Tomporowski, P.D. 96
Trembaly, M.S. 93, 103
Trois Rivières study 108
Trudeau, F. 108, 159
Tual, M. 139
Tungatt, M. 45, 48, 65, 126, 171

UK Sport 1, 26, 69, 72, 150
UNESCO 68–9
UNICEF 19, 72, 87
United Nations 19, 68–9
United States of America 18–19, 104–5, 107, 108, 109, 110–11
Urban Programme (1976) 10–11
urban regeneration, and contingent valuation method 140; and expenditure substitution 137; importance of sport 135–40; Indianopolis strategy 136–7, 138; intangible

benefits 140; location/context issues
138–9; and mega-events 135; and reimaging
projects 135–6; and sport plus approach 139;
and sports stadia 136, 138–40; and tourism
139; and veil of appearance concept 140
US Dept of Health and Human Services 40
Utting, D. 118, 123, 125, 130, 132

Value of Sport Monitor 1, 26
Van Bottenburg, M. 54
Van der Poel, H. 10, 12
Van Rooy, A. 71
Vance, D.E. 97
Vanreusel, B. 158
Veal, A.J. 9, 142
Videon, T.M. 102, 106, 129
volunteers 55–7
Volvo International Tennis Tournament (1998)
143
Voss, H.L. 125

Waddington, I. 9
Walsh, K. 13
Wang, C.K.J. 102
Wankel, L.M. 19
Warde, A. 48, 55, 56
Weiss, C.H. 2–4, 7, 26, 31, 37–45, 87, 88, 89,
90, 113, 117, 120, 141, 162, 163, 164, 169,
170, 172

West, S.T. 31, 38, 116, 117, 124, 127, 129, 132,
172
White, A. 17, 18, 24, 30, 43, 161
White, S. 16, 21
Wildsmith, J. 143, 146
Wilkins, N.O. 117, 131, 167
Williams, D.J. 130, 172
Wimbledon 149
Witt, P.A. 21, 30, 31, 76, 102, 116, 117, 123,
124, 125, 126, 128, 130
Wood, L. 18, 59
Woolcock, M. 58
World Bank 37, 72
World Commission on Culture and Diversity 71
World Cup 143, 148
World Sport Forum 68

Year of Sport and Physical Education (2005) 69
Yiannakis, A. 30, 102, 126
Youth Justice Board 116, 121
Youth Peer Leaders (YPLs) 82, 86, 89–90
YouthNet 76, 77

Zaharopoulos, E. 100
Zambia 69, 82–5
Zimbabwe 69
Zimbalist, A. 136, 137, 139
Zimmerman, M. 86
Zuzanek, J. 54